SACRED POSSIBILITIES

Life in its purest form defies all logic.

*The most beautiful and profound emotion we can
experience is the sensation of the mystical.*
—Albert Einstein

An open heart is an open mind.
—the Dalai Lama

Lucille DancingWind

BALBOA.
PRESS
A DIVISION OF HAY HOUSE

Balboa Press books may be ordered through booksellers or by contacting:

Balboa Press
A Division of Hay House
1663 Liberty Drive
Bloomington, IN 47403
www.balboapress.com
1 (877) 407-4847

Because of the dynamic nature of the Internet, any web addresses or links contained in this book may have changed since publication and may no longer be valid. The views expressed in this work are solely those of the author and do not necessarily reflect the views of the publisher, and the publisher hereby disclaims any responsibility for them.

The author of this book does not dispense medical advice or prescribe the use of any technique as a form of treatment for physical, emotional, or medical problems without the advice of a physician, either directly or indirectly. The intent of the author is only to offer information of a general nature to help you in your quest for emotional and spiritual well-being. In the event you use any of the information in this book for yourself, which is your constitutional right, the author and the publisher assume no responsibility for your actions.

Any people depicted in stock imagery provided by Thinkstock are models, and such images are being used for illustrative purposes only.
Certain stock imagery © Thinkstock.

Printed in the United States of America.

ISBN: 978-1-4525-9677-8 (sc)
ISBN: 978-1-4525-9679-2 (hc)
ISBN: 978-1-4525-9678-5 (e)

Library of Congress Control Number: 2014907679

Balboa Press rev. date: 5/23/2014

You can view photos that complement the stories included in this book, by going to:

www.sacredpossibilities.com/portal

You'll also have the privilege of seeing what was revealed to the author, after the book was completed (directly related to the last chapter, 11!). It's truly *amazing*!

Dedication

I dedicate this book to

DIVINE LOVE

CONTENTS

Special notes about this book

In order to respect the privacy of those who have shared the experiences included in this book, names have been changed and certain details are not mentioned (with the exception of one name, which is used by permission, in the last chapter).

The Divine refers to the One also known as God, Great Spirit, Creator, Supreme Consciousness, Higher Power, etc.

Spirit refers to all those who support me (and all of us) in various ways, from beyond the physical plane. They include the Divine, ascended masters, archangels, the higher self, deities, angels, elementals, star beings, spirit guides, power animals, ancestors, etc.

Nature refers to the entire natural world, which includes environments, physical beings of all kingdoms and elements (excluding humans), Mother Earth, and Father Sky.

All refers to everyone stated above, including human beings.

INTRODUCTION

Expect the unexpected

Because you are alive, everything is possible.
—Thich Nhat Hanh

If we did all the things we are capable of, we
would literally astound ourselves.
—Thomas A. Edison

Life is truly extraordinary—so much more so than we can even imagine. I've learned firsthand to always expect the unexpected and to anticipate that the "impossible" will manifest. It doesn't even matter what "laws" we believe exist in the universe. I know that *anything* is possible, regardless. Throughout all my experiences, ranging from ecstatic ups to despairing downs, life has continued to fascinate me.

When we dare to pay attention to our hearts, and we consider that there might be more to us and our world than what we've been taught, life takes notice. We receive invitations, often in surprising ways, to experience the possibilities that reside in the unknown parts of our paths. Our hearts (our sacred hearts that are beyond emotions) have always known the truth of what's possible, and they yearn for us to experience this. They entice us to accept the invitations through our true desires—all of them. It's only through personal experience that we're able to know anything beyond doubt, including what's possible for ourselves and this world. Our experiences become our personal, indisputable truth. They empower us as we navigate our paths through life. The more we're willing to trust and experience, the more life reveals its divinity to us, as well as our own.

I've always been a seeker of truth. From childhood, I was curious to know whether what I sensed about our world was accurate, since it differed from what I was being taught. I had a mysterious *inner knowing* that life was so much more than what I was learning from the figures of authority. I didn't understand why I had a different perspective than everyone else did; it made life more difficult. While I didn't mean to be rebellious, my unwavering loyalty to what felt true within my heart gave me such a nature. I was discouraged from questioning the things that didn't feel true to me, so I questioned within instead and remained open to receiving validation.

I was raised in a very religious family and community. Going to church at least once a week was mandatory. However, this never resonated with me. I experienced the Divine directly in Nature. Since I felt misunderstood while I was growing up, I spent as much time as I could in Nature, where I felt free to be myself without expectations or judgment. Here I experienced endless, miraculous wonders. I always left my natural refuge so awe-inspired and overflowing with joyful, pure love. It was an aspect of our world that so many seemed oblivious to. What I didn't realize then was that my heart's openness and expansion enabled me to experience the Divine this way.

Through Nature I understood that miracles were a natural part of life, not an exception, and that the Divine's love was pure, creative power beyond all logic and limitations. It created everything miraculous, magickal and awe-inspiring. Through the openness of my heart, I experienced the immense power of love with all my senses. I wished that everyone could experience this empowering state of being and awareness instead of having constricting fears that caused so much unnecessary suffering.

I was born with a very strong sense of having a mission to fulfill, yet it seemed to come with amnesia. I spent so many years feeling frustrated with this relentless calling within me and wondering how I was supposed to live a purpose I couldn't remember. It didn't make any sense to me whatsoever—until I had experienced four decades of life! Then the veil unexpectedly lifted, and I finally understood my purpose and the reason that things had been obscure for so long. Unbeknownst to me, I had already been living my purpose here on Earth!

Since I've always been committed to living my life to the fullest, I've been willing to experience everything I've felt called to—including the unknown at its most extreme. It has enabled me to know that anything *is* possible in this world of apparent limitations. While I wasn't consciously aware of the extent of support I had from Spirit until my late twenties, my personal commitment has allowed me to always let my heart lead, regardless of circumstances. With every experience, I have deepened my trust in myself and life. This trust has pulled me through my scariest challenges (including a test of faith that felt as if it would never, ever end!). I've discovered what's divinely possible when we go where the pressure of resistance is the greatest.

In my search for clarity about my purpose, my life has been like a series of multiple movies lived all over our magnificent world. I finally see how they're all divinely linked together, now that I can look back and "connect the dots"! Through my various studies, jobs, volunteer work, relationships, homes, online networking, and travels abroad, I've connected with all sorts of people from all over the world. Through my mystical experiences and tests of faith, I've connected more deeply with myself and with beings of Nature and Spirit. Through all these connections and experiences, I finally gained clarity about my unique path. *Timing is everything.*

I've learned from my own journey—and many others'—that everything is always perfect for us on our particular paths, no matter how it may seem. Amidst the waves of experiences, we all have our uniquely tailored processes to go through. While some people know their purposes earlier in life, I could not know what mine was until later, when it was time. It was necessary for me to go through decades of experiences, to gain what I needed to fulfill my calling. It was all preparation, and it was brilliantly orchestrated by Spirit, through my heart's guidance. When I realized I had actually been living my purpose all along, I couldn't help but laugh at the genius of it all. There's always so much more to our journeys than meets the eye!

I know from a wide range of personal experiences that we *always* have endless support, in countless forms beyond the physical, available to us. At all times, there are great orchestrations going on behind the scenes on our behalf, that we're not aware of. However, it's always up to us to ask for, accept, and receive this support—we do have free will.

I've learned that life in its purest form defies all logic—and that is such a wonderful thing! It makes all things possible. We're limitless by nature, and through our love and desires we have access to an infinite number of sacred possibilities. Life is amazing beyond words or measure, and the more we trust that it is, the more we experience it—even through the more challenging parts of our journeys.

Now I'm being called to fulfill the next phase of my purpose—which includes this book. I'm sharing what I've experienced, with great love and as much transparency as possible, while still respecting the privacy of those involved. I've included *everything* that Spirit guided me to share. Transforming my fear of being fully seen was paramount to being able to do this! As I wrote the book manuscript, I was perplexed at times about certain stories I was being guided to include—until I revisited my journals and recalled the full details. Then everything not only made perfect sense, but I was amazed all over again by my own experiences. These reminders encouraged me further as I was guided to write this book through my most extreme test of faith. That experience became the last chapter of this book, written as I was experiencing it in real time! There really is always a higher purpose to everything.

My personal stories are examples of what's possible in all life situations, for everyone, regardless of how impossible your circumstances may seem at times. When you feel inspired or required to fulfill a desire, regardless of what it is or what it involves, you always have everything you need to make it manifest. Nothing is impossible, and the Divine delights in demonstrating this when you open up to the possibilities.

In order for this book to be of greatest service to you, I looked at what has been the most inspiring for both men and women when I've shared my stories with them. I discovered recurring aspects that were empowering for them to experience through me. I've divided this book by chapters that feature these key aspects, for they are invaluable to living an empowered life from the heart. Each chapter also includes personal stories and insights that emphasize the featured aspect. The last two chapters are extreme examples of all key aspects combined and used together in real life situations.

I feel there's nothing more important than being able to live from a place of love instead of fear, for ourselves and for our world. To do so we must be able to rely on our *own* inner divine guidance, with absolute trust. When we become aware of these key aspects that work together, we're able to confidently live through all experiences, knowing that everything is exactly as it should be, even if we don't understand it at the time. None of these key aspects are surprising – they're fundamental parts of who we are as human beings. It's simply a matter of remembering who we are.

Throughout my stories I also openly share my interactions with my essence language, Spirit and Nature (invaluable allies). These interactions will show you how easily you, too, can further empower yourself and deepen your trust in yourself and life. As you read through my experiences, you'll clearly see why complete self-trust is invaluable.

As you venture through the chapters, I invite you to notice which emotions you feel and observe them with an open heart and inquiring mind. Our emotions are powerful teachers, indicating what resonates with our true essences (divine souls) as well as what desires to be transformed. They give us the ability to understand ourselves with greater clarity.

Please also keep in mind that everything you read is from my perspective and based on my personal experiences. You don't have to accept or believe any of it. I encourage you (as I do with everyone) to always tune in or check with your inner knowing, to see what feels true to *you* about all information— *no* exceptions. Regardless of the source, information is *always* from someone else's perspective, so it's not necessarily true for you.

From my heart, I offer you this gift of sharing. May you experience *everything* that's possible for you on your sacred path!

We Are Sacred

**Every aspect of us ("weird" and all)
is a gift with possibilities.**

Let us accept truth, even when it surprises us and alters our views.
—George Sand

Everybody is a genius. But if you judge a fish by its ability to
climb a tree, it will live its whole life believing that it is stupid.
—Albert Einstein

Many of us grow up not knowing who we *really* are. We know who others think we are, or should be, and we know we're different than everyone else. We feel as if we don't fit in. We might even feel as if we've ended up on the wrong planet somehow or wonder why we're here.

However, we all gain the clarity of really knowing ourselves through life's ongoing journey. It's through our continuous daily experiences that we notice and remember our true essences—who we are at our divine spiritual cores—and discover our reason for being here on Mother Earth at this time.

Each one of us is a miraculous creation of the Divine and related through divine love. We're all connected through this sacred energy as part of one vast family, regardless of our physical forms.

We're also unique expressions of our Divine Creator. No two beings are created exactly alike. Anyone who knows the basics of astrology quickly realizes that we each have our unique soul blueprint. Its accuracy is astonishing! It clearly demonstrates how not one of us is like another: the way we think, feel, learn, and process things. We each have different tendencies: how we're inclined to evolve in this life, our unexplainable quirks and particular characteristics on all levels.

If we all learned the basics of this ancient science from a young age, we would have much less conflict with each other. We would be aware that we're simply all different for a reason. We are *meant* to have our own individuality—we were designed this way! We're here to shine who we are, peculiarities and all. No part of any of us is a defect or mistake. Every aspect has a beautiful reason for being, even if some reasons are less obvious and some aspects more questionable than others.

It's liberating to know that we're exactly as we are meant to be. It enables us to be at peace with our desires so we can also benefit the world in our own ways. We have different experiences, qualities, personalities, talents, and perspectives. Our gifts, skills, knowledge, wisdom, strengths, and attributes are a unique combination. There is a divine purpose for this. If our world didn't need each of us exactly as we are, we simply wouldn't exist here.

We also all have specific heart desires. They're within us to guide us to experience more of who we are. They invite us to discover, acknowledge, accept, and embrace every facet of our magnificent, true essences. Our heart desires act as catalysts. They are destinations that require us to embark on different inner and outer journeys. When we do, we get to know ourselves on a deeper level and realize that we're *so much more* than we thought we were.

The more you know and honour yourself and your true desires, the more possibilities you invite into your life. These support you to be the best you can be. Your sense of well-being and fulfillment expands, because you're able to contribute to the world as you were meant to, instead of as how others think you should. Ignoring and denying aspects of yourself creates disharmony on all levels. This is inevitable.

Every one of us also has a particular path that enables us to continuously evolve into greater expressions of who we are. We get to choose on a daily basis how much of our own path we desire to experience. No paths are alike, and there's great purpose to this. When we compare ourselves and our lives with others, especially in a self-deprecating way, we diminish ourselves. Having a clear sense of who we are enables us to honour our paths and feel fulfillment with our unique experiences. What feels like a leap of faith for one may feel natural for someone else or feel impossible for another. It's all perfect—no one is greater or lesser for it. We are here to learn and teach through experience. When we celebrate who we are, it's a beautiful act of loving appreciation to the Divine. Everyone feels that energy, and it benefits us all in more ways than we can imagine.

When we commit to simply being ourselves, we reclaim our natural state of being and our personal truth. An enormous amount of energy is liberated when we stop hiding parts of ourselves. Greater energy flows freely when we stop being or trying to be someone that others expect us to be. This shifts our energy in incredible ways, and we begin to notice an increase in synchronicities, opportunities, and different forms of abundance that support us on our journeys. Even when we shine just a little bit of our divine essences, others take notice.

It has taken me a long time to feel safe to be my true self regardless of where I am or who I'm with. Throughout my childhood, and even as an adult, I have drawn criticism, bullying, or accusations (from all sorts of people) for not being willing to conform to one thing or another. Rather than face judgment on a regular basis, I learned how not to attract attention. However, it seemed that even when I thought I was blending in, certain people always took notice. They made comments about my eyes and my smile. Throughout the years, more and more people seemed to naturally gravitate towards me, and I eventually realized I was never meant to fit in.

I'll never forget one time when I was just a teenager and I went to an annual festival with my family. During the teenage years I definitely did not want to stand out from the rest. At one point, we visited a tent where there were Native American dancers beautifully dressed in their traditional attire. The drumming instantly ignited my spirit, and the dancers mesmerized me. I listened to the drum beats and chanting with great joy. After several performances, the master of ceremonies announced that the dancers would each choose a volunteer from the crowd to join them onstage. They all found someone, except for one called a "grass dancer".

4

As the MC proceeded to look through the crowd, he suddenly locked eyes with mine. With a grin, he said into the microphone, "How would you like to join us up here, smiley?" All eyes turned towards me, and I just about died on the spot! I had always gone out of my way to avoid the spotlight, and I'd hated being the centre of attention. Now I not only was the focus of attention but I was also being invited onto the stage to dance with the group of performers! Since I didn't want to offend the dancer, I reluctantly accepted the invitation. Once up on that stage, however, I was amazed by how good it felt to dance to that drumming with the group. I just made sure I didn't look at the watching crowd, and I focused on my dance partner instead, fully enjoying myself.

Our paths of self-discovery always follow their unique courses, and the Divine applauds when we courageously decide to stand out as individuals—as we are meant to. Spirit is always more than willing to support us. Life continuously encourages us to see ourselves as we truly are beneath the layers of conditioning, expectations, and false identities, accumulated throughout the years since birth. As we recognize and peel away those layers, we reveal more and more of our true selves. We're never lost, we simply forget. Awareness helps us to remember.

Whenever you experience something that feels inspiring, uplifting, or blissful, it's an indication of your true essence resonating. When you take note of what resonates with you— through people, experiences, environments, etc.—it clarifies who you are as an individual. This is very powerful.

We broadcast who we are through our energy. The truer to our essence our energy's frequency, the more we attract people similar to us at the soul level. Nature demonstrates this beautifully. This is how plants attract their perfect pollinators, even when they're in the middle of "nowhere!" I observed this firsthand for seven years while living in the city. At the time, I had transformed my backyard's lawn into gardens of plants native to the area, and this is one of the greatest teachings I received from Nature. I was in absolute awe, every day, at how the tiniest butterflies and bees somehow found these plants in an urban environment. In a moment of clarity, I realized that it's all about energy. Plants broadcast their energy without reservation. They radiate who they are in the purest form. In doing so, they attract exactly who is looking for them, and they mutually benefit from this. It's a divinely brilliant system that works for everyone, since we're *all* energy beings, and energy has no boundaries.

The recent years have brought even greater numbers of circumstances and experiences into my life, enabling me to further discover and remember all aspects of my true essence. In embracing these opportunities, I've connected with those that I call my "soul family," who live all over this beautiful planet. These connections have been the key for me to gain the confidence to openly share who I am with others. Every year since 2007 I've been guided by Spirit, through my sacred heart's inner knowing, to join different mentorships and networks; to attend specific events, workshops, and courses; to become visible through different types of social media; and to travel to specific places. Thus I've connected with people that I feel an instant soul recognition with, whether we meet in person or otherwise. When we connect for the first time, it feels as if we've always known each other and we're actually experiencing a joyful reunion. We share a similar knowledge of reality, so we "speak the same language." We feel fully acknowledged and accepted in each other's presence (physical or virtual). We also celebrate and understand each other in ways that others can't. It's such a liberating gift!

While we're all part of one grand divine family, we do have a variety of people that we relate with in different ways throughout our lives, for reasons specific to our paths. Sometimes our interactions are very brief, and other times they last a good part of our time on Earth. These people can be teachers, acquaintances, co-workers, friends, family, mentors, and service providers, or they can be those that we relate with in more deeply significant ways.

One simple way to describe this dynamic is to imagine that we're each in a circle. We share our personal circle with others we feel a very strong connection with—a connection beyond logic. This is our soul family. It's our inner circle. Then there's another circle around this, like a ring. It includes people like friends and family that we connect with in special ways, but the ties feel less intense or direct than with those of our inner circle. Then a larger ring circles this one. It includes different people that we interact with, but to a lesser degree of connection than the previous circle. On and on, ever-growing rings surround our central, personal circle and continue to expand like ripples until they include our entire divine family—everyone in existence. We might never be aware of those we have a connection with past the first dozen rings; however, they *all* count. We're all interconnected, and we affect each other in more ways than we can imagine.

Every one of us has a soul family that belongs in that inner circle. These people make us feel fully empowered when we connect with them. It's our birthright to feel safe and free to be completely ourselves, without judgment. Our soul connections are invaluable. Knowing that we always have each other's loving support strengthens our sense of self-assurance. This enables us to then confidently be ourselves with anyone, in all situations. Through *all* connections, human and otherwise, and by spending quiet time within our sacred hearts, we deepen our understanding of ourselves. The more we do, the clearer is the energy that we broadcast.

Our true essences also all have some aspect that others would judge as being "weird." Anything that's different than what someone is familiar with or understands, is deemed as being weird—or, in some cases, as something to fear. We've been conditioned to feel this way. In general, we naturally judge everything and everyone in our awareness (usually unconsciously). To do otherwise requires diligent practice.

When we realize that we are being judged based on someone else's personal experience and *their* perspective, we're better able to not let it affect us. The more comfortable and confident we are with our "different" aspects, the less we broadcast them as being something not right. They are what uniquely defines us as ourselves. No part of us is meant to be hidden or ashamed of. We were meticulously created, with loving care and purpose. Regardless of who conceived us as parents, ultimately the Divine brought us into being. When we honour all that we are, simply by wholeheartedly being our genuine selves, we become radiant beacons of light for others. We allow them to feel safe to remove their false identities and courageously shine their authentic selves. The more of us who do this, the better our world is for it.

Until 2012, there was one aspect of myself that only a select few knew about. It's something very personal and actually indescribable. Most definitions pertaining to the mystical and mystics mention that it has to do with direct experience that can't be explained or described in any way. I fully agree. However, Spirit started guiding me to share this aspect of myself with soul family, as best I could. It felt like a giant stretch beyond my comfort zone, for it dealt with a sensitive subject. I didn't understand why I was being guided to do so. Yet, when I found the courage to share as I was guided, I discovered that many needed to hear my story, for various reasons! It surprised and empowered me to see the beneficial effects of my sharing; this is what Spirit wanted me to experience. Now I'm also sharing it with you as best I can.

Nothing is too weird about any of us. I've realized there's always a reason for every aspect that makes us who we are, even if we might not initially understand it. I never could have imagined, nor expected, what I suddenly experienced, seemingly out of the blue, one fateful evening.

On the 2010 winter solstice, I was still living in the city with my former husband. I was in the kitchen on the main floor of the house, preparing for a love-and-appreciation ceremony to honour All on this special day, including the beings of Nature residing in the snow-blanketed yard. No other person was with me.

I've never followed a religion or particular belief system. My spiritual way has always been based on what I feel and personally experience as a *knowing*. I've always simply practised love and appreciation from my heart and a sacred relationship with All (this has always been much easier with

9

Nature and Spirit for me, than with people). I've also created different inspired ceremonies and rituals for various occasions, usually on my own and sometimes with others. I eventually discovered that shamanism (see glossary for a full definition) best described my way of being.

As I stood in the kitchen, silently chopping different dried fruits, nuts, and seeds, I went into a light meditative state and tuned in to the energies of Nature and Spirit. After a while, I suddenly, and quite unexpectedly, felt an incredible wave of blissful energy flow through my base chakra, up to my crown chakra, and through my entire body, giving me what I can only describe as a full-body, cosmic orgasm! Every part of me felt "blissed-out," including my heart. It was a very different experience than a purely sexual orgasm. This was solely energetic, yet I also physically felt its effects profoundly throughout my entire body. It was extraordinary—expansively sublime beyond what words can describe. It was like the purest love energy; it felt so sacred. My heart overflowed and tears filled my eyes.

I had never heard of anything like this, probably due to being one of those things that you can't really describe—it has to be experienced. I felt it was best to keep it secret unless I was guided to do otherwise. I was well aware that anything related to sensuality and sexuality brought up different things for different people. Sexuality is something that has been intensely judged, condemned, and abused over the course of history, and it can trigger many different emotions, reactions, as well as controversy. Growing up in a highly religious family and community, with multiple organized religions within the family, I overheard and was told repeatedly that experiencing anything related to sexual or sensual pleasures (determined by the figures of authority) was sinful or even damnable. Despite that, I never agreed with this belief system myself, for my heart knew a different truth than this. My sacred connection with Nature and experiencing the Divine through it, had taught me something else.

All of Nature is sensual and sexual, and as humans we're no exception. We are creations of the Divine's love, and everything created from that love is sacred. We're *all* sensual and sexual beings by nature and were created this way with purpose. To be sensual and sexual is to fully experience life through all our senses (physical and spiritual). Innocent pleasures perceived in all ways are another means for us to directly experience the Divine in the physical forms that we've been given. To reject these aspects of ourselves is to reject our natural state of being and not accept all of who we are. We can't fully love ourselves if we believe that these parts of our nature are bad. This leads to ill-being from disconnection.

There is nothing more sacred on Earth than experiencing the Divine's gifts—our own divinity and that of others (human and otherwise)—through our human experiences. It's about experiencing everything from a place of divine love and taking the time to fully appreciate it all—our water and beverages, our foods, our bodies, our environments, our relationships, our activities, our co-creations, our connections with others of all races and species. In doing so, we realize that we're not separate from the Divine nor from each other—*we're all sacred.*

To selectively decide that it's shameful or sinful to experience certain things related to our own sensuality and sexuality is an insult to our divinely created existence. The creation of this belief system in recent history has denied people of many forms of direct, empowering connections with the Divine. Anything that has reminded people of their own divinity has been condemned. Even Nature became something to fear, dominate, and control; its sanctity was abandoned. This has caused people to forget their own divine interconnectedness with All and to think that a middleman has been the only way to reach the Divine. This, of course, has given the intermediaries all the power.

Denying our true nature and taking away its sanctity has caused an epidemic of dysfunctional and highly damaging obsessions, addictions, and behaviors. We see this everywhere, including among those in positions of authority. I know an astonishing number of women who have experienced some form of sexual abuse by family members, authority figures, or others they trusted. Many men have also experienced this type of abuse. Most of this abuse was experienced before these individuals reached the age of adulthood. So much healing— for the past, present, and future—is needed regarding this. Only by bringing the truth into our awareness and restoring the sacredness of it, can we begin to heal this on all levels, from individuals to nations.

You cannot change your divinely created true essence to fit what others consider to be 'right' or 'wrong'. While you can do your best to hide it, you are as you are regardless, and you are perfect in the eyes of the Divine.

As I was growing up, I always wondered why I was immersed in a belief system that felt so contrary to my true nature. I have always been highly aware of my sensual nature, regardless of my upbringing. I've always delighted in how feathers, rain, plant leaves, and sunlight felt on my bare skin … how the illuminated colours of a sunset changed like a living painting before my eyes … how the sweet scent of flowers danced in the faintest breeze and infused me … how soft mosses, warm sand, cool grass, and smooth stone felt beneath my bare feet … how the melodious songs of birds uplifted me no matter what I was feeling … how a heartfelt hug with another person felt mutually wonderful. I've always greatly enjoyed being immersed in the water of lakes and oceans, feeling my entire body unite with its flowing environment. I've always been a slow eater, savouring every bite of food and sip of beverages that I've ingested. The countless colours, forms, textures, scents, sounds, and flavours of our natural world have always highly pleased me. They're all direct, miraculous expressions of the Divine. Beautiful manmade creations born through divinely gifted talents and inspiration, including various works of art, music, gardens, meals, jewellery, furniture, etc., have also always highly pleased me. It's such a sacred gift for us to experience it all. When we do so with reverence, it's an act of appreciation to our Creator.

I've also had a keen awareness of my sexual nature from a very young age. Since anything related to sexuality was a taboo subject when I was growing up, I made sure I hid this aspect of myself. I learned a lot about sexuality from Nature itself (in its divine, innocent form—not people's defiled version of it). However, nothing in my awareness could explain the orgasms I began to experience when I was 10 years old. I couldn't ask anyone without risking possible punishment, and I didn't even know there was a word for these experiences until I went to university. I didn't become involved in a sexual relationship with a man until my university years.

Despite everything that was preached from my childhood days onward, I listened to my heart's truth. It made *no* sense to me that something as natural and innocent as those experiences was condemned by the religious figures of authority and those who believed them. Interestingly, I began hearing more and more stories that revealed how these figures of authority, throughout history and into the present, had committed horrific sexually related acts involving the innocent—despite what they preached. This validated my heart's inner knowing that no matter what others believe or say, our sacred hearts *always* know the truth (whether we choose to listen to them or not).

Due to my special relationship with Nature, I always remained in touch with my true nature and treated my sensuality and sexuality as something sacred. I just never imagined that one day I would experience something like what I did on that winter solstice. It seemed as if I had now been initiated into a more expansive level of myself—for things were never the same after that day.

Just over a week later, I was hiking on my parents' property in the country when I felt *called* by a beautiful red pine. This tree being was an uncommon species for that area, and it was nestled among jack pines, quite a distance from the trail. I had to trudge in thigh-high snow to get to it, but it was calling me strongly enough that I accepted the invitation. As I silently sat in the snow with my back against its trunk, simply observing my natural surroundings, I went into a state of deep relaxation. After a while, I felt a wave of beautiful love energy flow through my entire heart area from the pine. I consciously sent it my own love energy in return, which I also felt as a wave emanating from my heart. We shared a glorious exchange of love like this for some time; I physically felt it within my body's entire core area. I had never experienced this type of connection with a tree before—I felt so blessed to have received this gift so freely! Then I suddenly felt that same wave of blissful sacred energy like I had experienced on the solstice, flow through my body from the ground up! It was pure ecstasy!

In that moment, I received a teaching from this wonderful evergreen. I learned that tree beings are always in this state of blissful energy that I felt, for they are pure channels for the sacred energies of Mother Earth and Father Sky (our Sun and the Cosmos) that unite. It's a sacred union of flowing, pure love energy directly from the Divine. That's why trees are such pure healers. Anyone who walks through their immense aura fields or spends time with them feels the benefits from their energy. It's a well-researched and known scientific fact. As humans, we're also natural channels and healers ourselves, but our minds interfere with that powerful ability.

Since that solstice, this sacred love-energy experience has become a part of my life, highly enhancing gifts I had but didn't understand. While I've always sensed energies, this specific ability has been greatly amplified and continues to evolve and refine all the time, in unexpected ways. During the last months that I was writing the final chapter of this book, I experienced a whole other dimension of this gift, which continues to amaze me every day. An ability that used to be mainly a mystery to me has become invaluable and so important in ways I couldn't have imagined. It's among my most dominant senses now, including the physical senses. It had held the potential to be so much more all along and I was completely unaware of it! When the timing was divinely perfect and I was ready for it, Spirit ignited it. I was in a state of absolute love and appreciation when I received the manifestation of this sacred possibility.

A while after my solstice experience, I inquired with Spirit about my purpose in channelling this divine-love energy. I was told it was sufficient for me to know that, through me, it affects others' energies—people, all Nature beings, environments, etc.—in beneficial ways, whether we're aware of it or not. I'm like a lightning rod for this energy, to channel and transmit it in a more potent form on this earthly plane. I know there are other people who do this in ways unique to them. I found it interesting that my parents named me Lucille when I was born. It's a rare name for my generation and it means "light." I've always felt a strong connection with lightning and I actually feel this sacred energy even more intensely in the presence of lightning. Also, for years now, some people who've known me for decades have been asking me to send them my "Lulu vibes" when they need encouragement, positive energy, or healing. They've always reported favourable outcomes. I don't even remember how that got started, but it made me realize that I've always been involved in transmitting beneficial energy in some way or other, even when I wasn't consciously aware of it. The solstice initiation amplified it that much more.

Along our paths, life continuously reveals how every detail about us truly does matter. When you're able to connect the different aspects about yourself and your life like dots, you gain a greater perspective of who you are and understand why things have had to be this way. However, it's only by looking back that you see all the dots connecting. Experiences are the key to uncovering the more complete picture of who you are.

As I revisited my journals to include the stories in this book, I saw even more evidence that everything was purposeful and orchestrated by divine wisdom. It was just so amazing and confirming! When I was guided to connect with many more people in 2012, I realized that Spirit was right about the effects of me sharing my energy. Since then I've had so many people comment about how they perceive or experience it. It has affected them in various, beneficial ways—even from a distance. I can share it in person or virtually through writing, voice recording or video—those are simply different means for me to transmit my energy. When I do channel this sacred energy for conscious healing, I hold the intention in my heart that, with the Divine's guidance, it will travel with my love to where it is needed.

This was a significant example of sacred possibilities for me. I learned a valuable lesson about comparison. In my late teens, when I first became aware of intuitive abilities, I had felt that everyone I read about had more useful ones than I did. I tried to acquire abilities like theirs, and I ended up quite disappointed. I obviously wasn't meant to experience what they did. Now that my own abilities have developed and evolved, I feel blessed to have them. Each of us receives *exactly* what we require for our specific sacred paths.

I've seen from my own experiences and observations with so many, that the more you embrace your true essence and express it in everything you do, the more you allow yourself to experience your personal potential that wants to manifest. *This* is how you discover your gifts and divinely given purpose! While the process may take more time for you than it does for someone else, it's always perfect for each of us.

I've learned that if we're meant to have knowledge about something, we will receive it when the time is right for us. I've also learned that being impatient doesn't speed up the process one bit—even when we have the highest intentions! Every aspect of our beings is tailored for our unique paths and reveals its higher purpose with impeccable timing—governed by the Divine. There's always great wisdom at play, and everything is orchestrated with precision. None of it is redundant, and at some point it *will* make perfect sense. We just have to patiently trust the process.

Our sleep dreams can also teach us more about ourselves. They are like reminders guiding us on our paths. Some particular dream experiences feel very different than the usual ones. They have a different quality to them. When I have such dreams, they feel as real as my physical experiences when awake, and every detail is imprinted in me. Interestingly, many of my physical experiences become forgotten or dreamlike, whereas I never forget these special dream experiences, and they *always* open the door to so much more!

One night, in May of 2007, I had one of those vivid dream experiences. I suddenly found myself swimming in the ocean, at great speeds. I was leaping out, using what I realized was a dolphin tail to propel myself! I felt great joy as I leaped high above the waves and dove back into the water. Then, abruptly, I was walking in human form, in a forest of giant evergreen trees in a community of Native American people. A wise elder was serenely watching me from where he sat. I walked up to him, and he showed me a dolphin tattoo along the inside of his right forearm. It looked like a black line drawing. As he pointed a finger to it, he looked at me and said, *"You* are part of the Dolphin Clan." Then I woke up.

Months later I had another brief, profound dream experience. This time I found myself floating in the universe. Suddenly, I was in the presence of a radiant, luminescent female star being. She gracefully greeted me, forehead to forehead, and told me simply, "Your star name is *Aylani*." and then she vanished. I saw its spelling in my dream and then woke up. I felt guided to research this name on the Internet and was surprised to discover that it did exist on Earth and its origin was Hawaiian. (It was spelled with an *i* instead of the *y* that I had seen.) I also discovered that this method of greeting, forehead to forehead, was highly significant among Polynesian cultures. I was in awe.

With our dreams comes the awareness of certain things. After I had this dream, I began to notice dolphins showing up consistently in my physical environment, in the most unexpected ways. They were obviously making sure I paid attention. Months later, I suddenly felt guided one day to research the relationship between dolphins and the star system of Sirius. I had learned to not question my intuitive guidance, no matter how unusual it might seem. As I searched online, I simply allowed myself to go where I felt guided to go, with no conscious navigation. I discovered a woman who lived on the island of Hawai'i and she was organizing two weeks of swimming with wild dolphins in the Caribbean ocean, off a tiny island called Bimini! My soul quickened at the idea of doing this. I knew that if I was meant to go, I would receive clear guidance and everything would work out somehow. And against all odds, it actually did!

By the winter of that year, it became clear that I had to go. I knew it in my heart and had no doubt in my mind. However, it was understood at the corporate office where I worked that vacation in the summer months was strictly reserved for employees who had seniority of 25 years or more. I had 12 years of service, and since this dolphin experience was scheduled for the end of June and beginning of July, logically I would be completely wasting my money to book this trip. But I felt strongly that I had to do so, and the dolphins made sure I did. By this time, they were showing up in my life every day, in every way imaginable. I felt guided one day to look at flights on the Internet and discovered a seat sale—with dolphins advertising something in the sidebar of the website. I booked my flight and then reserved my space for the dolphin journey of two weeks. I had *no idea* how everything would work out, but I felt so excited! I had always felt a loving connection with dolphins, and just the thought of seeing wild dolphins in the ocean—never mind swimming freely with them in their natural environment—felt so very special to me. I also appreciated that the organizers were so respectful of these magnificent beings and all ocean life. I was more than happy to support their work.

Then a series of unanticipated events occurred at work, enabling me to apply for a job with the government. Due to jobs being abolished and rearranged within the corporation, I had felt for some time that I would need to change jobs. A woman I knew at the office ended up working in my department for a few weeks to substitute for someone on vacation. She sat only a few desks away from me, and she overheard me mention that I was looking for another job (I wasn't hiding it). One of her close friends happened to be high up in the government and was looking to fill bilingual positions in her department—which I happened to qualify for! Under regular circumstances, I would never have been able to apply for this job. However, because of my co-worker's connection and the fact that she knew me personally, I was able to easily get around the regulations and submit my resume.

I passed all the required tests and the interview, and by the beginning of 2008 I was handing in my resignation and starting a new job! I had been a corporate customer service representative and was now going to be a governmental information officer (still working in a downtown office and assisting clients every day). The best part of getting this new job occurred during the hiring process. I mentioned that I had an important trip already booked for the summer and would require those two weeks off. I was granted this request without question! Everything just flowed and worked out so miraculously—better than I could have ever imagined! It was phenomenal. I was bursting with love and gratitude!

Since I like to journal, I desired a special notebook for this trip. I discovered one on the Internet that had a metallic photograph of the face of a dolphin on it. It was perfect, except for the shipping costs, which were three times more than the journal itself! I felt I just had to notify the company that I loved this journal but wouldn't purchase it because of the shipping fee. A customer service representative replied to my email and asked for my mailing address, which I provided. Within a week I found this journal in my mailbox as a gift from the company! I expressed my joyful appreciation to them. What a wonderful surprise! Now I was all set—snorkelling gear, fins, and all.

This experience with the wild dolphins was so profound. The first day I went in the ocean I was mesmerized by just how magickal it felt to effortlessly swim with my fins in such buoyant, warm, clear, turquoise-blue water, with no land in sight! It felt as if I were in a universe of crystalline water and sunrays—so awe-inspiring! As instructed, I swam leisurely near the surface with my arms respectfully to my sides. I was looking through my mask and breathing through my snorkel when I heard the clicks and squeaks of many vocalizing dolphins. One moment I couldn't see them, and the next moment I was suddenly surrounded by a pod of beautiful Atlantic spotted dolphins!

They swam so close to me, some only inches away, that I felt as if I were part of the pod. They all made eye contact as they slowly and gracefully came from behind and passed me. I was spellbound by their presence and agility. Then the three oldest dolphins of the pod (they had the most spots on them) turned around a few yards away from me and floated motionlessly side by side at the surface, facing me. As they did so, they looked so deeply into my eyes that I felt they were seeing me at the soul level. I felt so much pure love flowing to me from them, it touched me to the core. Then, one by one, they swam slowly towards me and passed by me again, maintaining eye contact and almost touching me. I felt so honoured, welcomed, and profoundly moved by this experience. My heart burst wide open and overflowed with absolute love for these magnificent beings. I felt my connection with them even more deeply. When I surfaced and pulled off my mask, I realized that my salty tears tasted like the ocean water. We're all so interconnected.

I made beautiful heart connections not only with the dolphins but also with precious soul family—it felt like a reunion of many. I had clearly been meant to go there at that specific time. At one point I treated myself to a massage. During this treatment, I unexpectedly remembered the fall of Atlantis, experiencing it as one who had been there. Instead of drowning, I had actually shape-shifted into a dolphin being and had dolphin spirit guides with me throughout this memory vision. I released so much deep grief related to that experience that I hadn't even known was within me. On one of the nights on that small tropical island, I also experienced a very intense thunderstorm, with spectacular lightning. As the group left the island on the last day, I saw a beautiful rainbow (also very significant to me). My journey there ended up catapulting me into a new level of self-discovery and remembering, on multiple levels. Had I dismissed those significant dreams and the intuitive guidance that led me to this experience, my life would have been very different. This opportunity was a gift orchestrated by many, seen and unseen.

When you acknowledge everything about yourself (even the most seemingly "bizarre") and act according to *your* personal truth, magick unfolds on your path so you can experience and be everything you're meant to.

Honouring our individuality also means that our personal relationships are as unique as we are. We're here to experience life to the fullest. Personal relationships, with ourselves, others and those of union between two individuals, offer us incredible opportunities for personal growth. They offer unique learning experiences. When we treat our relationships with others as sacred soul contracts between two unique individuals, it enables us to honour these journeys together with awareness and without judgment. Relationships of union are also not meant to fit a mold of expectations dictated by others. How we choose to celebrate a union doesn't make it more or less significant than what others might deem to be acceptable. It doesn't matter what it looks like or how long it lasts—each union can be sacred when we hold that intention in our hearts. It's not dependant on others' approval. While our relationships of union play highly significant roles, all relationships are invaluable to our personal evolution. Awareness enables us to make the most of these connections.

One morning in 2012, I was contemplating what it means to be individual souls who are also part of a greater whole—a family that is much vaster than we can comprehend. I was to be involved in an event and asked Spirit what would be a good analogy to share with those present that evening. I received the vision of a vast, sunny landscape covered by a blanket of freshly fallen snow. The white snow was twinkling like millions of radiant diamonds, reflecting sparkles of rainbow colours (light in its purest form contains all the colours of the rainbow). Then I was shown individual snowflakes, and I admired the perfection of each one. Crystals that are so intricately detailed with no two alike—that is a miracle in itself.

As individuals, we're just like the snowflakes that are created from the same source. We're miracles of magnificence unique to each of us, yet all related through that same Creator. We also all have something special to contribute here on Earth, for our inner light shines more visibly and more brightly when we connect with each other somehow. Every connection we make refines who we are and gives us the opportunity to be our best. This allows us to shine our diamond essences, which are pure, divine love-light. Snowflakes on their own don't sparkle the way they do when they're with many more, just as I saw in that landscape. When we connect with each other through our loving sacred hearts, we all shine more brilliantly and create together a world of incomparable beauty.

The Messy and the Miraculous

Our hearts always defy the "impossible".

Love and desire are the spirit's wings to great deeds.
—Johann Wolfgang von Goethe

Darkness cannot drive out darkness; only light can do that.
Hate cannot drive out hate; only love can do that.
—Martin Luther King Jr.

At every moment we make decisions. We choose either love or fear, empowerment or disempowerment, trust or doubt, our own desires or someone else's, faith or worry, possibilities or impossibilities. The choice is always ours, and it's not always easy to make. The choice that feels right, is often the most difficult one to make.

We can't know what we're actually capable of or what life is really like if we don't step outside our familiar spaces—and that requires courage. Our courage comes alive when we step over the boundaries of our comfort zones and leave behind what our minds feel is secure. Our heart desires continuously invite us to do just that. We all have what can be described as divinely connected, sacred hearts, intimately linked to our essences and to Spirit. Our hearts have access to higher knowledge and guidance as well as desires aligned with our unique purposes. They always know what's true to our souls' paths, regardless of our emotional states and physical circumstances.

Sometimes our hearts call us to do something that feels absolutely impossible. It hurts just to think about it. We might successfully ignore it for a while, but it only makes things become slowly unbearable. Eventually, it becomes more painful than the fear itself. When we make the decision to honour that call and embrace the journey of the unknown—no matter how terrifying it might feel—we discover what's possible.

Towards the end of 2010, my way of life began to reach its completion point. Through a series of eye-opening incidents in every area of my life, I clearly realized that the apparently perfect status quo was unfortunately based on controlling conditions and superficial expectations, instead of being based on love. Everything was conditional, regardless of how much I had wholeheartedly invested of myself in every aspect of that life. What had been a dream come true almost a decade earlier had slowly evolved in the opposite direction of where I knew I had to keep going, to keep my commitment to my sacred path. Due to multiple factors, conditions had become damaging instead of empowering. It was truly heartbreaking.

It became painfully obvious that I had to take full responsibility for my own well-being. Every aspect of this life no longer supported my love-centred values and desires at all. I felt profoundly disappointed, for my job, husband, and home had all resulted from incredible chains of events that only the Divine could have orchestrated. All my heart desires had manifested then, even better than I could have imagined. Clearly they had all been necessary at that time in my life. I just had never considered that they were not meant to last for the rest of my life. Because of this, I had believed that somehow things would get better if I held on just a bit longer—and I held on to that hope for as long as I could, mostly for the sake of our families. Things got worse, however, in every way possible, and I had to see the situation for what it was. What used to fill me with loving joy now only filled me with great heartache.

By early 2011 I knew without a doubt that that chapter of my life had served its sacred purpose and had reached completion. I realized that, as painful as it was, everything was actually working out exactly as it was supposed to. I didn't have evidence of this, yet I knew it in my heart. It was time for me to leave it all behind: the security of my government job, my marriage, my home, and the city! While all the signs confirmed this to me, just the thought of it felt overwhelming, to say the least. The most difficult thing for me was the sorrow I felt for having to leave a family that was dear to me and for the hearts that would break. Fortunately, we didn't have children together. I felt so very grateful for that. My energy level had reached its lowest point ever—physically, emotionally, and mentally. For the first time in my life, my excellent health took a plunge. This was actually a gift, for it clearly showed me how things really were. I knew that by choosing to honour my true essence and sacred path I was also honouring my husband Adam, and his chosen path.

Now that I knew what I had to do, I was desperate for a solution. To avoid a worst-case scenario and prevent further stress, I chose to not tell anyone—not until I had a plan. I could have chosen the typical path that would have served my own needs and provided me with a lot of money in more ways than one. However, after a lot of deep contemplation within my heart, I chose what felt best for everyone involved, trusting that somehow things would work out for me. Since we had always done things our own way (despite others' expectations), Adam and I had never had a typical marriage ceremony and never exchanged vows nor signed papers that bound us to each other. We were considered a common-law marriage. This was now a blessing—we could part after nine years without having to go through a divorce process. That greatly simplified things. Yet, if I was to leave the way that I felt was best for both of us, I knew I couldn't do it on my own. I needed a tremendous miracle from the Divine to achieve the desired outcome. It was one that I couldn't even imagine myself.

Before I resigned from work, I went on stress leave (without pay). I spent time daily in a local park filled with majestic cottonwood trees, so I could commune with Nature and Spirit, and freely be me. Every morning, when I did my ritual of love and gratitude to All, I asked Spirit for a solution that would benefit everyone involved. I received signs, which I recognized as encouragement, from my personal essence language. The numbers 33, 333, and 11:11 and rainbows became prevalent, appearing almost daily wherever I was. I also requested extra support to get me through this time, since I had never felt so alone.

I gradually became aware of the presence of the radiant light being known to many as Archangel Michael. He was supporting me with unconditional love and giving me the strength, courage, and hope that I so needed. This was a new experience for me. It seemed that as soon as I chose to honour my well-being in all ways and to fully commit to what my path required of me, it caused a significant shift. I had been initiated into channelling that blissful divine-love energy on the winter solstice, and from then on my intuitive abilities had quickly evolved. This enabled me to perceive much more beyond the physical plane than I could before. This expanded awareness was such an unanticipated blessing.

I felt guided to go through and organize all my things. I went through my collection of books, mostly non-fiction accumulated over the years, and donated half of my personal library. I kept the ones that were absolute favourites. I went through years of paperwork, shredding and filling many garbage bags for recycling. As I was sorting piles of papers one day, four beautiful monarch butterfly wings fell to the ground beside me! They must have been between some of the papers I was sorting. I often collected treasures that I found during my time spent in Nature. The monarch was a very significant symbol to me, so seeing those wings made me feel reassured and empowered. I pasted them in a journal so I wouldn't lose them. I also went through my personal belongings and donated a lot of them to different charities. I had done this to a lesser degree in previous years to prevent an accumulation of "stuff". That annual practice now enabled me to take these steps towards leaving without alarming anyone. I still did not know whether I'd be able to leave, but it felt good, while I maintained my focus on that desire for a great miracle.

It eventually reached a point where I felt I might lose all hope. Then, suddenly, my heart desire was unexpectedly answered in the most extraordinary way, in April of that year! Unbeknownst to me, a string of events had been divinely orchestrated during the past four months for this miracle to manifest the way it did. I realized with absolute amazement that so much had been going on behind the scenes on my behalf!

The previous December I had attended a crystal-healing certification course, after being on a waiting list for over a year. The first evening of the class, I arrived 30 minutes too early, as did another young woman—we'd both been told the wrong time. This was her first time attending something like this. I was surprised that she'd made it in, since the roads were very icy and she lived an hour's drive from the city. For some reason, I sat right next to her in that room of two dozen empty chairs. Normally I would have left some space between us, since I was sensitive to energy. However, this was different. We both felt an instant kinship, and we ended up talking until class started. It became clear that we had a very special soul connection— we were soul sisters. We discovered that we shared amazing synchronicities, one having to do with the farm I was raised on. When I was a teenager, my family sold the farm, which included two houses, to an immigrating British family. When Anna and her family immigrated to Canada shortly after that, of all the places they could have chosen in this large country, they came to live on that farm with their British friends! Most people I'd met over the years had never heard of the municipality where I grew up, never mind the actual farm. We were astounded and knew it was significant somehow, not mere "coincidence".

Then one day in April, when I was focused on receiving a miraculous solution, Anna suddenly told me that her parents' rental house (which neighboured her own home in the country) had mysteriously become vacant without notice. The tenants hadn't even told her parents—they'd simply moved out. Since she knew how much I loved vast environments of Nature and missed it in the city, she offered me the house as a "'Nature getaway" during weekends until someone moved in. Anna had no idea about my situation or my desire.

In that moment, I had a sudden clear knowing in my heart that *this* was my miraculous solution! I asked her what the monthly rent was, and it astonished me—with everything included it was less than what I spent bi-weekly on groceries! It also had wonderful well water, which was priceless to me. I asked if her parents would be willing to rent it to me as my home. Because of our connection, her parents gave me priority over other interested prospects. I didn't even feel the need to see the house first—I just *knew* without a doubt that I was receiving my greatly needed miracle. I suddenly felt so relieved and deeply grateful.

When I told Adam about this home, he could not believe I had found a place like that, and he stated matter-of-factly, "That's impossible." Yet it wasn't. And actually, I hadn't found it. *It had found me*, through the Divine's intervention and the guidance of many. And then more miracles followed.

I packed only what fit into a medium-sized U-Haul truck, leaving many things behind. I had never driven a truck before, never mind one this size. I couldn't even adjust the seat nor see anything in the blocked rear-view mirror, but my determination was stronger than my fear. I just knew that I had the support and protection of Spirit and I would be fine. Although it was a day of torrential downpours, it didn't rain during the time that my belongings were packed and then unpacked over an hour later! My dear soul sister met me along the way to guide me to my new home. Anna was an invaluable angel of support at that time in my life. I felt eternally grateful for her.

When I finally stepped inside that old two-story house for the first time, it felt like an outer reflection of how I felt inside. It needed a lot of transforming love and appreciation. It felt good to have a brand-new place to call home. I told the "spirit of the place" that as long as it took care of me, I would take care of it. I suddenly felt guided to open the door of one of the kitchen cupboards. When I did, I knew with certainty that I was exactly where I was meant to be at that time. Adam had a single draft glass of clear glass that was my favourite to use for all beverages. I had chosen to leave it behind with him. Now, facing me on a shelf in that kitchen… was a single glass *exactly* the same—not even as part of a set, just *one*! I stared at the glass with absolute astonishment and picked it up to make sure it was real. It felt like a home-coming gift and clear sign from Spirit, to let me know that everything was working out exactly as it should be. I was indeed following the right path—my sacred path—which meant that my difficult decision had been made for the highest good of everyone involved (regardless of what others might initially have thought or felt about it). I overflowed with loving appreciation for this wonderful, and so unexpected, confirmation.

After I told everyone about my drastic life change, I received many donations from family, friends, and my wonderful new landlords. They gave me appliances and furniture to completely furnish the house, as well as curtains and other useful household items. The main floor had a large kitchen and dining area, a bathroom and two living rooms. The upper floor had two bedrooms. Life was so abundant, and I felt so grateful! I was even able to buy primer and paint in lieu of the first month's rent, and I transformed the *entire* house. I covered the dirty-white colour of every wall, cupboard, and fridge in rich, vibrant colours. I gave every room a different theme and energy, so enjoying this creative and physically demanding endeavor. The month-long process assisted me in releasing all the deep emotions I was feeling and allowed me to grieve at the deepest level, so I could move forward with clear energy.

Once the house transformation was complete, all that was missing was a sofa. I had painted the living room a warm-purple colour, and I envisioned a copper-orange, Victorian-style velvet sofa to go in that room. It would complement a goddess painting I had with those vivid colours in it. I had left behind my black sofa set—I now craved colour. Shortly after deciding what type of sofa I desired in my living room, I felt guided to browse a local website that worked like an online garage sale. As I did, I was absolutely amazed to discover a sofa and matching armchair that were *exactly* what I desired, even including rows of velvet buttons on the backs and arms! They were in excellent condition for only $130. The couple was selling them to make space in their basement and lived in the city, conveniently close to the highway. Anna borrowed her parents' truck and off we went to get my "new" furniture. The sofa set fit in perfectly—that room looked so regal and complete with it, I couldn't stop smiling at the magick of it all! Every single thing I had brought with me had found its perfect place and purpose in that house.

My new home felt like an oasis to me. Friends and family who visited later, commented on how good they felt in that house, with its wonderful, peaceful, and nurturing energy. By completely transforming the house with love and appreciation, I also transformed myself. It was profoundly healing. It was a divine gift that was perfect beyond anything I could have hoped for myself.

Another deep heart desire also manifested in the process of this miracle. The house was on beautiful rural property surrounded by forest and clearings. It had large windows that faced every direction, letting in a lot of sunshine and allowing me to see so much wildlife. Being over 100 years old, it had been built flush with the ground, so even indoors I felt like I was a part of the forest. Magnificently large trees, like oaks, elms, and balsam firs, stood protectively around the house. Interestingly, many were marked by lightning. The place felt so sacred and very powerful with energy. I was now immersed in Nature which my heart had yearned for over so many years!

I even had a pair of great horned owls that spent time from dusk until dawn in the large trees around the house, calling out near my second-floor bedroom window. This remarkable species of owl became one of my primary spirit guides (a power animal), along with its diurnal counterpart, the red-tailed hawk. The hawk even spent time in my bird bath one day—it was so impressive, standing only a few feet away from me! The strong presence of these power animals, represented in their physical forms, felt so comforting to me. They were like special guardians, night and day. I also had my soul sister Anna and her wonderful family as my perfect neighbours; this included children and various pets full of sweet, loving joy.

My new-home situation opened me to learn great teachings on multiple levels, including my first important lesson of being fully open to receiving. Having always been a natural giver and ultra-independent person, I found this a tough one to learn. However, along my journey through the unknown, I learned what an invaluable lesson it was. Anna and I also became significant teachers to each other in ways we hadn't anticipated. I discovered that I was also an answered heart desire for her. As with other soul family members, it was obvious that on a soul level, we had arranged for this before we incarnated. We were a mutual blessing in each other's life. I felt incredibly blessed and so liberated. For the first time in my life, I lived in a home and environment that resonated with me in all ways. It fully supported my true essence so it could freely emerge and express itself. This more than made up for all I had left behind.

A year later, when people started asking me about the seemingly impossible manifestations that I had experienced in my life, I reflected on the fact that I'd received one of my greatest miracles when I was at my absolute lowest level of energy. I certainly hadn't been feeling vibrant with positive energy or radiant with higher frequencies at that time, nor was I able to visualize anything. This seemed contrary to the laws of manifestation that I had been hearing about. It seemed like a miracle in itself that I had received my heart's desire. Clearly, nothing was impossible where miracles were concerned.

When I inquired with Spirit to better understand how this great miracle had manifested under those circumstances, I was lovingly reminded about the power of our sacred hearts. Despite everything, my desire and intention were always from my heart and firmly rooted in love. I was letting my heart lead instead of my mind or ego. Even though I felt at my absolute worst, my heart still held and radiated the high frequency of love like a vortex—which manifests miracles. I also allowed the Divine to create this miracle for me. Instead of trying to figure out a solution on my own, I fully surrendered the situation to Spirit and asked that the outcome be for the highest good of all involved. I also had absolute faith that this was possible. I was told by Spirit that had I chosen a different alternative (which most people felt I should have for financial compensation), the result would have been less than desirable. I was reminded that ultimately the Divine has the final Word on everything, regardless of what "laws" we believe exist. Everything in existence is governed by the Divine and can be changed at will, instantly.

Nature itself demonstrates the power of love. The existence of everything natural, including every living being that originated from tiny seeds, is a miracle. We, as human beings, are also miracles. By nature, we're meant to do things that defy logic every moment that we're alive. We're all co-creators of miracles. We've all been created by divine love—the substance of our sacred hearts. This love makes everything possible. It links us as humans with all other beings, including Spirit. It also allows us to connect with greater depth and transparency with each other. It's a far-reaching energy that has no boundaries. It creates infinite potential for our world.

We never know what's *really* going on. For the most part, we have a limited perspective on this physical plane and can't see the full picture of our experiences with others. This does have its divine purpose. However, when we shift from a perspective of judgment to one of love, empathy, and curiosity, the bigger picture does reveal itself, in unexpected ways. When we dare to open our hearts to others, human and otherwise, we energetically invite them to do the same. While not everyone accepts this invitation, more often than not our silent invitation is received. When we do this without expectation, we also allow ourselves to expand on a personal level and experience more of life's wonders.

In 2007 I was working for a large international corporation, in a huge office downtown. There was a particular employee who no one wanted to work with. Sam didn't do his share of the work, and others had to work more to make up for this. No one addressed the issue, but instead everyone talked behind his back. When his co-worker went on vacation for a month, I ended up working with him as a substitute. Everyone made sure I knew about his reputation. Because of my own experiences of feeling misunderstood, judged, and rejected when I was growing up, I had always given people the benefit of the doubt, regardless of what others might say. I was aware that there was always more to a person or situation than meets the eye.

I personally knew Sam as an eccentric fellow and had had many interesting conversations with him during lunch breaks. However, I had never worked directly with him before, and after a week of doing so, I realized why everyone said what they did. My stressful workload quickly became considerably larger than his every day. It didn't take long before I was out of patience with him. I had always despised gossip, avoiding it as much as I could, so I kept this to myself. Instead, I started wondering how I could best handle this situation in a way that would benefit both of us. I wanted to treat Sam like the adult that he was rather than having a manager talk to him like a child. I didn't feel that telling a manager would solve anything—it could actually make things worse.

On the second Monday morning, after a week of working with him, I noticed once again that he wasn't doing any work, while I was already overwhelmed by the workload. Monday was always the busiest day of the week. I could feel my blood pressure rising—which rarely happened. Before I got angry and did or said something I might regret, I took a little break from incoming calls and breathed deeply, tuning in to my heart. I asked Spirit how I could approach this delicate situation so that it benefited both of us, if possible. Feeling calmer, I suddenly just knew what to do. I turned around to face him, addressed Sam by his name, and simply asked in a nice tone of voice, as though I were asking a friend, if he thought he could help me with the work that morning. I added that I would greatly appreciate it. I kept it lighthearted and asked with curiosity rather than accusation.

Since we worked in open-cubicle work spaces, I could almost feel all ears in the area tuning in to what I had said. Everyone within proximity was waiting with anticipation for drama to unfold. What resulted instead was a surprise to us all. His reaction was so unexpected. He seemed startled out of his own world, looked at me with surprise, sincerely apologized, and went immediately to work! I later sincerely thanked him and explained that I couldn't handle the stressful workload on my own. He said he fully understood—and Sam was a wonderful co-worker with me from that day forward! We were able to work well together and even enjoyed each other's company. It was quite amazing. People were also very impressed by how I had handled the situation, saying they would have strangled him instead. I would have preferred that no one witnessed it, but in that office setting there wasn't another option without making a big deal about it. The day after I had addressed the issue with him, he confided something personal to me that fully explained the behavior that had been driving everyone crazy. I realized it had taken effort for him to help me out first thing when he arrived at work, and I felt even more appreciation for him.

What surprised me even more about this situation was that a month after it occurred, I saw a friend who was highly psychic. I hadn't told anyone about what had happened with that co-worker, yet she described how I had recently transformed a lot of karma between me and a co-worker. She described him perfectly, so I knew who she was talking about. She proceeded to tell me that in the past we had shared a life in ancient Egypt, where we had both been slaves. We had been part of a group of workers who were building a large temple with bricks. In that life, he had always done less work than the rest of the group, so I had covered up for Sam to prevent him from being punished. Unfortunately, we had been found out, and as a result we had both been punished by death.

I was astonished, for we now had found ourselves in a very similar situation in modern-day life! However, by nicely asking him to do his share of the work instead of covering up for him or reporting him to a manager, I had unknowingly cleared up that karma for both of us. I had actually felt the energy shift in a significant way between us when that happened—as if a density between us had lifted and the energy had become clear. The negative tension had transformed into positive harmony.

Simply being aware that previous lives are possible, or that there's more to our existence than this current life, can give us a much greater perspective about the relationships we have. Regardless of the type of relationship, our awareness can explain certain dynamics that we can't explain with logic. This enables us to handle certain situations differently. Our hearts and Spirit always guide us to connect for a reason and their language isn't based on logic.

It made so much sense to me to hear that my experience was related to more than the present circumstances. I realized on a deeper level how our relationships are much more complex than we can imagine—and why that is. My unexpected situation with this co-worker was an opportunity to clear the energy between us. When we did so, it completely changed the dynamics between us—for the better.

When I later resigned from that company, I was so touched by the loving surprise farewell I received on my last day. So many that I had worked with in different departments gathered at my desk to share hugs. They had all contributed towards purchasing a very thoughtful card, which had monarch butterflies on it(!), and beautiful gifts, as well. I also discovered that the one who had organized it, and gone shopping on behalf of everyone, was Sam himself! It made it even more special for me to know this. There's something indescribable about the feeling that fills you when you realize that you've touched others in a meaningful way, simply by living from your heart. While I've never seen him since I resigned from that company, it all felt perfect to me. The purpose of us working together had been fulfilled.

We just never know how we might affect others and ourselves when we act from love. We're continuously encountering situations that give us the opportunity to act from a divine place within our hearts. Opportunities can be challenging to different degrees. However, when we do choose love, the beneficial effects are more far-reaching than we can imagine, including on a personal level. Even if I hadn't heard that past-life story from my friend regarding Sam, the result from our interaction in the present time would have been immensely rewarding in itself.

Often, when we choose love, we also discover the true meaning of courage. Courage can show up when we least expect it. It's a force that moves through us to accomplish something we never imagined we could.

Courage is experienced when you have a sudden desire to do something that might feel challenging or even impossible but you commit to it anyway, focusing on your heart's intention instead of the odds against you. You no longer think about yourself but about what must be done, and this is only possible through love.

In 2002 I did volunteer work in Costa Rica as an intern for a sea turtle restoration project. I not only managed the project with another intern but was also in charge of other volunteers who came to work with us. I worked for a dear friend, Raul. He was the Latin American director of a foundation with several projects like the one on which I was working. Most volunteers came for two weeks or longer at a time. However, Raul's nephew came only for a short visit, from a city in the United States. Luis was slightly older than I was, and he loved adventure.

The small village where we lived was literally at the end of the road, which terminated in the far southern tip of Costa Rica's rainforest. The nearest phone was a two-hour bicycle ride on sandy or muddy roads, and the nearest hospital was three hours by vehicle, including a river ferry crossing. The village had one vehicle only. Despite its remoteness, there was a rental house for tourists at the far end of the small village, owned by Europeans. It was for travellers who wanted a vacation off the beaten path. They also rented two-person sea kayaks and allowed the volunteers to borrow them when they were not in use.

One day, Luis decided to go sea kayaking. Since most of our work was during the night, we had a lot of free time during the day. I hadn't been kayaking yet, so he invited me to go with him. I was more than happy to join him, except for one thing—we couldn't find any life jackets. We couldn't even find any type of flotation device to bring with us! I was dumbfounded. The owners weren't around that day to ask about this. I knew that going out on the open ocean, or even a lake, without any of those was not an intelligent thing to do. It was even less intelligent when I knew that the ocean was highly unpredictable and had strong tides. I knew with every ounce of common sense within me that we shouldn't go out on the ocean unless we could find something to help us float if we fell in. Yet there was also an adventurous side to me that wanted to go out on the ocean that day. Luis figured that the kayak was a good flotation device in itself. Since the sky was clear and the waves were tame-looking past the rocky coral near the shore, I let him talk me into it. My parents had given me a small golden angel pin as a gift for my trip. So before we left, I securely fastened it at the hip of my two-piece bathing suit. Luis sat at the front of the large sea kayak, and I sat at the back.

We happily paddled together through the surf and out to the ocean, where the view was breath-taking. I was able to see the beautiful landscape from the sea turtles' perspective for the first time since I had arrived. The sun was shining above, and on one side of us was the shore of coral, sandy beach, and palm trees, while on the other side was the vast Pacific Ocean that spanned far beyond the horizon. I suddenly felt so grateful to have accepted Luis' invitation. We kayaked for a while, fully enjoying the experience at our leisure.

When we decided to return to the shore as the high tide began to move in, everything was going smoothly. Suddenly, out of the blue ocean, I saw a big wave coming towards us like a shallow, rolling wall! I instantly felt that this was definitely *not* a good thing. We were quite a distance from the shore. We manoeuvred the kayak to try and stay as aligned as possible with the wave, so it wouldn't hit us sideways. The wave grew larger and larger until it suddenly hit us with such a force that it sent Luis and his paddle flying off the kayak and into the ocean. I was absolutely astonished, for I somehow remained firmly seated on the kayak, as if pinned down, and literally surfed this giant wave all the way to the shore! The other intern and a volunteer had seen everything from the beach. I saw horror on their faces when we heard Luis screaming between waves far out in the ocean. I didn't even think—I snapped out of my state of shock and reacted to his pleas for help. It was obvious to me that I had to go get him or he would drown, for I was the only one in a position to do so.

Since I was only five feet two inches tall and weighed around 100 pounds, the odds were against me. However, I managed to turn around the bulky sea kayak in the waves of the shore, and then I paddled it alone against the incoming waves without tipping over, all the way up to a terrified and flailing man. When I reached him, he grabbed onto the kayak and immediately tipped me over! I asked for the protective presence of the Divine and archangels to get us safely back to the beach. We hung onto the kayak as I talked to Luis to calm him down enough so we could both get back on. Thankfully, I had managed to hold on to my own paddle. After a while of floating with the waves and spitting salt water, we were able to clumsily get back on. Since I was the only one with a paddle now, and he was in shock, I had to paddle the kayak up to the beach, without capsizing. I actually managed to do so. When we arrived, we both collapsed on the sand with exhaustion and absolute relief. Everything felt so surreal.

When we recovered, he looked at me squarely in the eyes and was silent for a while. He then told me I had saved his life and sincerely thanked me multiple times. After another moment of silent contemplation, he told me that what I had done was impossible—he couldn't understand how I had done it. I knew without a doubt that I hadn't been alone. I couldn't have accomplished it without some form of Divine intervention. I simply told him I had had the assistance of many angels. I had always felt strongly protected, and that day I'd felt a strong, invisible force come to our assistance. My heart had called out and the Divine had answered. I was eternally grateful for that miracle.

When we act from a place of pure love, there's no limit to what we can manifest, in partnership with Spirit. I've experienced this so many times over the course of my life that it has become a personal truth. I don't just believe it, I know it.

The Magick of Receiving

Spirit delights in giving beyond our wildest dreams.

Everything for me is sacred, beginning with earth,
but also going to things made by man.
—*Paulo Coelho*

Look deep into nature, and then you will understand everything better.
—*Albert Einstein*

Most of us have experienced some form of heart trauma in our lives. This causes our hearts to enclose themselves in a protective shield to prevent further pain. Unfortunately, this armor also prevents us from experiencing all that our sacred hearts desire for us, including embracing who we truly are.

Many of us have been taught by others to expect that life is against us and to be suspicious of anything "too good to be true." We're taught to focus on limitations and worst-case scenarios instead of possibilities and positive outcomes. This causes us to constrict with fear, instead of opening up, expanding, and allowing.

We co-create daily with every choice that we make. Being willing to open our hearts and minds—even just a little bit—to something different, invites the abundance of the greater possibilities that are continuously being created for us. These include opportunities, connections, miracles, magick, synchronicities, wonders, and guidance. If our hearts, our minds, or both, are closed to what's possible in this world, we can't receive the wealth of possibilities that are available to us at all times.

I've always had a different view than most and unknowingly have practised an easy and safe way to open the heart and mind. Expressing loving gratitude on a daily basis has always been my way. It's how I begin every day. This combines the awareness of the mind with the emotion within the heart. It's as simple as noticing and acknowledging all that we have and feeling love and appreciation for it all—those we cherish (human and non-human), Spirit, Nature and all who support our way of life. This includes our nurturing Mother Earth, protective Father Sky, life-giving sunlight, air, and water, our bodies, food, homes, clothing, material possessions, environments, suppliers of products and services we use, modes of transportation, etc.

By regularly practicing love and gratitude, you gently open your heart and radiate a higher frequency, allowing your mind to be more open to possibilities. This enables you to receive more of all that life wants to give to you. It's also a beautiful exchange of energy that requires very little time, and benefits you and those you feel appreciation for. Making this a daily morning practice keeps your channel for receiving wide open, so you can benefit from all the opportunities every new day creates for you.

Throughout my life I've experienced countless miraculous and amazing manifestations that would initially have seemed impossible to most. I've allowed the magick to manifest through the frequency of love, by opening my heart and mind to life's divinity. While I know that anything is possible, it seems that the Divine continuously delights in surprising me with even greater jaw-dropping, masterful orchestrations.

One such manifestation unexpectedly occurred when I was in beautiful Sedona, Arizona, for the first time. I definitely got tested on how well I had learned my lesson of receiving (receiving on all levels). I also became even more acquainted with Spirit's wonderful sense of humour and careful consideration to details!

It was the beginning of 2012, and I had finished rereading a book that my greatest (living) mentor, a master and elder on Earth, had written many years before. As I finished reading it, I suddenly felt guided to look him up on the Internet, to see whether he was teaching in person. To my surprise, not only was Drew teaching, but his classes were in Sedona—a place that had been calling me for years! As with all places (or beings) that had called me throughout my life, I always knew when it was time to answer that call. Spirit always clearly let me know, somehow. Now I was being guided to Sedona. I also felt I needed to attend Drew's wife's workshop, which he recommended. She was teaching it before his class, and it resonated with me. I had to submit an application before enrolling for both, which I did. Although I had thought of attending at a later date that year, I felt strongly guided to attend the one in May, so I applied for that month.

I received both acceptance letters by email at the same time, 3:33 p.m. Then I also noted in the address information that 333 was the street number of the centre where the classes would take place! The appearance of this significant number, three times, further confirmed that I had to go, even though I had no income (I had to use credit). Since I was clearly being guided by Spirit, I had to trust. I had begun a new journey into the unknown on my path, and it required me to fully trust myself and the guidance I received. I found the perfect-for-me hotel on the list of recommended places to stay. It was eco-conscious, had delicious breakfasts included, was within walking distance to the centre, and had a beautiful Nature trail that wound through the desert landscape and beyond majestic stone formations. I paid a bit extra to have my own room instead of sharing with someone else, since I enjoyed having my own space. I was all set and felt that something incredible awaited me.

Just having the opportunity to meet and thank this mentor in person for his books was something very special to me. Drew's books had confirmed my awareness of certain things about our world. They had also validated who I was at a time when I had felt like an alien on the wrong planet. That was priceless to me. I felt my soul quicken with excitement! I already felt the energy of Sedona's beautiful stone formations and was eager to be in their physical presence. I was finally answering their call!

Interestingly, I was assigned the seat C33 for my flight to Arizona. While 33 was also a very significant number for me, C was also a 3 (being the third letter in the English alphabet), translating my seat to 333! It was one more sign from my essence language, guiding me on my journey to the sacred lands of Arizona. I arrived in Sedona in the mid-afternoon and was in absolute awe at the sight of the majestic, rust-coloured stone formations. After settling in and eating an early dinner, I went hiking on the Nature trail until the sun was setting. I hadn't realized how perfectly timed my stay was until I arrived— it coincided with the blooming season! What an unexpected blessing. Every cactus and plant had beautiful blossoms. Despite having seen photographs, I had never thought much about desert landscapes having a season for flowers. I was so grateful to have followed my heart's inner guidance (from Spirit) to be there at that specific time.

The air was sweetly scented with the exquisite perfume of flowers along with the aroma of junipers and pines. Many of those tree beings stood like gnarled works of art on the desert landscape. I deeply inhaled this delicious scent and felt it infuse every cell of my body. The energy of the surrounding stone formations was intensely blissful to me. I was in heaven. I also had the next day to enjoy hiking that glorious Nature trail, which I did at sunrise, in the afternoon, and again at sunset. During that time, I noticed that I repeatedly received obvious signs from Nature that signified a special partnership. I even had a male broad-tailed hummingbird perform a mesmerizing courting display above my head! I felt so honoured and delighted. As I ended my evening hike, after not encountering one person during the entire time, I was surprised to see a young man standing at the entrance of the trail. He was just silently smiling at me and holding the gate open for me to walk through. I hadn't even heard him walk up to it. As I passed through the gate and thanked him, it felt like a premonition. It was uncanny.

The next morning was the first day of the workshop. I happened to meet my wonderful hotel neighbour with whom

I shared the balcony, and we felt an instant connection. We discovered that we were both attending the same classes. It felt so perfect to have Glenda occupying the room beside mine. We had a pleasant walk to the centre and the workshop took place in the largest room. After registration, I chose to sit in the row of chairs nearest the front stage, next to two older women. Most of the 100 chairs were still empty as people stood around and talked.

As I introduced myself to the two women, I saw from the corner of my eye a very handsome younger man, with black hair and tan-coloured skin, walk through the doorway. He briefly scanned the room, looked straight at me, and then walked all the way up to the second row and sat directly behind me! I immediately felt what I can only describe as electric energy between us. I couldn't help but think, "Uh-oh…." I had never experienced this type of energy before. It was incredibly tangible and impossible to ignore. I made sure I didn't look at him. The two women beside me were looking at pamphlets, when this man suddenly leaned forward very close to me and asked *me* where they had found the pamphlets! I had to look at him face to face to answer him, and when we made eye contact I felt an instant soul connection. Amir smiled at me with gratitude, and I suddenly felt that *something* was going on in the ethers. I thought to Spirit "Oh my—*what* are you up to now?" I could sense it so strongly that it almost gave me goosebumps.

When class started, we were instructed to form groups of nine and maintain these groups for the duration of the workshop. Amir ended up in the same group as me (of course!). I started feeling resistance about what seemed more and more like a divinely orchestrated set-up. Yet I was also intrigued, remembering all the signs I had received in Nature the previous day. I'd never been one to shy away from learning what I knew was a must, but it didn't mean I never felt resistance to it. I decided to simply observe with an open heart and mind.

After class, as I walked outside to leave, Amir quickly came up to me and asked if I was going to visit a vortex with any of the groups, to which I replied no. I was planning to go back to my hotel room to unwind. After being around so many people all day, I now preferred some alone time. He seemed alarmed when I unintentionally stated that I was "going back home," meaning my hotel room, which I quickly corrected. He smiled with relief, and we wished each other a good evening as we parted ways.

Shortly after that, however, I received an invitation from a group of three wonderful women I had met, who were from Germany, Austria, and Australia. They were going to visit the beautiful Bell Rock stone formation vortex. One of them had a car, and they were eager to include me, so I accepted this unexpected opportunity. I was grateful that I had. As we hiked at the base of this massive stone being, I encountered a little whirlwind on the trail that no one else saw. Whirlwinds were very significant to me, so this was a sign that something special and magickal was unfolding. I ended up going barefoot since my sandals weren't ideal for climbing rocks. The warmth and fine consistency of the sand and stones felt wonderful on my feet's soles. After fully savouring that impressive stone being's energy, I was conveniently dropped off at my hotel room. I spent some time alone eating dinner and writing in my journal. I felt exhilarated by everything that I had experienced that day.

The next morning I dressed up to reflect how sensually feminine and vibrant I felt. I wore a sleeveless crimson-coloured top with a full-length, flowing black skirt, and adorned myself with a beautiful rhodochrosite stone necklace and matching earrings (which I had purchased from my soul sister Laurie specifically for my Sedona journey).

It had been one year that month since I had left my marriage, and I felt very much at peace with that. It had been the best decision I could have made, for both me and my former husband. He also understood that—the energy was clear between us. Since my early twenties, when I had ended any relationship, I'd always taken time for myself to integrate everything I had learned and to simply fully enjoy being on my own. The longer the relationship, the longer my post-relationship "me time." I'd also never looked for a man. Interestingly, like a divine plan, *all* my relationships had resulted from the perfect-for-me man (at that time) unexpectedly entering into my life, due to a series of amazing chains of events. They had all felt destined. Needless to say, I had not invested much thought into men for a year. Now I suddenly found myself in a workshop surrounded by men on the same wavelength as me, with the most attractive one being in my group! I also knew that Amir and I shared a significant soul connection I couldn't logically explain.

After eating breakfast, I walked across the balcony to Glenda's patio door to ask her if she'd like to walk together to class. Both her doors were wide open, with the sheer curtain waving in the breeze, so I vocally greeted her. I knew her well enough already to know she wouldn't mind if I entered her room, so I pulled back the curtain to step in—only to come face to face with a standing *Amir*! His fit body *bare* like a beautifully sculpted Persian god, he was wearing only a white towel around his hips! I was absolutely stunned, to say the least, and speechless, as we stared into each other's eyes in *complete* disbelief. Time seemed to stop. What a sight to behold first thing in the morning. I felt as if I was watching a movie and starring in it at the same time. What a perfectly orchestrated "classic" scene—except that this wasn't a movie; it was very real. Standing only a few feet away from me, he suddenly blurted out, "Nothing happened!" Then, as though perfectly choreographed, Glenda innocently waltzed out from the bathroom and mischievously smiled when she saw me.

They proceeded to explain his story to me. Amir had enrolled for both classes at the beginning of the year but had missed the workshop back in February. He received a credit to attend any of the remaining workshops during that year. He had decided to attend the May workshop and driven from a city in California. On the way, his vehicle had gotten a flat tire, so he hadn't had a chance to get a room before the workshop. The previous evening he had joined a group to visit a vortex; the group had included Glenda. When the women found out that he needed a place to stay, they all offered him their rooms. However, Glenda's motherly, protective instincts took over, and she offered him her hotel-room floor, which he gratefully accepted. He had *no* idea that her room was against mine with a shared balcony, so he was just as surprised to see me as I was to see him. As he got dressed, she discreetly whispered to me (with a big smile) that he would need a new place to stay, because she was claiming her space back—adding that he *really* liked me. After hearing all this, I now knew without a doubt that this was indeed a divine set-up by Spirit, although I was oblivious to the reason for it. Even my hotel neighbour was suddenly a conspiring matchmaker and obviously greatly enjoying it.

That morning, it was a challenge for me to focus on class, and by our lunch break I knew that I had to get to know Amir better. I could almost feel my entire team from Spirit, whom I refer to as my "sacred circle," pushing me towards him—it was almost amusing. While I did have free will, I also couldn't help but feel intrigued by all this. I had to find out what was so important about this man that Spirit was so insistent about. Whenever I felt that sense of *knowing* about something, I accepted the invitation of the experience (even if it was just so I never thought "What if …?").

So we ended up going out for lunch together. We had such interesting conversations about topics that were anything but mainstream and highly enjoyable to both of us. We were both very surprised when we discovered each other's actual ages—I thought he was much older and, like most people in the workshop, he thought I was much younger (which delighted me!). However, we weren't concerned by our age difference and enjoyed ourselves so much that we lost track of the time— and actually returned late for class! I laughed with disbelief. I hadn't done something like that in a very long time. We actually happened to arrive during an exercise that required everyone to have their eyes closed! As I walked up to my chair, I silently thanked Spirit for this divinely perfect timing (and I didn't dare make eye contact with the teacher).

After class Amir, Glenda, and I went out for dinner together, since we all got along so well. Then we returned to her room to visit until, without warning, she suddenly dismissed us with an exaggerated, "Go-o-o-o-od ni-i-i-i-ight!" claiming that she was very tired and needed to sleep! As we slowly walked back to my room, I decided to focus on the view. The balcony had such a gorgeous overlook of the surrounding stone formations, and their shadowed silhouettes were visible against the twilight sky. I could see the planet Venus shining brightly.

I had so many thoughts going through my mind as I debated why I should or shouldn't offer to share my room with him—it was maddening. I had always been very selective about which man I allowed into my sacred space, and I had always known them long enough to feel a connection. This was something completely new to me. Amir and I had just met, yet I felt such a strong connection. He felt it too. My mind was in overdrive, evaluating everything from my principles to what I sensed from Spirit and my heart. I realized I had to examine what those principles were based on regarding men and relationships, and I had to decide what was fundamentally important to me. It was apparent that I was being handed a gift by the Divine, delivered to my door, and I had a choice to make.

I finally managed to quiet my mind and tune in to my sacred heart—my inner knowing, free of judgment. I clearly knew that on a soul level we had agreed to be together at this specific time to teach and heal each other. It was obvious that we had a soul contract together. I also understood that we would part ways afterwards. I could either embrace this opportunity of transformation to see what possibilities awaited, or I could decline it. I had the freedom to choose, and it was entirely up to me. I had always lived my life in such a way that I never had regrets. When I had that feeling in my heart of a higher knowing, there was always great purpose to it, and I *had* to find out what it was. I knew that if I chose to not receive what I was being offered, I would definitely always wonder about its higher purpose and feel regret.

While all this was going on within me, Amir respectfully stood a distance away from me in calm silence, giving me the space that I needed without trying to influence me in any way. I greatly appreciated that. I felt his kind heart and spirit, and I knew I could fully trust him. I finally asked him if he'd like to share my room with me, if he didn't have another place in mind. He smiled and accepted my invitation, offering to sleep on the floor. I was impressed by his level of respect and gentlemanliness, qualities that I highly valued in a man.

Instead of having him sleep on the floor, I created a border of pillows down the middle of the king-sized bed, so we each had our own side. I laughed at myself as I placed the pillows— he did too. I knew that agreeing to explore our soul contract was an empowering decision to make, and that we were mutually attracted to each other on all levels. However, despite that, I required a greater heart-to-heart connection before even contemplating kissing (for kissing in itself was sacred to me). I was open to just seeing how things would naturally unfold, as they were meant to. As we went to sleep, within my heart I lovingly applauded the Divine with great appreciation for completely amazing me once again. It felt so surreal. No one else could orchestrate something like this with such perfection and attention to details—towel scene included!

We spent four days and nights together, since he extended his stay after the workshop was completed. During that short period of time, we learned so much from each other. Coming from such different lifestyles, we taught each other the best of both our worlds, and we enhanced each other's experience of Sedona and life to new heights. I expanded his awareness of energy and our beautiful natural world as I experienced it through my senses. I brought him on hikes and introduced him to helpful beings of Nature and Spirit. He reminded me of many things I had forgotten about myself over the years, including my playful nature. He also reawakened the passionate, sensual goddess within me that had been dormant. Due to multiple factors during the last months of my old life, my body had undergone significant changes which included unwanted weight loss and detoxification through my skin. Needless to say, I had acquired a negative self-image that I needed to overcome. The Divine used a beautiful man's genuine, loving heart and eyes to help transform this for me. We shared so much wholehearted laughter and fun, incredible wonders, out-of-this-world conversations, and sweet bliss. We were mutual catalysts, each providing exactly what the other had unknowingly needed at that time.

Months after we parted ways, I realized that Amir had opened me to feeling ready to receive my beloved (my sacred "twin-flame" man). I will always cherish this divinely fated rendezvous that manifested for us in such a sacred place. I never could have imagined that this awaited me in Sedona!

I also did not miss any classes with my mentor and was fully present for them. It felt so wonderful to finally connect with Drew in person and express my wholehearted gratitude for the books he had written. He was so humble and fully appreciated what I shared about his books. The first time we exchanged a love-filled hug, I had never felt so fully seen by a person, at a heart and soul level, as I did with him. It reminded me of my first encounter with the wild dolphins in Bimini. On the last day Drew unexpectedly manifested a little heart desire I'd had. Giving hugs was part of my nature, and I had desired to give him one last big one after class was over. However, Glenda and I decided to leave the crowd instead. As we walked by the parking lot we were surprised to see him alone by his vehicle, getting ready to leave. Despite my little desire, I decided to give him his space, since he was usually surrounded by so many people. We continued to walk back to the hotel instead. A few minutes later, we suddenly heard a vehicle pull up behind us on the road and heard him ask us whether we'd like a ride! We happily accepted his offer, and as he dropped us off at our destination, we exchanged one last loving hug. When I saw the big smile on his face and sparkle in his eyes, I felt that he knew about my secret little desire. I smiled back with great love and appreciation.

I received more than I could have ever dreamed of when I answered the call to journey to Sedona. It was all so amazing—beyond words. The Divine is infinitely loving, wise, creative, and aware of *exactly* what each of us requires at specific times to continue evolving on our own path. We might need to see ourselves from a different perspective through the Divine's eyes, so that we can embrace our whole selves without judgment. We might need to let go of certain self-limiting beliefs or attitudes that sabotage our true potential. Maybe we need to let go of fears, so we can experience more of life. Or it may be that we simply need to experience something completely different, in order to keep expanding our personal truth and knowledge of this world (and beyond).

When you're ready and have the desire to evolve further, even if you're not consciously aware of it, the seemingly impossible is orchestrated in the most divine ways to give you the opportunity to choose. You can deny yourself these opportunities or you can say yes to them—and discover (or remember) that you're *so much more* than you thought you were and that our world is divinely extraordinary.

After my mentor's class had ended, I went on a very special organized tour to the sacred lands in northern Arizona. Our small group of five had special privileges because of Drew's connections with the Southwestern Native American tribes. I experienced incredible beauty that photographs just don't do justice to. I chose to hike one of the Nature trails of the awe-inspiring Grand Canyon on my own, which took half the day and was so spectacular it almost seemed surreal. The next day a very special encounter awaited me when we visited the Navajo lands.

Instead of the scheduled private tour to a popular canyon, our young Navajo guide brought us to three other glorious canyons that enabled us to savour them without other tourists. It was such an unexpected gift. At the first canyon, the rising sun's golden light was shining through and transforming the undulating walls into shimmering sculptures. It was breathtaking! As we silently walked along the sandy corridors, we suddenly found ourselves in the presence of a beautiful great horned owl! It was perched atop a stone inside a large crevice, with the sunlight illuminating its space and shining on its head. It looked so regal as it silently observed us. I had not expected to encounter an owl in this arid landscape. It felt like such a blessing for me to see this special power animal there. That canyon felt so familiar to me, and as our guide played the flute, the music echoed hauntingly throughout the canyon. It touched me deeply.

As I left Arizona, I had a strong feeling that I would be returning to Sedona before the end of the year. I had no idea what would bring me back, but those feelings were always accurate, whether they made logical sense or not (they usually didn't!). I simply acknowledged it, with curiosity and without expectations.

When August arrived, it brought an unexpected invitation to attend an event the following month. This event was taking place just south of Phoenix, Arizona, which meant that if I attended, I would be very close to Sedona. While I felt strongly guided to go to this event, I felt quite hesitant about spending any more on my credit card (without knowing how I would pay for it). It was completely illogical. However, I was continuously being tested by Spirit and asked to trust my sacred path. I *was* committed to my path. Therefore, only a couple of weeks before the event, I checked to see whether there were any flights left through Air Miles—and there was one! When I contacted the event organizers, they had two free tickets left, so I claimed one and booked my flight.

When I realized I would be back in Arizona and so close to Sedona's sacred landscape, I felt overjoyed! I decided to book one night in Sedona at the same hotel I had enjoyed the first time I'd been there. I also booked the same reasonably priced shuttle service I had used from the Phoenix airport to Sedona. I'd enjoyed that convenient transportation service, for it allowed me to fully savour the scenery instead of focusing on driving. Unbeknownst to me, I was going to be even more grateful this second time, to have that service!

The morning of my flight, as I did my love-and-gratitude ritual outside a friend's house, where I had spent the night, a great horned owl called out from a location nearby! I was amazed to hear one in the city—it felt like a blessing for my trip. I knew I was doing exactly what I was being divinely guided to do.

When I landed in Phoenix, I felt elated to know that I would soon be in Sedona again. Halfway to our destination approximately one hour north of Phoenix, I started feeling the wonderful energy of a thunderstorm! It had been hot with a sunny, clear sky in Phoenix, and clouds were starting to appear the further north we went. I suddenly started seeing storm clouds, and I mentioned them to the shuttle driver. He told me the clouds were signs of the ending monsoon season, but he didn't believe that they were storm clouds. Since I was a little girl, thunderstorms had felt comforting to me. I had always slept peacefully through intense night storms. Lightning had captivated my spirit in a way I couldn't explain—I'd simply always felt a connection with it. Now I was able to feel the storm energy in ways I hadn't known was possible. Regardless of what the driver said, I felt ecstatic at the thought of experiencing an unexpected thunderstorm in Arizona. It wasn't something I could have planned for.

What followed was one of the greatest gifts I could have received from Spirit—I ended up experiencing *seven* glorious thunderstorms! As we drove closer to Sedona, I saw lightning strike from the dark clouds, touching the landscape around us. As the rusty-red stone formations started to appear in our environment, I was filled with wonder at the sight of the lightning making contact with them. The contrast between the stones' rich colour and the black-blue clouds with lightning streaking the sky was such an awe-inspiring sight. Never in my life would I have imagined I'd be experiencing thunderstorms in Sedona one day, much less such intense ones! I felt absolutely ecstatic by this surprise. I hadn't even known that this desert landscape had a rainy season, never mind storms.

I ended up experiencing five storms just on the way to Sedona. Then, as I checked in at the front desk of my hotel, another intense thunderstorm rolled in. It completely drenched me in a matter of seconds as I walked outside to my room, accompanied by flashes of lightning and deafening, cracking thunder. I felt fully infused with blissful energy! I felt so welcomed again by this sacred land, and I was grateful to Spirit for guiding me back here on this specific day. As I settled into my room, showered, and changed into dry clothing, the storm passed. It was impressive to see such intense storms pass through so quickly and then have the sun shining brilliantly hot again afterwards.

I decided to get some dinner at my favourite Mexican restaurant nearby, and while they worked on my order, I decided to go to a specific store that sold Navajo rugs and jewellery. It was only a short walk away. I had enjoyed looking at these beautiful, authentic works of art during my last trip here. Since then, I had thought about how wonderful it would be to have a small rug to use as an altar cloth for my ceremonies, indoors or outdoors. However, all I had ever seen were the original sizes that ranged from large to massive. As I talked with one of the owners, I laughingly expressed my desire for a miniature rug (not thinking they made them in that size). I was so surprised when she informed me that they actually did have a selection of those; they were the size of place mats! They all had certificates of authenticity included. As I looked through the small pile, I was amazed to find exactly what I had secretly desired—a miniature rug in the "Storm" pattern. They only had *one* with this pattern, and what a *perfect* day to acquire it, with all the storms passing through! It felt so significant; it was another gift from Spirit, while also being a test of my trust. This entire year had been about learning to further trust myself, Spirit, and my path, through experiences. I felt so blessed as I returned to my hotel room with this unique treasure and my delicious dinner—and *another* glorious thunderstorm rolling in! I placed the beautiful, little rug on my balcony to let it infuse this spectacular storm's intense energy (which I blissfully savoured along with my dinner).

After this last storm passed, I eagerly left my room for a sunset hike. I brought along favourite crystals and my Navajo rug. When I arrived on the upper trail, the landscape surrounding me took my breath away. The stone formations, desert sand, trees, cacti, and other plant beings were all freshly washed by the rain, and the sun now shone brightly on them all. Everything was blazing with colour! The vividness of the textures and rich colours was so surreal that I seemed to have highly enhanced eyesight! The aromas of the landscape's vegetation also permeated the air and infused me with bliss, as they had in May. I was so surprised to see flowers blossoming for a second time. I was later informed by locals that the recent monsoon season had brought enough rain to cause a second blooming season. It was another unexpected gift I received for returning at this time.

I also encountered more wildlife (which always delighted me) including a deer and a hare. At one point a large raven flew so close to me that its wingbeats sounded like a dragon's. It was very impressive, and I felt honoured by Raven's presence. (Just as I wrote that about Raven in my book manuscript, exactly a year later in Canada, two very playful ravens flew near me, calling out to catch my attention, as I sit on a veranda! It's a joyful, synchronistic reminder from Spirit that life is always fully aware of us, beyond time and space.)

The next day, I decided to skip early registration at the event and rescheduled my shuttle pick-up time for the evening instead, so I could make the most of my day in Sedona. I was allowed to leave my luggage in the hotel's locked room behind the front desk while I explored. Between hikes, I took breaks from the heat to refill my water bottle and visit stores that felt inviting to me. I had a desire to find a photograph of lightning striking the Sedona landscape. I did find one, which also had a rainbow with the lightning—it felt very special. This shopping also resulted in wonderful connections with locals.

I was able to hike at sunrise, in the afternoon, and again in the early evening before my departure. At sunrise I did a love-and-gratitude ceremony on the sacred landscape with my miniature Navajo rug and special crystals. I placed the rug directly on the rust-coloured ground as an altar cloth. On my afternoon hike I was able to savour a glorious thunderstorm occurring just north of Sedona, above a large stone formation that I was told is called Thunder Mountain. I sat in the shade of a pine for a while and silently experienced the storm and my surroundings with all my senses.

During my last hike, I decided to walk part of it barefoot, where it was a level sandy trail. It felt so good to connect with the sacred land this way. As I continued walking, savouring every moment, I suddenly felt guided to look straight above me. I was always aware of my surroundings, including the sky— there's always so much going on in our celestial environment.

In that moment, however, I was wearing a brimmed hat, so my perspective of the sky was limited. As I did look up, I gasped with astonishment—a radiant rainbow that looked like the stroke of a paintbrush was shining directly above me! I wouldn't have noticed it had I not been guided to do so.

Rainbows had always felt like the visible form of the Divine's love to me. As a child, I had loved to paint rainbows more than anything else. They had always been a special essence sign for me. I had felt a tiny heart desire to see a rainbow after all the storms that had passed through Sedona since I'd arrived. Now my desire had been granted in the most unexpected way. Under this radiant rainbow, I declared to Spirit, with Nature as my witness, that I was ready to reunite with my beloved, "the one," in divine timing. I felt so blessed and so deeply in love with All and life itself. I fully savoured this moment as long as I could before departing.

My attending the event near Phoenix was also obviously divinely guided. It took place at a resort owned by Southwestern Native American tribes. I discovered that even a building created for commercial use could exude sacred energy—even more than many places of worship I had set foot in! This absolutely amazed me. I had never considered that as a possibility until I entered this unique building. It was a soulful co-creation in all ways and this could be applied to anything. The beautiful grounds and hotel complex were meticulously designed, created, and decorated to honour the cultures of the land. Every single room and decoration felt infused with purpose and blessing. The traditional music that played through the intercoms was so enchanting. The entire place was filled with spirit, and it profoundly touched me, the way natural landscapes do. I felt so privileged and grateful to be there.

In 2011, shortly after one of my brothers created my business logo, I had received an inspired vision for what Sacred Earth Connection™ was meant to be—as a physical centre. The first time I was in Sedona, the details had been revealed to me. Now I also understood its full potential with this greater awareness.

For that alone, the event was well worth it to me. My third-floor hotel room also faced the sunrise over a mountain range and had a large tree with branches that drooped over my balcony. Beside it was a large saguaro cactus with a pair of flickers (a species of woodpecker) living in it. It was such a perfectly assigned room for me. I felt so blessed, and the gifts kept unfolding.

I realized that this event was actually an enticing lure to bring me back to Arizona's sacred desert lands, to experience so many more wonders, to receive greater insights, and to make additional soul connections. While I had initially thought I'd been guided there to network with everyone at the event, I quickly realized that I'd felt overwhelmed by the group of over 200 people in attendance. Instead, I followed my inner guidance to spend the breaks connecting with Nature, barefoot on the gorgeous grounds, and allowed those I needed to associate with to come to me. It worked brilliantly. I ended up connecting with more wonderful soul sisters as well as a soul brother. This soul brother was also an answered heart desire. A few months earlier I had expressed to Spirit my desire to connect with soul brothers as well as soul sisters.

To me, each gender has its own energy and perspective, which is equally important to me. I've always felt in greater harmony when my personal circle includes a balance of women and men. My own business logo depicts a sacred geometry symbol that signifies the balance of male and female energies, among other things. To me, this applies within and without.

This new soul brother I met wasn't even part of the event. He was an employee of the hotel and a member of one of the local tribes. I just happened to encounter him on the third evening, when I was walking the grounds with my soul sister Aurora. I felt an instant kinship with him. He was one of the several dear soul brothers I ended up meeting through travels during the following months. I cherished every heart connection I made.

On the last night, after the event was over, I had the pleasure of watching a glorious thunderstorm that hovered above mountains in the distance, with the silhouetted saguaro cacti standing tall on the desert landscape. It was such a beautiful lightning show which I joyfully shared with Aurora. Then, the next morning before my airport shuttle arrived, I went for a sunrise hike on the Nature trail that extended out from the hotel into the desert. During my hour of hiking, I met very few people and saw three different rainbows appear in the sky above different mountains! So magickal!

This second trip to Arizona, like the first one, was filled with so many unexpected gifts. Had I given in to financial worries instead of trusting higher guidance, I would have missed out on heart connections, new perspectives and extraordinary experiences that have imprinted in my heart. I would not have experienced all that was there for me.

It's not being irresponsible when you do what you feel truly *called* to do. It's honouring yourself, no matter what that calling looks like. When you know your heart is inviting you on a specific journey, regardless how illogical it might seem on the surface, there's *always* a higher purpose for it.

In my case, Spirit was teaching me a new level of trust and faith on my path, in ways that repeatedly challenged me to stretch beyond my sense of security and comfort zone. Yet, with every courageous leap I took, I was able to receive experiences that strengthened my faith and deepened my trust. They opened me to experience greater expressions of divine love in all forms. The divinely designed consequence was that my own ability to love fearlessly kept deepening.

Throughout our lives, we're continuously being invited to experience things. This also includes the different landscapes on our glorious Mother Earth. Each one radiates specific energies that benefit us in various ways. They facilitate harmony within us when we become out of balance, enhance our sense of well-being, promote healing on all levels, accelerate our personal evolution, or simply provide a sacred space for us to be aware of our true essences. Whether deserts, lakes, forests, mountains, meadows, oceans, valleys, or prairies, every type of environment offers its unique gifts.

Even though we're rarely conscious of it, as Nature beings we're finely tuned in to the energies of these environments, on all levels. We know when it's time to immerse ourselves in a specific environment. Whether we act on this inner knowing or not is up to us. There are always many benevolent entities working together behind the scenes to initiate our connection with these different landscapes, whether we simply visit or take up residence. It's just as possible to have soul contracts with places as we do with people and other relationships.

When you feel a calling to spend some time in a certain environment, accepting this invitation is a gift you give to yourself as well as to the landscape. There is a mutual benefit when you connect with any environment through your heart. You give it doses of high frequency in the form of joy, love, appreciation, and reverence in return for what you receive. Just as you benefit from the higher frequencies yourself, so do the landscapes and all types of beings that inhabit them. Nature radiates the Divine's loving, sacred energy and is always available to you if you're willing to receive it.

Our Supportive
Mystical World

Life (seen and unseen) is always fully aware of us.

The supernatural is the natural not yet understood.
—*Elbert Hubbard*

I love to think of nature as an unlimited broadcasting station, through which God speaks to us every hour, if we only will tune in.
—*George Washington Carver*

When we choose to let our hearts lead the way, it can feel quite unnerving. Sometimes what our hearts lead us into is so easy that we barely notice their leadership over our minds. We experience this most strongly when we spend time in Nature or we do something we truly enjoy doing at the soul level. It naturally induces us to think less and experience more of our true nature, from our hearts. Other times, however, our hearts lead us into the highly unfamiliar. Then our minds panic and fill us with uncertainty, doubts, and worries. Fears disrupt our natural state of being. Nevertheless, when we realize we're never alone, since the Divine permeates all life, we're able to navigate our heart-led paths with more confidence.

Life, seen and unseen, is always fully aware of us in all ways. It receives our energies in the form of thoughts, emotions, and light, which create a universal language of frequencies. We're always broadcasting to life, just as it's always broadcasting to us. We have more allies than we can imagine—there's no such thing as being alone. When we open our hearts to these allies, they provide us with support, guidance, and assistance in countless ways, from the subtle to the extraordinary.

One summer's day in 2007, I was in the city, riding the transit bus home from work. Things had become very stressful among the employees, managers, and customers. Jobs were being abolished constantly since a new president had taken over the control of that large corporation. This made every day a challenge. Most employees couldn't see themselves changing jobs, so they were miserably counting the years and days until retirement. That day on the bus, I was letting my thoughts wander to other possibilities for me. I knew there was no way I would be staying with that company much longer, never mind until the age of retirement.

I was sitting beside the window and had opened it a few inches to let in more air on that wonderfully hot, sunny day. Suddenly, as I was thinking about leaving my job, what appeared to be a leaf flew in through the small window opening and landed on my shirt. Surprised, I picked it up to have a closer look and saw that it was actually a beautiful butterfly wing! The butterfly had always been special to me as a personal power animal, signifying beauty and great transformation.

This was such an unexpected gift, received in a very incredible way. I felt so grateful for that clear sign from Spirit. It confirmed to me that changing jobs was the next step I needed to take on my path of life. It was very empowering.

Regardless of our states of being, we always have infinite support—we simply have to ask for it. However, the more we notice and lovingly appreciate the divinity that exists in all of life, the more life also responds to us. We create and nurture sacred relationship with All. We automatically and naturally align with our true essences' high frequency and experience even more of our world's wonders. All life is more receptive to the frequencies of appreciation, joy, inner peace, reverence, and love. Life is also much more expansive and multi-dimensional than we can imagine (as we ourselves are).

When we're in alignment with our true nature, we're able to recognize the miraculous everywhere. We realize that miracles are a natural occurrence. Our heightened perspective allows us to receive even greater demonstrations of the mystical and the possible. We experience the realm of our sacred hearts.

A few weeks after beginning my new life in 2011, I received a wonderful opportunity to fulfill a desire I'd had for some time. I happened to come across a friend whom I had met at the crystal-healing course in December. I asked her if she knew anyone who could teach me to construct a frame drum. She giggled and informed me that *she* was about to give such a workshop in only two weeks. Talk about divine timing! I was amazed as she described her workshop to me—it was even better than what I had desired. I felt so supported and guided on my journey. I made plans to attend with my soul sister Anna.

During her drum-making workshop, my friend taught our group according to her Native American tradition, as taught to her by her elders. She also told us that we might receive our own spirit name, so we should pay close attention, especially to our dreams. It was a name given directly from Spirit. Our small group learned wonderful lessons as we created our frame drums together, working with a sense of community. By the end of the workshop none of us had received a spirit name, but we all left with beautiful drums and new wisdom.

Two weeks later, I stayed overnight with my sister at my parents' country home. On the Sunday morning, they had all left early for various reasons, leaving me alone at the house. I had brought my new drum with me, to start the day with my usual morning ritual. It was a glorious sunny day, so I walked outside to a large secluded clearing at the end of the property. It was surrounded by forests made up mostly of two species of tree beings—trembling aspens and jack pines.

Barefoot on the grass, with the wind blowing in my hair, I drummed while expressing my love and gratitude to All. The weather was so beautiful, with puffy white clouds floating across the sunny, blue sky. I just kept drumming and dancing for the sheer joy of it. After some time of doing this, I suddenly received my spirit name—I intuitively heard the phrase "dancing wind"! At that point, it was rare that I actually received information through my intuitive sense of hearing, so this surprised me. I wondered whether I'd heard right. The wind gusted, making the pine branches whisper and the aspen leaves rustle and shimmer around me. Since it was so unexpected and I loved the name, I wanted to know that it was an authentic spirit name and not just something I had imagined. I needed a confirmation that my mind couldn't dismiss. I asked Spirit to show me a clear sign that day, to let me know without a doubt that *DancingWind* was in fact my spirit name. By asking Spirit for a sign outside of myself, out of my control, I was ensuring that my mind couldn't dispute it.

I drove back to my new rural home shortly afterwards, which was almost two hours northwest of my parents' property. The weather was now extremely hot, with barely a breeze. When I arrived, I decided to take a walk around my environment with my camera to photograph Nature's splendour in full bloom. I loved using photography to share the beauty and wonders of Nature with others, as I experienced it with all my senses. I eventually ended up at a crossroads near the property, where two gravel roads led off in all four directions. I silently stood there for a while, wondering why I felt guided to this isolated location. It was away from anything obviously interesting to photograph.

All of a sudden, a beautiful dust whirlwind, approximately my height, appeared directly in front of me on the gravel road! It twisted around, picking up dust and bits of dried grass and leaves—it seemed so playful. I had not seen a whirlwind for years. I stood in awe. Moments later, just as it had appeared out of thin air, it disappeared. I knew immediately and without a doubt that I had just received my sign from Spirit, confirming that *DancingWind* was indeed my spirit name. I smiled wide in my heart. What a truly special gift it was, empowering me on my new journey into the unknown!

The following year, I felt the desire to honour my special spirit name by legally changing my surname to DancingWind. A few weeks after I confirmed this desire in my heart, I woke up one morning and knew this was the day I had to submit my name-change request. I didn't feel like driving to the city, especially not downtown where the government office was located. However, I felt so strongly guided to go, and I knew better than to dismiss that nudge. It was later than I preferred by the time I left the house, but more and more I was realizing how everything was always divinely perfect when I honoured myself. Feeling I *should* have left earlier was my mind being at odds with non-linear time. I ended up experiencing a beautifully magickal flow, which might not have manifested had I left sooner.

As I drove down the long driveway, a little whirlwind appeared, spinning with sandy dust only a few feet ahead of my car. One hour later in the city, I found a perfect parking spot downtown and had just enough coins to park for one hour. It was windy as I walked to the government office, and I encountered three beautiful white feathers blowing towards me. Feathers were very significant to me, and white represented the colour of Spirit in Nature. As soon as I pulled a number ticket at the office, my number was called, and within 20 minutes the forms were filled out, signed, and ready for processing! Six weeks later, on November 3, 2012, DancingWind officially became my surname. I felt as if something powerful and sacred had occurred.

What's been interesting to me is that this name seems to affect people with a special energy of its own. All sorts of people regularly compliment me about it. Their spirits always light up with joy when they express their comments to me. Even if it's not in person, I hear it in their voices or feel it in their written words. It even affected a very large, serious-looking airport customs officer who was questioning me. He looked at my passport a moment ... then he looked at me ... and suddenly he exclaimed, "You have an *awesome* name, Miss DancingWind!" and he smiled the biggest smile as he returned my passport to me!

I realized even more through these interactions that names and words have powerful energy and vibrate at certain frequencies. Although I've known this for some time, to actually witness this in action is quite amazing. I understand more clearly why I felt it was so important for me to honour my name legally. Everything has a greater purpose than we can imagine, and I feel honoured to have received a name from Spirit that touches others this way. I had never thought before how a person's name could have such a positive effect on *other* people as well as on the bearer of the name. This was another demonstration from Spirit of the infinite number of possibilities available to us that can have benefits that reach beyond time and space. (The benefits are not bound to a moment nor to an action itself.)

This experience with my drum and spirit name showed me once again how supported we are on multi-dimensional levels. The support we have from Spirit, Nature, and beyond, far exceeds what we're aware of. When we're open enough to invite it into our lives, magick manifests. The more open we become, the more of it we experience. It continuously amazes and delights me.

Some forms of support are clearly little miracles just to demonstrate that the Divine's will can manifest *anything* for us, even our smallest heart desires, simply out of great love for us.

One summer's day in 2013, I was at my parents' house with all my siblings and their families, visiting for almost two weeks. At one point while everyone was busy I decided to work on this book's manuscript for a while. I settled myself on the open-air veranda with my lightweight Ultrabook. Anyone who knew me well also knew how special feathers have always been to me. As I typed away, one of my brothers walked up to me and gave me a gorgeous, little feather he'd found on the ground. I was so touched by such an unexpected, thoughtful gift. Since it was a balmy evening, I worked late outside until it was time to sleep. It had been extremely windy all day, and as I gathered my things, the small feather suddenly blew away with the wind! I had my hands full, so I brought everything indoors. I then grabbed a flashlight and returned outdoors to look for the little feather. It was logically obvious that the wind had blown it away, but I kept looking anyway. I felt sad to have lost that precious little gift. I finally gave up the search and went to bed, since there was nothing but furniture and incessantly high wind to be found on the veranda.

The next morning, the wind was still blowing full force, as it had all night. Despite that, I went outside and looked again for that little feather by daylight. I didn't find anything—the wind had swept the veranda clean. I paused, and from my heart I expressed to Spirit my desire for a small miracle that would somehow bring me back that gift—if I was meant to have it. I then sat on a lounge chair and wrote in my journal while everyone was slowly waking up in the house. Suddenly, a gust of wind blew some of my journal pages over. A large feather I had found and placed between the pages flew away! I jumped up to retrieve it, but it had already disappeared, back in Nature with the strong wind. I couldn't believe it! The wind was having a lot of fun with my feathers! As I slowly walked back to the chair, feeling a bit disheartened, I had to pass over an electric cord that ran along the veranda floor to my parents' water fountain. I suddenly felt guided to look down at the cord in front of my feet. To my absolute amazement, I saw, there on my path, in plain sight and securely tucked underneath the cord, the little feather my brother had given to me! Spirit had miraculously granted me my desire. I burst with so much joy and gratitude for this wonder.

I was reminded once again that nothing is impossible and *all* desires are heard. When we believe in possibilities instead of impossibilities, we invite life to respond accordingly, and magick and miracles manifest in greater ways and with greater frequency. When we choose to experience miracles every day, that's what we will experience, in countless forms. One of my favourite quotations from Albert Einstein, an iconic genius well aware of the mystical, reminds us that we can live life as if everything is a miracle—or not. It's up to us, and it's always a matter of perspective. (The actual quotation appears in the afterword.)

What you might perceive as impossible might simply be a question of timing. Sometimes you have to go through a process before you can believe something is possible and can experience that possibility. The types of manifestations that you experience are a good indication of how open you are to life and possibilities. The more open you are, the more you will experience the mystical along with the mundane, for life is mystical by nature.

At the beginning of 2012, I felt guided to go to my favourite crystal store in the city. It was just a feeling I had that was nudging me to go. I took the opportunity to run some errands, saving the crystal store for the end. When I walked into the store, one of the store owners told me they had just brought in a wonderful selection of new crystals and stones, including moldavite of many sizes, for very good prices.

Moldavite isn't a crystal or a stone but a beautiful, green textured, glassy material that was created by a meteorite's contact with our planet. In a sense, it's a manifestation from the merging of Father Sky with Mother Earth. Its energy is very powerful. It resonates with the element of storm (all elements combined), which I also consider to be my personal element.

It had been calling me for a while, but I had never seen a piece that I really liked or that wasn't overpriced. That day happened to be different. I didn't feel the desire to spend time with the crystals and stones of the store the way I usually did. Instead, I walked right up to the display case that held the moldavite, intuitively knowing where it was. It just called to me so strongly, and I felt a wonderful resonance with it. The store owner was right—the pieces were gorgeous and reasonably priced. I felt all sorts of sensations as I held several of the larger pieces, knowing that one of them was for me.

After I purchased the piece that felt right for me, I started my one-hour journey back, north of the city. The entire night sky was brightly illuminated by stars and familiar constellations—I had a great view since I was facing away from the city lights. As I drove on the highway, I suddenly had a thought about how I had with me a treasure of the vast universe related to the stars and everything beyond our magnificent planet. As I thought of this, I felt a wonderful wave of energy flow through me. Then, as soon as I finished that thought, I watched as a large, glowing meteorite fell slowly through the starry northern sky ahead of me, perfectly aligned with the middle of my field of vision, until it disappeared near the horizon. I was completely astonished! I had never seen a meteor before (only "falling stars," which were much further out in space). What an unexpected, beautifully synchronistic gift it was to see that. It gave me goosebumps and felt like a cosmic wink from Spirit, confirming my thoughts with perfect timing. It also made my piece of moldavite that much more special to me.

Throughout the years, I've experienced firsthand the multi-dimensionality of our world. What we see as the third dimension is just one of many that exist. While this isn't news to shamans, scientists, or people who use their spiritual abilities (beyond the five commonly known senses), it's still not part of mainstream consciousness or conversation. However, at times it can actually be quite easy to perceive these different layers of existence from our physical plane, even with our physical senses. We are evolving so that our special intuitive abilities are becoming common abilities. These abilities are allowing us to experience more things—such as seeing benevolent beings from other dimensions. It's quite natural, actually—as humans we *are* multi-dimensional beings. All we require is to be open with awareness and to accept what we see. The more aware we are, and the less we dismiss things as imagination, the better we're able to perceive what resides beyond our physical dimension.

Plant and tree beings are familiar to us, so we usually see them as their physical forms, and might also perceive their multi-dimensionality. However, sometimes there's more to see. Beings from other dimensions use them to become more visible to us. For most of us, physical sight is the most dominant sense.

Taking this into account, these beings use foliage as another means for us to see them and be aware of their presence. It's the same concept as those special images that are created with other images within them (stereograms). Our regular vision sees the dominant two-dimensional image immediately as a clear picture. However, when we keep looking at it and our gaze slightly shifts, we suddenly clearly see the other image come through, usually as a detailed three-dimensional one. We see a completely different image than the first, yet both are just as real, and the previously hidden image is created by the first image. It's the same with the apparitions of these beings from other dimensions. While we initially see foliage, we then clearly see a being appear, in detail, created by the foliage (it's not a physical being hiding among the vegetation). The more we notice them, the easier they are to recognize. If I'm not already looking at a specific area of vegetation, I'm usually guided to look there. I'm not aware I'm being guided until the being slowly appears or I suddenly see it there with every detail clearly visible. Sometimes they simply appear where I was already looking.

One afternoon, I was talking on the phone with my soul sister Anna about a particular spirit guide that we both knew. I walked around the house then decided to sit in front of a large picture window, facing the surrounding forest. Through the window, I could see a large section of the foliage and trees. After we had been talking for a while, I suddenly saw the head of the spirit guide we had been discussing, with very clear facial features, appear through the foliage! It was giant—as large as the first story of the house—and very serene-looking. It was so impressive to see how every leaf had created its fine features. Since Anna was highly clairvoyant, she knew what he looked like, whereas I felt his energetic signature without knowing about his physical appearance. This was the first time I had clearly seen him, so I described his appearance to her. She was amazed by my description and confirmed it was him. I saw him perfectly with my physical eyesight. The giant size of his head reminded me how easily physical appearances can be changed beyond the denser, physical third dimension.

I've seen many faces appear through foliage this way, always where there are layers of leaves, as in a forest of deciduous trees and shrubs. They've appeared in various locations where I've resided or visited in my travels, and they are mainly spirit guides, ceremonially dressed shamans, elementals, and star beings. I've also seen these beings appear through the trunks of large trees or stones like boulders and cliffs. I know of other people who have seen them this way as well. Different beings might appear to different people. Regardless, out of respect, they usually only appear this way to those who are open on some level to seeing them. For people who are curious yet uncertain, these beings might appear in dreams or through clouds instead, as a way to initiate interaction. Dreams and clouds feel more distant and less real than apparitions through vegetation, trees and stone. When people feel more comfortable with the idea of these beings' existence, then they might become more visible in their surrounding environment.

Clouds also display a level of consciousness and can mirror our own back to us. They're highly influenced by us, as weather shamans especially know. They respond to our focused attention, emotions, and thoughts in incredible ways.

One particular spring day I decided to go for a walk down a busy street in the city. The only Nature to be found there was the sky above me, so I brought my attention to the billowy white clouds that filled the sunny, blue sky. At one point I decided to focus on two very large clouds in my field of vision. As I focused on them, I set an intention in my heart to send all cloud beings love and appreciation for their presence. I filled myself with those emotions and radiated this energy out to them all, focusing on the two large clouds ahead of me. After a moment, I paused and briefly closed my eyes, mentally asking these cloud beings if they could feel my loving energy flowing to them. When I opened my eyes, these two large clouds had separated into four and formed a giant, detailed happy face, complete with two eyes, a nose, and a curving, smiling mouth! I was astonished by their immediate response and smiled back with joyful delight. Shortly afterwards, they merged into one big cloud.

Over the years I've also interacted with storm clouds, and they always respond using lightning, thunder, and waves of immense energy. Of course, life respects that we're all different and responds to us in very individual ways, according to our energy. Since I've always had a special connection with thunderstorms, they know how much I enjoy their response to me in that particular way.

When we appreciate Nature so that we see every aspect of it as a being instead of a mere thing, we honour its existence and invite connections and relationships. Through our loving hearts we can open ourselves to experiencing all of life in various ways. We are able to receive interactions from all beings of Nature and beyond, including the elementals, with our common senses. When we use our intuitive abilities, our connections and relationships expand even more (I discuss this in detail in chapter 6).

When I began to openly describe the little twinkly lights I see (with my physical sense of sight), I discovered that other people also see them, but often don't know what to make of them. I felt guided to mention it here so anyone who sees them can acknowledge them for who they are. These small lights are not the same as what we see when we feel light-headed. They may suddenly appear anywhere around us, regardless of what we might be doing. (I even had a blue one appear just now, in front of the screen of my Ultrabook, as I was typing this text! It obviously wanted to make a point!) They can have a radiant colour or be similar to a miniature sun. These ones all light up like stars. Most often I see small blue ones or clear ones like the sun. I've also seen other colours. They're usually solitary, but I've occasionally seen the star-like ones in clusters. They're like tiny bursts of starlight that appear and disappear, as if they're travelling from one dimension into our physical one and then back into the other.

These twinkly lights feel like different forms of what I refer to as *elementals* (governors, guardians, and co-creators of different aspects of Nature). While I don't remember, I obviously used to see them as a child, for I discovered one of my paintings from kindergarten that depicts nine equal-armed, small crosses of varying colours clustered beside a very large tree. I've seen them sporadically throughout the years, and then they began appearing consistently to me when I chose to leave the lifestyle I knew, in order to fully align with my sacred path. Their appearances let me know when I'm on track with my purpose. Since the beginning of 2013, they've been appearing every day. Their energy feels very joyful, innocent, and loving. They provide confirmation and celebration on my path. They might signify something different for someone else. I always appreciate their presence and thank them for it. I've also seen variations of these joyful elemental lights including some that look like tiny flames and orbs of different colours. The more we acknowledge them, the clearer they become.

As human beings, we all know the language of energy. We know when energy feels good to us and when it doesn't. It's so natural to us that it can be difficult to have a conscious awareness of it. As soon as we start thinking about it, it distracts us from the experience. Our minds have been conditioned to analyse everything and they complicate things. Even children, as they grow older, fall into the state of overthinking everything. I've had many ask me how I'm able to connect with Nature. Connecting with any being of Nature or other dimensions is not a process of thinking but rather a process of being—being love within our hearts.

When I used to *try* to communicate with beings of Nature during my teens and twenties, nothing happened. I always had a special connection with Nature, and had infinite patience. Yet, my expectations were intellectual—I was trying too hard. My mind was in control, waiting for something to happen.

That's how we're trained by society to do anything. To get results, we must do something intellectual, step by step. However, Nature is completely different—it requires us to completely embrace and be love, without reservations. One way of learning focuses on the mind, while the other is all about the heart. The heart's energy allows and receives, while the mind's energy analyses and chases. Nature responds favourably to a heart-centred way.

My first significant connections were with tree beings. By significant I mean it was clear that those beings were energetically extending themselves, to make a conscious connection with me. These connections occurred quite unexpectedly when I wasn't trying. I was simply immersed in Nature, fully out of my head and into my wide open heart. I was in a state of great love, reverence, and appreciation—and life naturally responded. Those connections were effortless, as a result of mutual resonance.

Whenever you're in Nature and a particular being suddenly captivates your attention among many, it's extending an invitation to connect with you. Your frequencies resonate with each other. It could be a certain tree that you suddenly notice out of an entire forest, a specific flower within a large area of vegetation that seems to stand out from the rest, a motionless and silent bird perched on a branch catches your eye, a stone on a beach captivates you, etc. When you shift your perspective from one of merely seeing a tree, a flower, a bird or a stone, to one of being in the presence of someone who is fully aware of you, your heart opens to this being. Simply spending some time in silence with this being, and feeling a loving sense of wonder for this individual, is accepting the invitation and opens the channel to communicate further.

It's a language of the heart that we simply need to remember how to use. We all know it—it's part of our nature. It's a matter of opening ourselves to connections by feeling love, appreciation, reverence, gratitude or admiration, without expectations. It's about really *feeling* these emotions within our hearts, *not* thinking that we feel these emotions. There's a big difference. Our intuitive senses can then perceive and interpret the connection into messages that we understand on a personal level. While the means of perception and interpretation is unique to each of us, it invariably starts with *love*. At times, communicating is solely an exchange of the sacred gift of love energy, and that in itself is divinely fulfilling on all levels.

This type of heart interaction has always been a fundamental part of us as conscious human beings—until a multitude of factors discouraged it and it became our downfall. We shifted from living predominantly in our hearts to living mostly in our minds, and we forgot about our sacred relationship with All. We forgot how sacred everything created and experienced from love is. The destructive repercussions of this are very apparent with the countless losses (of all forms of life) that our world has experienced and continues to.

As babies we all live from our natural state of being and experience much more than the average adult—we experience the truth of life. Our pure hearts and innocent minds broadcast the frequency of the Divine's love, and everyone responds favourably to that, including beings beyond the physical realm. The more we live from that space of absolute love as adults, the more we're able to interact with others of all species, in a mutually beneficial way. We switch from the relentless frequency of overdrive (beta) to the harmonious frequency of Nature (alpha). At this frequency, Nature doesn't feel alarmed around us, and we're able to coexist in a beautiful way. This is most apparent with animals.

One very hot summer's day when I still lived in the city with my former husband, I was spending some time in our backyard, a Nature oasis we had co-created five years earlier. On this sunny day, the dragonflies and butterflies were present in great numbers. While I was familiar with the butterflies that visited, I had never seen so many species of dragonflies. Dragonflies of all sizes and colour combinations had been visiting the gardens all day. Every colour of the rainbow was present, as well as white and black. I hadn't known that so many different types of dragonflies existed, and I couldn't help but feel that the Divine must have immensely enjoyed creating them all. Many hovered above the vegetation, while others sunned themselves, perching on plants, stones, and garden structures throughout the yard. I was filled with wonder and loving appreciation for all the gifts that Nature was providing for me through this urban ecosystem. Then I received a magickal and unexpected gift.

Since I love the energy of stones, I was silently sitting cross-legged on a flat granite stone of the path between two of the gardens, simply observing in silence. Some time passed, and I noticed a medium-sized ruby meadowhawk dragonfly perching on a nearby blade of wild grass, facing me. It remained motionless and watched me. I knew it was acutely aware of me, in ways beyond my understanding. We looked at each other for a while, neither of us moving. I suddenly felt the desire to lovingly connect with it even more, so I slowly raised one of my hands, palm facing up, towards it. Then I extended a finger as a potential perch. I kept looking at it with a smile—it was so beautiful. It had a ruby-red body, brown eyes, and wings that glistened rainbow colours in the sunlight. To my delight, it suddenly lifted off from the blade of grass and hovered over to my finger, where it perched, still looking at me! Resting briefly, it then flew in a wide circle in front of me and perched back on my finger, looking at me again. After a while, it flew in another wide circle and returned to perch on my finger, facing me again. It was so endearing; my heart was bursting with pure joy. What a special connection. Eventually it flew to another area of the garden. I felt overjoyed and honoured by this display of ultimate trust.

Many times while in Nature, I've had animals continue to behave as they were before I arrived—they don't seem to mind my presence at all. In fact, many don't even seem to recognize me as a human being. I know many people who have also experienced this. It's all about energy. It's one of the greatest compliments we can receive as humans, since animals are pure truth. They immediately let us know what frequency we're broadcasting, whether they're wild or domestic animals. They sense our energy long before we see them, so if we're not in a state of harmony, they want nothing to do with us. We either don't even see them, because they've hidden, or we see them fleeing. If our energy is chaotic, they might even react defensively or with aggressive behavior.

However, when our energy is harmonious, it's common for smaller varieties of wildlife to either interact with us or simply accept our presence. I've had many butterflies, bumblebees, and dragonflies perch on me while I've been hiking or sitting in Nature, for no apparent reason other than spending time on me. Various mammals and ground-dwelling birds have walked by me without noticing me sitting on the ground at the base of a tree. Birds have also hovered or perched beside me when I'm fully in tune with my natural surroundings, and occasionally they have even briefly alighted on me (with no food being present). These interactions always make me smile. I never underestimate the power of loving interactions. Consciousness isn't just a human aspect.

We always have the ability to choose every single moment. It's easy to fall into unconscious patterns of choice and simply repeat these patterns of reactions. With awareness, we have the power to change our lives. When we choose a different reaction than what automatically comes up from our conditioning, we suddenly change a pattern, and that's a very powerful thing.

I woke up one morning to find a magnificent and intricate spiderweb hanging between my sofas. It was shining in the rising sun's light—the spider had spun this large masterpiece overnight! As beautiful as it was, the location wasn't ideal, for the web itself was in the middle of an area I walked through a lot. After admiring it for a while, instead of destroying it, I chose to lovingly communicate this predicament from my heart to the spider. I simply asked it to move its web to a safer place where it wouldn't get accidentally damaged. A few hours later, when I returned to the living room, I noticed the spiderweb was gone. I found it safely behind the sofa, a perfect replica of the first one! I thanked the spider with joyful appreciation, for I didn't mind its presence—it ate insects that found their way into the house.

Love has no boundaries, and when we radiate love's high frequency, it affects everyone around us—people, wildlife, plants, environments, and beyond. It benefits everything beyond what we can understand. A soul sister texted me one day; she had seen a quotation that reminded her of me: "Miracles are love in action." It felt like a gift to receive this. From my own experiences, I couldn't agree more. One year I received a very unexpected, quite visual, demonstration of this.

It was 2002, and I was living in a downtown apartment near the corporate office where I worked. At the time I had many indoor tropical plants, which had graced a few of my homes during the past five years. One particular plant was a double cane palm, and it was just a bit taller than me. It was lush and healthy. I had enjoyed two years on my own since my last relationship, and then it all unexpectedly changed quite suddenly. I entered into a relationship that was clearly destined, because of the series of incredible events that brought me and this man together. We were perfect for each other at that time and very much in love from the start. I'd always been a passionate person, so I felt all emotions deeply. I savoured love fully, and now I was feeling permanently high on love as we began our relationship; I radiated this energy everywhere I went.

To feel this level of love is to be in a heightened state in which everything in life is enhanced. Our senses seem to perceive things with greater clarity and depth. Everything seems to flow with greater ease. Seemingly negative things don't affect us the same way they might otherwise.

As I began this new relationship, I noticed a strange phenomenon occurring with my cane palm plant. Two spiny arms began to emerge out of the two crowns; they grew longer and longer every day. I marvelled at how quickly these mysterious protrusions developed, curving and growing downward. Then each spiny arm grew multiple branches, which in turn sprouted spheres at their ends. Within a couple of weeks since I had first noticed these odd growths, my cane palm had over a dozen clusters of beautiful, snow-white blossoms! They looked like exotic pompons and were extremely aromatic. In fact, they were so intensely scented that I could smell their perfume in the hallway outside my apartment! It was such a surprising manifestation, perfectly synchronized with my state of heightened love. When I researched the cane palm on the Internet, I discovered that there was no record of these plants blossoming indoors, never mind in an apartment without sunlight shining through. What my plant did was unheard of!

When we think about everything and everyone being comprised of energy, with love being the most powerful form, I'm not surprised that my plant responded in such a spectacular way to its highly love-infused environment. Life is always fully aware of us, regardless of its form. Our energies do affect each other, whether we're aware of it or not.

The Fears that Haunt Us

Gatekeepers of opportunities and transformation beckon us.

*I learned that courage was not the absence of fear, but
the triumph over it. The brave man is not he who does
not feel afraid, but he who conquers that fear.*
—*Nelson Mandela*

*God writes the gospel not in the Bible alone, but on
trees and flowers and clouds and stars.*
—*Martin Luther King Jr.*

Most of us harbour some fears, whether we're aware of them or not. They can be very obvious, as feelings of terror, or very well disguised, as anxiety, worry, doubt, possessiveness, panic, insecurity, control issues, obsessions, anger, judgment, criticism, etc.

However, fears also indicate the area where we're being called to grow and experience true liberation. Experiencing fear is a sign that we're being pushed to move beyond our comfort zone. This is how we can evolve past who we think we are or what we think we're capable of. This is a good thing *if* we don't let our fears paralyse us but instead see them as opportunities to transform ourselves into who we're being called to be.

During an early morning meditation one day, I asked Spirit to clarify, in a simple way, what it means to be in this physical world that is said to be an illusion. While I understood the concept, I felt it needed further clarification, since what we experience is very real in the moment. For most of us, if we pierce a body part with a large knife, or walk in front of a moving train, or jump off a cliff onto rocks far below, it doesn't matter how much we're told that our reality is an illusion, we will physically damage ourselves considerably—or worse. However, I also know from experience that nothing is impossible, that everything that exists is energy, and that many people have mastered the ability to manipulate their physical reality in extraordinary ways. So I wondered what the term *illusion* meant exactly, when applied to our everyday "reality."

As I was meditating, a bird suddenly crashed into the bedroom window—then again and again—near me! Spirit explained that what the bird was seeing was an illusion created by the window's reflection. It was seeing mostly sky between trees, and it was trying to fly through it. Regardless of how much it tried, the bird kept hitting the solid window. With our broader perspective, we could easily see that if the bird took a moment to look around, its perspective of the surroundings would expand. It would see that above itself and the window was the actual sky it wanted to fly through. If it remained fixated on the illusion it was seeing, however, it could either seriously harm itself or simply not advance anywhere. Ultimately, the bird had a choice. Also, if I turned on the light in the room, the illusion would suddenly disappear—the bird would see the room instead and the window for what it was. In this example, the window represented our physical environment, the bird represented all of us having human experiences, and Spirit and I represented all who have a higher perspective and a higher power to change things at will.

The word *illusion* isn't the most accurate word to use regarding this physical world. Rather, our world is a *perspective*. It's highly changeable, and designed for us to learn particular lessons through experiences. We see exactly what we need to see at every stage of our personal growth (which is really not a linear process). As we evolve, we see and experience things differently. As our awareness shifts, so does our perspective and physical reality. We experience more and more of the mystical along with the physical, and we realize that nothing is as it seems—it's always a matter of perspective. (Interestingly, as I wrote these last two lines in my book manuscript, I noticed the word count was 68,666. The number sequence of 666 relates to the physical reality and material illusions.)

The interesting thing about fears is that they're all created by our minds. In most cases, we imagine scenarios based on information we've received from others, and we think these scenarios are real. Anything in the past and the future doesn't exist, except in our minds. The only thing that does exist is in the present moment, *now*.

Our thoughts are extremely powerful, however, and they make our bodies chemically respond to these false realities and the fears we associate with them. We experience actual symptoms in reaction to these fearful thoughts; we believe they are as real as our physical bodies (for they feel that way). We create fears that live just on the other side of our personal security thresholds, thereby ensuring that we stay within our safety zones. However, we'll never discover what really resides in the outer limits unless we step over into that unknown.

It's no different than, as a child, hearing that there might be a monster in the darkness under your bed, yet never knowing whether it's really there, until you find the courage to actually look under there. Then when you do, instead of finding a monster, you find the favourite toy you thought you'd lost!

I must have been no more than five years old when I began to see a wolf watching me through my bedroom window, every time I went to bed and the lights were turned off. All I could see was its head and face. Due to so many big-bad-wolf children's stories, as well as what I heard adults say about how these animals were to be feared, I was terrified. I always slept with the covers over my head, leaving an opening just big enough to breathe through. I did this for years, since I didn't understand why I had a wolf watching me this way. I was told this wolf was my imagination. As a child, I had been taught about guardian angels and archangels but never about spirit guides. As a teenager, I no longer saw that wolf watching me and my fear transformed. Instead of fear, I developed a special love and admiration for these beautiful animals, the ultimate free spirits of Nature. I realized that it was a highly misunderstood and wrongly persecuted animal, based on people's fears. Then, as an adult living on my own, I began to see Wolf in very significant sleep dreams, always protective and loving, with wisdom to share. When I discovered shamanism, I understood that this was an ancient and wise guardian for me with a powerful presence—my oldest power animal.

When we're born as babies, we generally don't know what fear is. We're eager to discover and experience life, fearlessly. We trust that we're fully supported in all ways and we have all we need to accomplish anything. We have an urgent desire to experience all that life has to offer. This desire drives us to learn to walk despite the hazards it might present, so we can explore our world even more fully with our greater mobility.

We've all had occasions, especially as children, when we felt fearless and we accomplished and experienced things that seemed magickal or supernatural. We were able to do things effortlessly with the first attempt or with greater efficiency. We might even have played with animals that never harmed us, even though most people would have said they were dangerous. We felt almost superhuman and experienced extraordinary things.

Then we experience more of life. While some fears and phobias might originate from past-life memories, we generally learn fear through the perceptions of others. Without realizing it, in trying to protect us from the world as *they* know it, people teach us to fear things. We're taught to fear insects; judgment; death; Nature; failure; dark spaces; the potential loss of security; criticism; life forms beyond Earth; particular religions, cultures, and countries; and anything we don't understand. We're taught to fear the unknown, the Divine, walking barefoot outdoors, debt, "bad" weather, inadequacy, hell, sunlight, flying in an aircraft, imperfect produce, inconvenience, the unexplainable, and absence of evidence. We're taught to fear anything that others deem something to fear, based on their personal perceptions or intentions. (Fear has always been the easiest means for authorities and institutions to have control over people and nations.)

We also learn fear from our own or others' experiences, as well as through the media or entertainment. We lose touch with our natural state of being and become filled with fears that weren't ours to begin with. Few fears are our own from birth. If we do have past life fears, it's difficult to know unless we remember somehow or someone else informs us. Regardless of what the fears are, recognizing their source is the key to working with them and transforming them—if we are willing to do so.

I'll never forget one day when I was in Arizona and I felt the need to walk barefoot on the desert trails. As I proceeded to take off my hiking boots and socks, a local man known to be a shaman advised me against it. When I asked him why, he replied that the desert had some nasty spiders and snakes that could really harm me. I was astonished—not by this information but by the source of it. While I was fully aware of those animals, I didn't share his fear. I felt in harmony with the sacred land, Nature and Spirit and just knew I would be fine to walk freely with them. And so I did, multiple times, and savoured every moment of it. If I had felt it wasn't in my best interest to walk barefoot there, I would not have done it. It would have been easy for me to immediately assume he knew better than me, justifying his fear and taking it on as my own. I chose not to.

The shaman's fear could have been caused by one of many things. Maybe as a boy he had stepped on a stinging insect and now had a fear of walking barefoot, regardless of where he was;

maybe he had a phobia of snakes or spiders—or it might have been something entirely different.

My own experience has been that I've always felt at home in Nature and I don't share the fears that many have about it. Instead, I have an awareness beyond my physical senses of my environment (whether it be natural or manmade). I depend on this awareness to alert me if my safety is actually in jeopardy.

While having certain fears can keep us safe from danger, it's always important to tune in to our hearts and see whether these fears are our own or someone else's. It's interesting when we discover fears that we've accepted as our own—without any valid reason to hold on to them. Every day others' fears are being projected onto us. It's easy to unconsciously take some on as our own. When we examine each fear this way, we're able to decide whether it is benefiting us or limiting us.

Regardless of whether our fears are small ones or paralysing ones, opportunities continuously show up throughout the course of our lives that enable us to transform them in some way. With every fear that we transform, we further liberate and empower ourselves. The more we focus on our fears, often without being aware that we're doing so, the more we encounter experiences that invite (or force) us to face them. Our true essences desire us to transform whatever is holding us back from living to our highest potential.

When I travelled to Costa Rica in 2002 for volunteer work, I didn't fear any of the venomous animals that inhabited the area I'd be calling home for three months—that is, until I heard about how scorpions can hide in clothing and footwear. The thought of them hiding in my things is what planted the seed of fear in me. I had a fantastic imagination, and sometimes it didn't serve me well at all. Their physical appearance, as well as my knowledge that they had painful and potentially harmful stings, didn't help to calm that fear either. The more I thought of them, the more my fear grew. As soon as I arrived at the small village, I asked the local residents if they had any deadly scorpion species I should know about and how could I avoid them. I was informed that for a healthy adult like me, their scorpions were nothing to worry about. I was told that their stings were very painful and could temporarily cause numbness. While this wasn't the most reassuring information for me to hear, at least I knew they couldn't kill me.

Every morning before I got dressed, I would shake out the clothing I was going to wear, including the large, long-sleeved shirt I wore as a housecoat before and after my shower. I also always vigorously knocked my footwear upside down before slipping my feet into it. However, it seemed that I was meant to face this fear regardless what I did.

One morning, only five days after my arrival, I vigorously shook my housecoat shirt and put it on. I then walked down the winding stairs to the main floor to take my cold shower (the water flowed straight from the mountain through pipes). Before I reached the shower, however, I suddenly felt something sting my left upper arm. As I looked, I saw what appeared to be the shape of a scorpion moving underneath the sleeve's fabric! This was so unexpected first thing in the morning. While I was usually a very calm person, I freaked out and threw my shirt off onto the ground! I didn't care that anyone could see me if they walked by (since the house was built on stilts and was open-air). I looked at the shirt on the floor and, sure enough, saw a scorpion crawl out of the sleeve. I had been stung by a scorpion. I felt quite offended, for I had taken every precaution to avoid that! I had even hung my shirt on a metal hook behind the bedroom door, so how the scorpion had managed to get inside my shirt was a mystery. Now I had to wait and see what would happen. For the next few hours, my upper arm and tongue went numb, and my armpit throbbed—very bizarre. However, that was the extent of it.

I had officially faced, survived, and overcome my fear of scorpions shortly after my arrival. For the rest of my stay, they didn't bother me—I didn't even see any again! I couldn't help but feel that somehow it had been divinely orchestrated by Spirit so I could fully enjoy my experience there without worrying about scorpions. I had always been committed to doing all I could to fully live my life. Spirit knew that my door was always wide open to opportunities that allowed me to evolve further—and so the opportunities always showed up, usually in the most unexpected ways!

Many ancient cultures and wise elders of our world teach about the two polarities: fear and love. They emphasize that we can choose one or the other. All we have to do is look around us and see the wisdom and truth of this. Everything that has created chaos, suffering, and oppression in this world has had its root in fear. Everything that has created harmony, miracles, and beauty has had its root in love. Some ancient cultures even created complex structures and rituals dedicated solely to facing and transforming fears. They understood the great importance of this.

During one of my meditations when I was experiencing my first extreme test of faith, in December of 2012, Spirit shared this with me: "Love as though you've never been hurt.

Trust as though you've never been deceived. Leap as though you've never known fear." While practicing discernment is paramount, when we do feel divinely guided to love, trust, or leap, then having the courage to do so without holding back unleashes the full potential of the experience.

It takes a strong willingness and commitment to transform certain fears. Some fears are so ingrained in us that we don't even recognize them for what they are—we've learned them through observation. One of the most challenging aspects of choosing between love and fear is that the two may become blurred together. Love in its purest form is *not* possessive, jealous, controlling, judgmental, critical, abusive, disrespectful, blaming, suspicious, manipulative, competitive, etc. towards others (including all beings, ecosystems, and countries). Those aspects are all rooted in fear. If we don't recognize this, we might genuinely believe that our actions and reactions come out of love while they are actually coming out of fear. Some interactions can seem very innocent or well-meaning, especially with those dear to us, so we simply accept what we've been taught as being love. It takes awareness and diligence to practise love in the way that it is truly, mutually beneficial—for fear is our most primal emotion.

We live in a world where fear has unfortunately been the greatest driving force behind behaviors of individuals and nations (the media has played a big role in this and continues to). Over the past decades, I've connected with all sorts of people from around the world, through jobs, volunteer work, travels, courses, events, and networking. From my personal observations and interactions I've noticed that, in general, different environments automatically trigger either fear-based behavior or love-based behavior in us. Synthetic environments super-charged with electromagnetic waves (emitted by electronics) are very disruptive to our bodies in all ways, and don't promote states of well-being or heart-centred interactions. Natural environments have the opposite effect, as they are highly beneficial to us on all levels. It's easy to see the difference when walking in public places of high pedestrian traffic.

When I used to work in a city downtown, it was an area of concentrated corporate office buildings and stores, with small crowds of people streaming in the skywalks and on the sidewalks during morning, lunch, and afternoon breaks. I'd always been one to make eye contact and to smile at people, regardless of where I was. (I'd never been to places where this was discouraged due to safety reasons.) It was simply a warm gesture from one person to another that didn't cost me anything. For 15 years, whenever I went for walks on my breaks, I extended this gesture to others. It always amazed me that very few people returned the eye contact and even fewer the smile. Those who most frequently did return the gesture were the elderly, and they often seemed surprised to receive it. I could see and feel how they appreciated this unexpected, kind act acknowledging them. Their sparkling eyes and genuine smiles felt like mutual heart-to-heart gifts. Most people of the workplace seemed to go to great lengths to avoid eye contact or reacted in not-so-kind ways. I found, however, that when I extended this warm gesture to strangers in natural environments such as parks (even urban ones) or in crowds made up of people gathered with a common interest (related to the arts, Nature, or the spiritual), the gesture was returned and in a much more heartfelt way.

If we desire a more loving world, it's up to all of us to extend ourselves past our protective barriers and act from a place of love instead of fear. We're first and foremost creations of divine love. It's in our nature to express or receive love openly. When we don't, it creates *dis*-ease within us and disharmony among us. It's unfortunate that we require tragedies, storms, earthquakes, wars and other types of forces (natural or manmade) to remind us of our true tendency towards love. Whenever these events occur, whether locally or on a large scale with the entire world as witness, people suddenly forget their fears and act through their hearts' love and compassion to assist those in need— regardless of perceived differences. We've all seen examples of the power of love throughout history and into the present. It creates miracles. It makes the seemingly impossible possible.

When we transform our fears, we're able to connect with others through open hearts. It all starts with each one of us courageously choosing love. Simple acts of love and kindness, without expectations, go a very long way. Over the years I've had countless people express that just knowing me has benefited them, their families, and their lives in ways I could not have foreseen. All I've done is I've lived from a place of love to the best of my ability, regardless of whether I've risked getting hurt. Sometimes just freely giving love-filled hugs has been all it took to cause an incredible ripple effect. The more we courageously work on transforming our fears, the more others will take notice, and the effects will continue to spread in countless, beneficial ways.

For as long as I can remember, I've had a personal fear of being in the spotlight, whether I was just the centre of attention or alone in front of a crowd of people. Throughout my school years, just the thought of speaking in front of the class terrified me. I couldn't help it—it was an automatic reaction. As soon as the teacher announced that we'd each have our turns to read or say something to the entire class (even if it was just our names!), I would react as though my life was being threatened. My heart would immediately start beating harder and faster; it would be loud enough for me to hear it inside my head and feel it in my chest. I would become hot, my palms would sweat, my throat would go dry, and my breathing would get shallow. I would go into immediate fight-or-flight reaction and be unable to shift it no matter what I did. When I reached my thirties and still had this unshakeable fear, I was told that most people share this fear and that many even fear the spotlight more than death! This seems to be true. While this realization didn't assist me in releasing my fear, at least I knew I wasn't alone with this condition that was so utterly uncomfortable and inconvenient.

Then, when I became certified in certain energy healing modalities, I received a missing piece of my fear puzzle. I discovered that I had experienced a life in which I had addressed a large crowd of people from the outdoor platform of a temple, and been violently assassinated for it (a sword through my throat)! The trauma of that experience was still very acute in my subconscious memory. For me, the details of that experience deeply resonated and explained a lot. My new awareness did not make my overwhelming fear disappear. However, this knowledge did put things into perspective for me. This gave me the determination to not let it stop me from saying yes to opportunities aligned with my sacred path. Perhaps I could eventually even transform my fear this way.

From a young age, I've also felt a deep fear of being seen as my authentic self. I've always had a different experience of myself and this world than those I was surrounded by in my youth (and even into adulthood). I never met the expectations of family, friends, or society, so after experiencing various forms of rejection (being criticized, bullied, even turned into an outcast at school), I pretended to be like everyone else, as much as I could. Then, in my thirties, along with learning energy healing, I also answered the call of Stonehenge in England, which brought me to other specific places in that area. During those experiences, I recalled past-life events that shed more light on my fear of being seen. I remembered being persecuted, tortured, and killed numerous times, because I had had different beliefs than those in power and not been willing to conform.

Throughout history, it has never taken much to trigger persecution by people in authority. Anyone who lived in harmony and communed directly with Nature and Spirit, was regarded as a threat at some point and killed if he or she was unwilling to convert to a belief system considered by the "rulers" to be superior. Daring to have different notions than what was deemed true by those who claimed to know better meant risking losing your life—and so many did, in absolutely inhumane ways. Some people still live under these conditions. It's no wonder so many of us share this fear of standing out from the rest. Whether we have past-life memories or not, most of us have a memory that we've inherited from the collective consciousness (since we're all connected). It might not be a personal experience from another life, but we feel it as if it were our own regardless.

Once we identify the source of a fear, we then have the ability to work with it if we desire to transform it. Some fears can transform in very little time, while others require a lot of persistence and inner work. Sometimes we simply learn to live with a certain fear in a way that it no longer interferes so much with life. What makes all this possible is having something greater in importance than our fear—a desire that pulls us through and beyond that fear.

Since I've always had that strong inner desire to fulfill my purpose on Earth, I've been willing to do all I can to achieve this, including facing my fears and doing what I can to move past them. It has not been easy or comfortable; however, the rewards I've received from doing this work have kept me going every time these fears show up. Spirit always knows what we're ready to shift within us, and opportunities appear to enable us to do so, whether or not we consciously feel ready and able. We are never handed something that we can't handle.

When I self-published my first book, *Mending Mother Earth with Native Plants,* I dedicated it to Mother Earth. I wasn't brought up with this way of thinking (that our planet is much more than just a sphere of land and water with different habitats). It was simply born out of my sacred relationship with Nature and Spirit. Because of this, that dedication felt like a big step beyond my safety zone. I was openly expressing my love and appreciation, however, and I had to include it in the book for it to feel authentic and complete. To my surprise, I received so many incredible compliments about my book, and those whom I thought might have issues with my dedication were some of my greatest supporters. It made me realize that while my fear was justifiable based on my past, in the present it was based on assumptions and not actualities. That was a big lesson.

I did also have my fear of the spotlight, so I simply announced my book to those I knew, by email and word of mouth. After a long time of many people suggesting I get a Facebook account, I finally decided I would, as a way to give my book more visibility (for free!) on the Internet. Well, Spirit obviously had greater plans for me.

Just through word of mouth, I ended up being interviewed by an out-of-province magazine writer. I was featured in a monthly edition for my experience-based knowledge of coexisting with Nature in a city. Then the editor of another magazine contacted me. I wrote an article for him that highlighted the message of my book, which was featured in their 2011 annual issue. I also received an invitation to be a guest speaker on a popular Saturday morning radio show for the same reason I was contacted by the others. I wasn't even doing anything—these invitations were finding me! I recognized that these were invaluable opportunities, and my commitment to my path required that I say yes to every one of them.

However, the thought of the radio show terrified me. I accepted, however, to honour the purpose of my book. Its message was about the miracles of sacred relationship in Nature and what enables us as humans, to coexist in harmony as stewards of our natural world. The book itself was inspired by so many lessons and insights I had received from Nature, which were meant to be shared—even if it meant putting myself in the spotlight. And so I did. It felt quite unnerving to have a huge microphone in my face and know that countless people were listening to what I was saying. However, the host was wonderful as she interviewed me, and I discovered that I actually enjoyed it, despite my fear. When I heard a recording of myself later, I realized that I sounded natural, and my passion and knowledge came through louder than my nerves. Once again I had received an important lesson about perspective.

Having received those opportunities out of the blue, I shouldn't have been surprised when I then received an invitation that would really put me in the spotlight, face to face with a crowd! I had done the radio spotlight with a crowd I couldn't see, so this was the next level of stretching me beyond my comfort zone. The librarian of my hometown wanted to organize a book launch for me. I felt so honoured—and petrified at the same time. Just the thought of it brought up all the anxieties I had felt in my school years. Yet again, I knew this was an amazing opportunity to do my work as a messenger for something so divinely beautiful. I couldn't say no if I was committed to my path. So I graciously accepted her invitation. She was thrilled and so accommodating; she took care of all the advertising and preparation for it. I ended up in all the local newspapers. All I had to do was show up with copies of my book—and speak to a crowd. As the day approached, I felt more and more anxious.

On the day of my book launch, I experienced all the same symptoms I always had before addressing a group of people. To get me through it, I focused on the reason I was doing this, which was larger than me. I was simply being a messenger. I had prepared little notes for it, but I ended up putting them aside, choosing instead to speak authentically from my (pounding) heart. I would be speaking about something I knew intimately, so I relied on inspiration to guide me on what to say. I also made sure I had a glass of water and took my time speaking from the floor of the library. I was standing level with the crowd from an angle so everyone could see me. It was a very intimate setting.

The attentiveness of the people there and their smiles when I made eye contact were very encouraging. I made it through and was so surprised afterwards by the comments I received. So many thought I was used to speaking in front of a crowd! When I confessed how completely out of my comfort zone I was, they complemented me for looking so calm and for speaking so well. This really astonished me. It reinforced my new perspective about one of my dominant fears. What I felt within was obviously not visible to those watching, and while I didn't feel excited about speaking in front of a crowd, it hadn't killed me either. In fact, it had made me feel good to know I was making a difference. I greatly enjoyed meeting everyone afterwards. As I signed copies of my book that people purchased because they had been touched somehow, I realized that the public speaking had been well worth it. Knowing I had succeeded in inspiring so many just by showing up, gave me the courage to keep saying yes to opportunities, regardless of my fears.

I was later invited to be interviewed for multiple newspapers in the city, which I accepted. The journalist of one of the newspapers came to the house and took photos of me in one of my gardens after the interview was over. As requested, I provided her with photos from my personal collection of beautiful plants in bloom and wildlife. When the newspaper was published a week later, I was shocked to discover that they had featured large photos of *me* on the front page, as well as inside, instead of using my photographs! It was so unexpected, I felt betrayed. However, I received many compliments from people who saw the article, and I knew that once again Spirit was allowing me to work through my fear of the spotlight.

I worked through more of my fear of being seen when I started using social media and launched my website at the end of 2011. I felt I was leaping very far from my comfort zone again, for I was sharing a little bit more of myself that wasn't considered mainstream (I mentioned beings like elementals for example). Yet I received many wonderful comments from so many people, worldwide. I recognized the great benefits of being visible on the Internet. The more I connected with soul family, the more confident I became with being my true self in all situations with all people.

Eventually that fear actually transformed, and this book is the ultimate evidence! When I left my old life behind me in 2011, I could not have imagined talking openly with others about the things I experienced that truly ignited my heart and spirit in everyday life. I was so "outside the (mainstream) box." I discussed such things with only a select few. Now I've reached a point where I'm actually able to not only share my authentic self with the world, but also with transparency!

The transformation of one of my greatest fears definitely amazes me—it's a direct reflection of my own personal growth. I've realized along my journey of overcoming this fear that it's been mostly about not wanting to upset those who have known me for a long time; many of them have fears of what others will think. However, I now know I wouldn't be as I am if there wasn't a divine purpose for it. I also know I wouldn't have been guided by Spirit to write this book, exactly the way it is, if it didn't have a higher purpose. This book is the result of love overcoming fear. (As I wrote this last line in my book manuscript, I noticed the word count was 106,444. The 444 signifies that one is fully supported, guided, and loved by many surrounding angels, with nothing to fear!)

It is always possible to transform fear. It helps to know we always have the full support of Spirit to help us achieve this, each in our own way. As I've evolved more and more, greater levels of transformative opportunities have appeared, so I can keep liberating myself further of the constraints of my most dominating fears.

In 2012, an invitation of a completely different nature quite unexpectedly showed up. I was travelling to my business mentor's city, to work with her in person. I was also to do a photo shoot with her photographer. I had done so much work on my fear of being seen that having new photos done felt like a powerful, visual crystallization of all that internal work. A performing artist I had met in Arizona happened to contact me, and I mentioned my travel plans. Sarika lived near the area where I was going, and she surprised me with an invitation to do live "sacred art" at her special event in the neighbouring city. It would take place just before my scheduled time with my mentor.

I had never even heard of this artistic concept (never mind done it myself), so I was stunned, to say the least. It meant that I would be doing channeled art in the form of a painting, live in the moment, on a stage, in front of a watching crowd! In addition to this, I would only have a few hours to paint and would not know in advance what would come through. Of course, if I wanted to, I could think of something to paint ahead of time, but then it wouldn't be an authentic experience—it had to be a process of surrender to Spirit and the energies present. Fortunately, I had worked on my perfectionism for some time, and it was now an ally instead of a hindrance. Still, the thought of doing this felt quite intimidating to me.

Once again, I knew immediately that this was a divine opportunity to allow me to experience the spotlight, and in a bigger way than I ever had before. Declining was not an option if I was fully committed to my path. It became obvious to me that making friends with the spotlight was part of my work, for it kept finding me in the most incredible ways. I was grateful I wouldn't be alone on the stage; I would be sharing it with a musician along with Sarika. She was also going to take care of the supplies, the advertising, and the organizing of her event, leaving me with little to do except show up and assist with the set-up. It was such a gift.

The evening of this event, I did things that made me feel empowered. I spent some time outdoors, barefoot. I meditated, and danced to favourite music. I dressed up to express my true essence and chose to remove my shoes on the stage to feel more grounded. It was an opportunity that allowed me to be seen by others as my authentic self, while also in the spotlight. It felt like another momentous experience, orchestrated by Spirit, through so many. I set up everything in a way that enabled me to create a large painting on the canvas, while the crowd could also see it clearly. I then consciously placed my ego aside so I could just go along with the energy flow and freely create whatever wanted to manifest on the canvas.

During the event I simply tuned in to the collective energy, including the crowd and Spirit, and let that energy flow through me to become a painting. I had no idea what it would look like, but I released all thoughts and surrendered to the moment. I took my time and occasionally I even painted with my left hand, something I had never done before! I began by painting the entire canvas black and what emerged from this surprised me. It looked like a butterfly-shaped Earth cradled in the lap of a large, white spirit being, sitting in a half lotus position in the universe. It all went by surprisingly quickly. After Sarika finished singing, I signed the painting to mark its completion, and she handed me the microphone. I breathed deeply and faced the crowd from the stage. I found my voice and talked about a vision I had received that morning from Spirit to share with everyone. It felt simultaneously terrifying and exhilarating, for while my fear was still very present, I felt the connections I was making from my heart to those in the crowd. I also felt the power within me of overcoming my fear instead of letting it control me, so I could shine and be of service in the ways I was being called.

What followed absolutely amazed me and I knew this was Spirit's reward to me for braving the spotlight this way. People who attended the event came to exchange hugs afterwards, and they gave me such beautiful and genuine compliments, not just about my painting but about me personally. I noticed that both the women and men expressed a common thing—they were so inspired and moved by my energy and presence. This touched me deeply. I greatly appreciated how they took the time to share this with me, for through them I understood myself more clearly. I saw that Spirit was right about my energy affecting others in beneficial ways, without me having to do anything except be me. I only needed to be fully present, as a clear channel for the Divine to work through.

This is how it works for *all* of us. When we're doing something that fully resonates with our sacred hearts (our true essences), with or without fears, we brilliantly shine from a divine space. We radiate more of our divinity, which inspires others. Through this event, I also realized more than ever that what comes naturally to one is extraordinary to another, and it's important to know this. What we offer to others by being fully ourselves in this world is more amazing than we can ever imagine.

Watching me create a painting from a blank canvas mesmerized and inspired people in ways I had not anticipated at all. Had I let my fears of the spotlight and of being seen as my true self prevent me from saying yes to this opportunity, I would have missed out on an invaluable experience, as would the people I inspired. A few people even expressed that I ignited in them the desire to start painting! Working through our fears isn't just for our own benefit but also for the benefit of others we may not even be aware of. The ripple effects are incredible.

Sometimes fears we never had before can suddenly appear in a very big way, without advance notice. They confront us when we find ourselves in unexpected circumstances, such as tests of faith. Those fears become very powerful teachers. They're intense catalysts of deep transformation—if we're willing to face them and learn from them. What we may learn and become in the process can enable us to evolve on a personal level in a record amount of time! The last two chapters of this book are detailed, perfect examples of this.

I've learned firsthand the invaluable lesson of how perspective plays a vital role with our fears. I've had experiences that felt terrifying, yet they seemed so tame compared with experiences I went through later! When we learn things from experience we gain a deeper understanding, which becomes part of us and our personal truth—it becomes wisdom. Learning about perspective this way has been invaluable for me, for we all experience life through our personal perspectives. The greater is our awareness, the more our perspectives can empower us.

While I was in Hawai'i for a few months in 2013, I was taught another important thing about fears. Something interesting manifested that greatly reinforced how our minds play such a crucial role with creating our fears and therefore also play a key role in transforming them. I had been hiking at sunrise every morning for a few weeks, and I had never encountered a single dog. While I would hear some barking as I went by the countless driveways, they were always confined to the private properties. Then, one morning, my mind was particularly preoccupied by my empty bank account, despite Spirit's guidance to trust. When I went on my hike it seemed that every guard dog in the neighbourhood was waiting for me at the end of their territories, as I made my way back up the mountain! First I encountered a pair of dogs—each of which was larger than me. Both were actually standing on the road, beyond the driveway(!), and were fixated on me. They were already growling and barking, even though I was still a distance away. Although I love animals, I do feel apprehension in the presence of large dogs that I don't know (especially those who guard properties!). I find the behavior of wild animals easier to read, which allows me to act accordingly. These dogs were a complete mystery to me, and that made it difficult for me to trust them. I was also aware that all animals keenly sense energy, and fear was *not* an ideal one for these dogs to sense from me!

I didn't know what to do. I had already hiked the steepest part back up the mountain, so if I turned around I would be extending my hike considerably, and the sun was already getting hot at this point. If I continued, I risked getting mauled by two big, drooling dogs that were pure muscle with strong jaws! I remained as calm as I could and paused while I tuned in to my heart. I was grateful they didn't run up to me but were just patiently observing (while letting me know they knew I was there). Within my heart I sensed that this was another lesson for me about fear. This was also very symbolic of what I was facing in my life. These dogs were like physical manifestations of my fearful thoughts that day.

I slowly inhaled and exhaled deeply and sent a lot of love energy from my heart to both dogs. I asked Archangel Michael for protection and I decided to continue up the mountain. I walked with the most confident stride I could muster and focused ahead of me, avoiding direct eye contact with the dogs. They loudly barked and growled at me, with spit splattering, barely inches away from my body, but they didn't touch me. Absolutely relieved to pass through that ordeal unscathed, I then experienced the same scenario with three other dogs at different driveways (all were waiting for me on the road)! The others were individuals, so they seemed a bit less threatening compared with the pair. I did the best I could to ignore these dogs as well, while remaining heart-centred. I reached my destination unharmed and feeling *so* grateful. I also felt very proud of myself for facing that fear square on. After that day, I didn't see those dogs again. It was obviously another opportunity for me to learn more about fear in relation to energy.

We never know what our fears might teach us, especially about ourselves, until we decide to acknowledge them, face them, and understand them. It's always a process, and each one is unique. Within our hearts we always know what to do, and it's just a matter of whether we're willing or not. Every fear we have has a divine purpose to serve us in some way. Some fears can transform and vanish. Others might always be present within us. They teach us how much we've evolved to be able to coexist with them, doing what we feel called to do despite their presence.

While I was able to gradually transform my fear of being seen so I now feel safe with sharing my authentic self, I still have a fear of being in the spotlight. However, it's not quite as overwhelming as it used to be since I transformed my other fear. My commitment to my path and the calling of my heart are greater than my fears. (This was absolutely put to the test in 2013 and became my last chapter!)

An effective way to master our most intense fears is by allowing our heart desires to grow larger than our fears are. We then do what we feel we must, despite our fears. The rewards we receive from doing so are always more than worth it, and empower us to keep going with our divine purpose!

Absolute Trust

Fully trusting ourselves and life is true freedom.

All I have seen teaches me to trust the creator for all I have not seen.
—Ralph Waldo Emerson

The intuitive mind is a sacred gift and the rational mind
is a faithful servant. We have created a society that
honors the servant and has forgotten the gift.
—Albert Einstein

Absolute trust in ourselves is the most valuable attribute we can possess. We can't live empowered lives without self-trust, for regardless of what form of intuitive guidance we receive, ultimately it must go through our own personal filters. We all have personal filters through which every form of information must pass, before we recognize it as something specific, perceived by our senses. Our filters begin to form as soon as we are born, from our own experiences as well as through our interactions with people and our environment. We each have our unique way of perceiving and experiencing the world through our filters. It's easy to recognize this when we spend time with others.

A crowd of people could watch the same symphony in an outdoor stadium, and if we asked them about the experience, each would have a different story to tell, based on how they perceived it through their personal filters. While the music might have captivated everyone's attention, different aspects of this experience would stand out for each person. It could be the weather; the temperature; certain melodies or musical instruments; certain emotions that they felt; the crowd; the shoes, accessories, or clothing that musicians or people in the crowd wore; different scents; someone's hair or jewellery; the sky; the environment; someone's demeanour; sounds in the distance not related to the symphony; certain colours; the energy; the mood; conversations; someone's car; the location; the company; something mystical—just about anything!

Our filters give each of us a unique experience and also bring certain things to the forefront of our awareness, while other things are less prominent or not noticed at all. It's valuable to know this when interacting with others and our world. Too many people feel a need to be right, accusing anyone who perceives something differently than they do as being wrong. The truth is that, what each of us experiences *is true to us*, regardless of whether someone disagrees. This applies to all aspects of life.

If you feel cold when you're outside, it doesn't matter how warm someone else feels and how many times you're told that it's warm—it won't change the fact that to *you*, the temperature feels cold. Being respectful of each other's unique filters encourages empowering discussions instead of causing disempowering arguments.

Each one of us also has senses of perception that are tuned in to higher knowledge than the physical and the mental. If you have any doubt about the information that these senses receive, you end up questioning everything, and no amount of higher guidance will serve you. Without absolute trust in yourself, it's also impossible to make decisions based on your inner wisdom and remain steadfast when you're faced with challenges and adversity. Even more difficult than dealing with opposition from others is opposition from your own inner critic and self-doubts that your own mind creates.

Since our most powerful information comes from sources that aren't logical or tangible, with no proof that our minds can agree with, accepting that information is solely a matter of trust. It's very easy to dismiss it as nothing, but when we do trust and acknowledge it without analysing it, we're able to navigate through life confidently, regardless of what we experience.

Often intuitive information is time sensitive, and it's important to act quickly without thinking, which only trust enables us to do. It's not a logical process. When we receive these intuitive "hits," a sacred window of opportunity seems to open up for us. If we don't act without delay, we will lose that priceless opportunity. Being able to trust our ability to perceive information accurately is highly valuable for all areas of life, including our relationships and work. It enables us to live our higher potential by maximizing our time, resources, energy, and well-being.

When I was scheduled to work with my business mentor in person, I planned to stay at a hotel she recommended in her city, since it was near a large park filled with majestic trees. I thought I was booking early enough in advance, but I was mistaken.

When I went to the hotel's website to book a reservation, I was quite surprised to discover that they had no vacancies for the weekend I needed. All rooms were completely booked! I felt an *uh-oh* moment, and although it was clear from the calendar diagrams that no rooms were available, in that instant I felt I had to contact the hotel. Logically it seemed pointless and a waste of time, but I made the phone call anyway.

When the front desk clerk answered, I explained my situation. The clerk told me he had someone on hold on the other line with a cancellation. Would I mind holding while he took care of that first? I gladly agreed to hold and patiently waited. When he picked up the line again, he announced to me that the cancellation was for the weekend I needed—I had a room if I wanted to book it with him! My jaw dropped open. He even honoured the online discounted rate as he booked it for me. I was so grateful!

Had I not immediately followed through when I felt that sudden intuitive *nudge* to call, I would have lost that opportunity. The timing was very crucial. I could easily have dismissed it, since the website clearly showed every room was booked—that was the logical information my mind was stuck on. The higher information notified me of a unique window of opportunity and I had to act *right now*. However, I didn't know all this—all I received was a very subtle feeling, or sudden idea, that I should make that phone call. Over the years I've learned to not ignore even the slightest inkling. When we begin to recognize how our intuition works with us, we're able to perceive it for what it is and not question it.

Since so many of us have been raised in a predominantly logically-functional society and lifestyle, by the time we reach adulthood we might not even be aware that we have intuitive abilities (or that there is such a thing). They're not valued as much as our intellect, if at all, and yet they are invaluable. Many historical geniuses of science attested to this, including Nikola Tesla and Albert Einstein who both talked a lot about the mystical (I've included many of Einstein's quotes in this book). These intuitive senses perceive information beyond the logical. Due to our conditioning, we bury many of them under our dominating, louder thoughts as well as the noise of life. It can be challenging to perceive our higher guidance. It's usually so subtle that it's barely noticeable, with our physical senses and logical minds at the forefront of our awareness. It simply takes practice to notice when our minds reject this information and to recognize the self-doubts that show up.

By nature, as humans we *all* have intuitive abilities. While different factors can numb them or make them less obvious, some are just so natural to us that we don't even realize they're abilities or that we're using them. In the regular systems of society, we're generally not encouraged to use our intuitive senses as children and even less as adults. It's all dismissed as either being our imaginations (making it "wrong") or being irrelevant to "reality."

My own intuitive abilities were anything but obvious, even though I have many (as we all do). Even though I was using many of them every day, I couldn't recognize them in their subtlety. I didn't use them *consciously* until my late thirties. What I experienced until then seemed sporadic. I was never one who needed proof to know that something existed. Yet, since I didn't know what to make of these glimpsed things I couldn't explain, I dismissed them as bizarre, with no idea what role they played in my life or environment. No amount of reading and research enlightened me about my gifts and abilities.

Then one day, I felt guided to have my palms read, and my intuitive gifts were actually named to me. My ability to feel and interpret energies remained a mystery to me (until it was activated further, on that 2010 winter solstice). However, with this new awareness I was able to develop and use my other abilities simply through practice. I began to notice that the flashes of insight I received had a different quality than mere sudden ideas. I also realized that in order to receive intuitive information and make that link stronger, I had to share or implement what I received. I quickly realized that nothing could replace personal experience. The more aware we are, the more we can practise, and the easier, stronger, and clearer it becomes for us.

When I started to consciously notice these intuitive hits, it was so subtle that I wondered if I had perceived anything at all. I had just enough awareness to know I had perceived *something* different. This something stood apart from my familiar thoughts and sensations, or physical surroundings, just enough to catch my attention. To help me trust the information I received, I began to either express what I perceived or act on these nudges. Whenever I had conversations with soul family, I would share any "downloads" of information beyond my physical senses, no matter how subtle or bizarre they seemed.

A lot of the intuitive information we receive can seem unusual or can be perceived out of the blue. It's important to grasp it before our minds blur it. Writing it down can be very useful, especially at first.

Since the members of my soul family were also open to the unusual with awareness, I felt at ease sharing anything with them. By doing this, I was able to practise differentiating between higher information, my usual logical thoughts, and creative imagination. The more I practised, the more information I received. The more I acknowledged the information through sharing or action, the greater were the validations that what I perceived was accurate. Like exercised muscles, my intuition and trust became stronger.

Synchronicities are some of the most powerful confirmations. They're like winks from Spirit (commonly dismissed as coincidences) that show up through our environment and experiences with others. When I'm with people who have also developed their intuitive abilities, everything suddenly becomes amplified in wonderful ways for us, and this is also useful to know. The only way we can become confident with anything is by doing it until it feels effortless. When we're completely at ease with it, then we're able to continuously expand with experience.

You might recognize in yourself some of these most common intuitive abilities and experiences that most of us share. You might have "gut feelings," "hunches" or "nudges" that guide you somehow, and you might recognize them only after you receive some form of confirmation. You might feel a clear *knowing* about something with no logical explanation for this knowledge (which you didn't learn through regular means). You might receive flashes of insight or a sudden impulse of information, relating to something that will assist you or someone else, and it may be unrelated to what you were thinking at that moment. Déjà vu, when you recognize your current experience as one you have already experienced, is another example. Telepathy may be experienced with others in various ways, such as when you speak someone's thoughts, or you manifest someone's wish without consciously knowing they had it, or you suddenly think of someone you haven't thought of in a long time and then receive communication from them or bump into them in an unexpected way. You may have a premonition, a sudden and strong feeling that something is about to happen, and it does. Dreams or visions might give you information about yourself, someone else, or some aspect of our world or your personal life. There are also spiritual counterparts to all your dominant physical senses; they enable you to perceive and experience things beyond what your physical senses usually can. You're able to suddenly see, smell, feel, taste, or hear something clearly, with no logical or physical explanation for it. You might have an experience when you suddenly feel shivers and you sense a presence around you or feel that you are being watched, even though you don't logically perceive anything in your physical environment that could cause you to feel this way.

These are only some of the most common ones. Remembering that we all perceive differently liberates us to honour our abilities as they are, so we can work with them more efficiently. For instance, while I know many people who can see spirits with their spiritual sense of sight, I have never seen one as of the writing of this book. However, I've clearly perceived spirits with other intuitive senses when they're around me. I've heard their footsteps, voices, and laughter. I've also felt their energy, and I've even smelled their perfume and smoke from cigars and cigarettes (when there was no one in the room or building but me).

At one event in 2012, I heard a speaker refer to over 50 different intuitive or spiritual senses! Regardless of the actual number, they greatly outnumber our physical senses, and it's obvious we have these gifts and abilities to assist us in incredible ways. The more we use them, the more we recognize their immeasurable value in empowering ourselves. Perhaps this is one reason we haven't been taught or encouraged to value these divine senses, for an empowered person is difficult to control, by anyone or by any means.

It's common to have certain intuitive abilities that are stronger or more obvious than other ones. However, it's also possible to experience all our spiritual senses. The tricky thing about using them is that our minds love nothing more than to interfere, using logical thinking. Our minds have the job of rationalizing everything and keeping us safe from all harm, including the potentially harmful *unknown*. When we receive information through illogical means, our minds instantly analyse it and try to make sense of it. If they can't, the information isn't considered worthy of our attention (since it won't contribute to our immediate safety), and it gets discarded. However, until we strengthen our abilities and gain the confidence required to trust them as much as our other senses (if not more), we also have another invaluable attribute to assist our navigation of everyday life and the unknown.

Since life is always fully aware of us (through the Divine's all-knowing presence), it communicates with us at all times in ways unique to us. Whether we need confirmation about information that we intuitively receive or extra guidance as we make decisions, we have our own *essence language* that life communicates to us. Even our minds can't dismiss it, for it's outside of ourselves and perceivable by our physical senses in our immediate, tangible reality. It's a language that's completely unique to each of us, transmitted from Spirit in partnership with that part of ourselves that's always tuned in to higher, divine knowledge. It could also be called *sacred heart* or *soul language*. It's not based on logic. It's a priceless ally as we learn to use and strengthen our intuitive abilities, especially until our minds no longer hinder us. When we gain a certain level of trust in our abilities, we're able to recognize our minds' interference for what it is and work with it. While our minds are necessary, they are much more useful when they focus on realizing our full potential rather than sabotaging it.

I use my essence language as much as all my other senses every day, to get a greater perspective of my life's journey. It's especially helpful when I have difficult decisions to make, experience challenges, or go through tests of faith and need extra encouragement. It's a gift we've been given that is always available to assist us on our paths—it only makes sense to use it.

Our essences, which are that purely divine and infinite part of ourselves, speak a different language than our minds do. Our essences speak to us in symbols, colours, shapes, sounds, feelings, words, metaphors, numbers, songs, impressions, poetry, scents, and everything abstract and mystical. Only *you* know your personal essence language. What you recognize as a sign or message means nothing to others, and it's important to trust these personal signs and messages with that understanding.

When our heart desires beckon us to fulfill them, we end up navigating territory that feels unfamiliar to us. Whether it's slightly or extremely unfamiliar, we know the desire but we don't know the outcome. That can feel very intimidating or terrifying. Yet the unknown is where endless possibilities await us, and we always have everything we need to move confidently through it. We wouldn't have those heart desires if we didn't have what it takes to achieve them.

Your personal essence language lets you know when you're on the right path, regardless of how things seem or what others might say or think. It allows you to remain steadfast in the face of adversity, especially when you make decisions no one agrees with or understands. It also enables you to withstand your own self-doubts, which is invaluable when you experience ordeals or tests of faith. At times, your essence language might be the only thing that keeps you from giving in to doubt, worry, and fear. It might be the only thing that enables you to keep your commitment to yourself and your path instead of giving up.

The best way to identify your own essence language is to think about what signs feel special, lucky, or significant to you. Think as far back as your childhood. Some signs are familiar and easy to recognize. You usually interpret their meanings in a personal way, and the same sign can have different meanings under different circumstances. If you're unsure about the meaning of certain ones, you can look them up through various resources, under symbol, colour, or number, for example, and see what resonates with you. You may feel a connection with a specific number or number sequence, a song or word, an animal, a symbol from Nature or something artificially created. Some signs might suddenly become obvious during certain experiences and be added to your conscious knowledge along your journey.

Rainbows have always been very special to me; they are part of *my* essence language. As soon as I began to draw and paint as a child, rainbows were my favourite thing to create. I never tired of them. Throughout my life, they have guided me in various ways. By simply noticing the circumstances surrounding the appearance of these glorious light manifestations, I've learned to interpret their messages. The same goes with feathers, butterflies (especially the monarch) and lightning. They've been special parts of my essence language for as long as I can remember. The numbers 11, 33, and 333 have also been very significant to me for a long time, and at different times other number sequences have become prominent. However, whirlwinds and other spinning winds, including tornadoes, only became part of my essence language after I left my old life behind me and even more after I received my spirit name, DancingWind. As recent as they are, they have become a very significant sign for me; they often appear in vivid dreams when I'm going through certain experiences. The spiral is another symbol that has been part of my essence language for as long as I can remember, and interestingly, it now also has a connection to the spinning winds for me. The hexagon is an even more recent addition to my essence language, yet it's very prominent as well.

When our essence language communicates with us, the signs appear in unusual or repetitive ways to get our attention. They're not signs that we chase or look for—*they* find *us*. That's how we know they are authentic signs communicating with us and not just a part of our environment that we've happened to notice. They go out of their way to be recognized. They can also show up and we simultaneously just *know* they're signs meant for us (if logically it's not quite obvious enough). They use any means or form to communicate with us, including our natural and artificial environments, reading materials, television, radio, people's conversations or clothing, advertisements, Internet, vehicles, stores, household items, email, social media, synchronicities, etc. We simply have to be aware and open to receiving. Spirit takes care of the rest, in partnership with our essences.

I've received signs in the most mysterious ways and in the most unexpected places. I remember being in a huge, foreign airport once, and although I felt as if I were going in the right direction to my gate, I wasn't sure, and I didn't have a lot of time before my flight. I hadn't encountered any airport employees to ask either. As I questioned this more and more in my mind, I suddenly noticed a large feather on my path! There were no areas open to the outdoors, so its appearance was quite a surprise. It looked as if it had been placed there, perfectly aligned, like an arrow pointing in the direction I was walking. I couldn't help but smile as I picked it up and thanked Spirit. I then found my gate a short distance ahead of me. (As I was adding this personal story to my book manuscript, I happened to glance at my word count and saw that it was 62,333! The timing of the personally significant 333 showing up was reinforcing how essence signs communicate with us.)

Since so many of us now spend more time in artificial environments than natural ones, many symbols incorporate numbers, as these are so prevalent with technology. They can show up on digital clocks, licence plates, barcodes, billboards, advertisements, Internet information, phone numbers, page numbers, etc. The same numbers will show up repeatedly in different ways to get your attention, or you will see them with a sudden knowing that it's a message for you. There are various published resources that interpret numbers, many of which are associated with angels. More often than not, you also just intuitively know what they mean to you. A reference can simply provide you with a more complete interpretation of their numerical message.

When you see certain numbers, especially master numbers (sequences of doubles), take note of what your thoughts are at that moment or were just before you saw them. Sometimes those numbers simply serve as a flag to bring attention to your thoughts. Alphabet letters can also translate into numbers, such as A=1, B=2, etc. and L=12 or 3 (when you add the digits together), M=13 or 4, etc. Generally, master numbers, such at 11, 22, 33 and so on, don't combine to reduce to a simple number, but there are always exceptions. As with everything else, it's important to always listen to your inner knowing—your own personal wisdom. What might be true for someone may not be true for you, and vice versa.

Our essence language can also provide guidance during our journeys by confirming what energies are currently affecting us or by making us aware of them. Knowing what energies are influencing our journeys at any given time, can assist us to more efficiently navigate our paths. Instead of living from a reactive state of being, we're better able to go with the flow from a state of co-creative awareness.

One morning at the end of June 2013, it was getting close to my departure date from Hawai'i Island, and I was having a sunrise hike. I hadn't been guided to accept any of the jobs that had been offered to me, and I just knew I had to leave. But, that morning, my thoughts wandered to what I might experience once I left the island. For the first time in my adult life I was officially without a place to call home, my own sanctuary. Due to unusual circumstances, I'd had to leave the house I'd been renting for the past two years, and all my possessions were now in storage at my parents' home. While I knew that things were meant to be this way, it all felt quite surreal regardless.

Interestingly, the number sequence of 555 showed up multiple times within a few hours. It was obvious that so much more was going on than I could perceive. I saw 555 on the licence plates of vehicles three times. I also felt guided to go back up the same road I'd used to come down the mountain, instead of looping up on the other road that I usually returned on. I didn't understand it, but I felt so strongly nudged that I gave in to this peculiar guidance. After I'd hiked uphill awhile, I was surprised to see a large white label sticker, stuck on the concrete, in the middle of the road. I hadn't seen it coming down. On it was a scribbled phone number, clearly showing xxx-x555! So bizarre! Then, later, when I logged onto my Facebook page to post a "Miracle of the Day," a sidebar advertisement appeared, displaying $x,555 on it. I also received an email from a soul sister who lives in Europe with the time 15:55 showing in my inbox. This particular number sequence signifies huge changes throughout one's entire life as well as higher consciousness. (As I wrote this text in my book manuscript two months later in Canada, I suddenly noticed that the word count was 39,555. Another month later, as I was editing this paragraph, I noticed the word count was 62,555! Since I hadn't been writing or editing my manuscript in chronological order at that point, receiving the 555 twice at this section felt very purposeful—which is why I mentioned it.)

As I wrote and edited my manuscript for this book, the timely appearance of specific triple numbers was a constant reminder that Spirit transcends time and space. Linear time is a human creation and doesn't affect Spirit or Nature. Our essence language is also not affected by linear time. It is governed by the mystical.

We can also use our essence language to assist us with important decisions or with intuitive guidance. I use this form of assistance whenever I need to reassure my basic, logical self that everything is okay, as I'm navigating the unknown at its most extreme, taking a giant leap of faith, or going through a test of faith. At those times, when the circumstances can greatly alarm my mind, I even specify what kind of sign I desire to receive.

Two months after moving to my new rural home in 2011, to fully follow my heart's calling, I was navigating the complete unknown. I had left everything that felt secure to me with no evidence that things would work out. It was a *giant* leap of faith but one I just knew I had to take. Now I needed more reassurance that I was on the right path and fully supported by Spirit, as I focused on my burning desire to fulfill my purpose. It was one of those days when a lot of self-doubts were harassing me, and there was no better way to put an end to that than through tangible, symbolic signs from my essence language.

In the early evening, I decided to go for a long walk "around the block," the block being a one-square-mile area in the country created by four gravel roads among forests, ponds, and pastures. As I stepped outdoors, I asked Spirit for a clear sign that would give me the reassurance I needed. I specifically asked for a feather—and not just any feather, but the large feather of an eagle or owl. Since the feathers of birds of prey were very rare and considered sacred, this felt like an appropriate sign to ease my panicking mind. Logically, the chances of finding such a feather were slim, even more so considering the blowing wind.

It was a beautiful day of tropical heat and humid weather common in that area of central Canada in the summer—the kind of weather I had always loved. The sky was clear and bright blue, the sun was shining radiantly, and the wind was swaying the trees, grasses, and abundant blossoming wildflowers. Everything was a feast for the eyes and so wonderfully fragrant. As I walked, countless butterflies fluttered and glided nearby, and hundreds of dragonflies hovered and perched around me with every step I took. It was an incredible summer for dragonflies. They were everywhere, in the thousands, perching together on top of blades of grass and looking like exotic flower meadows themselves, their wings glistening gold and rainbow colours in the sun. I had never seen such an abundance of dragonflies. They mesmerized me and I greatly enjoyed the presence of these magickal beings. Birds were also present in great numbers, singing a delightful symphony from the forest trees and fields. All my senses were filled with bliss as I fully savoured my surroundings.

Before I reached half a mile on the road going east, I suddenly felt guided to look at the ground in front of me. As my gaze moved from the forest to the vegetation bordering the road, I was moved to tears. A large, beautiful, and perfect feather from a great horned owl was resting motionless on the ground just ahead of me, despite the wind! As I picked it up, I thanked Spirit with all my heart. After my walk, I respectfully tied this sacred gift onto the back of my special frame drum.

The more we learn to trust ourselves, the more we're also able to trust in the divinity of life and know that we're supported in all ways possible—especially when we commit to our hearts' desires. Our self-trust becomes our greatest "superpower," as it enables us to make empowered decisions with more efficiency than when we only use our minds. Our experiences are also much richer for it, since we're able to confidently let our inner guidance lead us to experience things that our minds wouldn't know about or approve of us venturing into. When we allow our hearts to lead, we're trusting in their higher wisdom and our inner divine guidance.

I use my intuitive senses, including my essence language, in sacred partnership with Spirit and Nature, as much as I do my regular physical senses. They're just as valuable with practical things as with mystical things. They assist me with finding perfect parking spaces; knowing what to write or what images to use in service to others (whether on social media or in publications); finding the highest-quality items I desire for the best price (for travel, clothing, food, or body care); giving someone the absolute perfect gift (not knowing in advance that it was a perfect gift!); knowing who to contact and when, where to travel, what event to attend, who to connect with—and so much more. They've also enabled me to avoid unfortunate outcomes by notifying me somehow. We all have these sacred tools to assist us with everyday practical living. The Divine gave us these gifts to be used. The more we use our intuitive abilities, the more empowered we become. They enable us to experience more favourable outcomes in all situations than if we didn't use them.

I've always been able to somehow find my way to a destination even when I logically have no idea how to get there. It's like an intuitive navigation system, and we all have it. Many of us have also experienced it while surfing the Internet, with no thinking involved, just allowing for higher guidance to lead us—and magick unfolds. While I've experienced my intuitive navigation system's effectiveness countless times, with driving in the city and in the country, I really put it to the test when I felt called to attend a shamanic retreat in Wisconsin, in April of 2011.

I decided to drive the 13 hours to my destination, with only occasional breaks. I had borrowed a GPS system from a soul sister, but once I arrived in the countryside where my destination was, it became useless to me. I was in the middle of "nowhere" on a road, around midnight, and I had not seen a vehicle for the past two hours. Then the GPS voice announced, "You have now reached your destination"—and its map marker concurred! There were no lights in sight except for the vast star-filled sky above me, and I was surrounded by fields and forests. It was close to the new moon, so there was no moonlight. I turned off that technical GPS and turned on my intuitive one instead, asking my navigator angels to assist me. All I wanted at that point was to sink into a bed and sleep. I did have printed directions to my destination, but they weren't helpful from where I was at that moment—in pitch darkness, on rural roads I had never driven on, with tiny, barely legible road signs. I had a sense of where the closest town was, so I drove in that direction and actually found it. It looked like a ghost town at that time of the night. After a few turns and passing several streets, I was able to find the highway mentioned in the directions and went from there.

After what seemed like an eternity—of winding, hilly, pitch-dark country roads bordered by forests, several deer, and raccoons and only my vehicle headlights lighting the way—I actually found the road to the lodge where I would be spending a week! The entire trip felt like a shamanic journey in itself. Earlier that day, only a few hours into my journey, I had seen a beautiful bald eagle soar across the highway ahead of me in the radiant sunlight, near the visible, tiny crescent moon. It had felt so significant and empowering to see that.

While our intuitive abilities are spiritual, our essence language is like a merging of the mystical with the mundane. It blends the spiritual with the physical. It enables us to remember and experience our spiritual natures. We're souls experiencing the physical, emotional, and mental aspects of life on Earth. When we use every aspect of ourselves as a unified team rather than as separate parts that compete with each other, we're able to navigate life with greater ease and grace. Our life experiences are also enhanced in countless, incredible ways.

Innumerable benevolent beings reside in the spirit world and desire to support us on our journeys through life. When we acknowledge our spiritual senses and use them, we also have greater access to these teachers, guardians, and guides of the spirit world. When we signal our openness to work in partnership with them, they respond.

One of the most common forms of spirit guides are animals, since we're all familiar and comfortable with them (therefore less resistant). Regardless of their forms, they're all equally beautiful and have important wisdom to share with us. Sometimes they show up simply to reassure us that we're still aligned with our sacred paths, regardless that things may seem uncertain, chaotic, or downright crazy. Sometimes we already feel a connection with the ones who show up at those times, and we feel an instant sense of comfort and encouragement in their presence.

I've always loved owls, and throughout the two years that I lived in the divinely gifted rental house (when I'd made those drastic life changes), both Great Horned Owl and Barn Owl had a very prominent presence in my life as power animals. When I moved and answered the call of Hawai'i in 2013, I was delighted to find out there was one endemic species of owl on the big island, where I was—the *pueo*. I had a heart desire to see one, if possible. One day during a forest hike, I found a feather on my path and sensed immediately that it was from the pueo. What a treasure! The next day I woke up before sunrise and felt the need to go for a long walk on the road that wound downhill and uphill on Mauna Loa, surrounded by Nature. At one point, I unexpectedly saw the word "pueo" written in bold letters on a mailbox by the road—it felt like a confirmation about the feather. Then, in the late evening of the following day, I had a glorious walk along the sacred Honaunau shore and I watched the sun set with soul family. As we drove along the highway afterwards, we suddenly encountered a low-flying pueo right over the vehicle! It hovered momentarily with its broad wings, letting me see it so clearly through the rear window. It was so beautiful and graceful, I was in awe. I discovered that the pueo was considered in the Hawaiian culture to be an *'aumakua* (ancestor spirit). It felt so sacred to have encountered it for three consecutive days in various forms and in very different locations. I felt blessed for this manifested heart desire and watched over by another owl guardian on my journey.

Having an awareness of all the different ways that we are supported by Spirit enables us to receive these empowering gifts instead of missing out. All animals, plants, and environments have different teachings, energies, and messages for us at different times. The heart connections we cultivate with each other have ripple effects. The more sacred relationships we have, the more everyone benefits.

When a particular animal becomes a messenger or desires to work with you as a teacher, healer or guide, it appears in unusual ways or three times within a short period of time. Some become prominent spirit guides such as power animals and can work with you your whole life; some briefly show up at specific times during your journey. Many published resources can advise what these particular animals bring to you, if you don't intuitively know or you desire more information. They're all beautiful allies to have, no matter what their forms are. Whether they're a small insect or a large predator, it's wise to acknowledge them and to not underestimate their power.

In October of 2011, a new teacher and power animal was assigned to me; he showed up in a way I couldn't miss. I was driving into the city one day, when a majestic bald eagle suddenly flew across the highway, just a few feet ahead of my vehicle at windshield height, ensuring that I saw it—in full detail! The road was surrounded by wide-open fields and sky, but it chose to appear to me this way. I was stunned and so relieved I hadn't hit it with my vehicle. Then, as I was driving within the city, a truck passed me, and I noticed that its license plate had a bald eagle on it. I had never seen one like it before. Later, on my way back home, a large moving truck appeared in the lane beside me at a red light, and (of course)—it had a large perched bald eagle painted on its box. Intuitively I sensed that Bald Eagle desired to work with me, but I couldn't believe that he had chosen me! I let my mind fill me with doubts instead, so I wouldn't have to acknowledge and accept him. This teacher brought tremendous responsibility and discipline for the spiritual path. I decided to respectfully dismiss these three encounters, thinking that Bald Eagle would leave.

I should have known better. Bald Eagle was on a mission and very persistent. For the following three months, he showed up in some way or other almost every day! He was always in my awareness. I finally surrendered to the fact that he wasn't leaving me and I needed to acknowledge that I was ready for this teacher, whether I felt it or not (for *he* obviously felt I was). Just to make absolutely sure, however, I made a request. On the last day of the year, at the dawn of 2012, I asked Bald Eagle to show me a clear sign that day to confirm that he was indeed a new teacher and power animal for me. I made a promise that if I received this sign, I would honour him with a ceremony. On my way to the city for a New Year's Eve celebration, as I drove near downtown, I suddenly noticed a large semi-truck drive past me in the lane to my left, which gave me an excellent view of the side of the truck. I was completely astonished when I saw that, stretched over the entire length of its long trailer box, it had the image of a giant, soaring bald eagle, its extended wings spanning from one end of the box to the other and its eyes gazing at me! I had never seen such an impressive image on a trailer box! It was spectacular and undeniably the sign I had requested. It was also accompanied with a strong inner "knowing". I thanked and honoured Bald Eagle, as promised.

I've learned so much from this teacher and ally since then and continue to do so. I also recognized Spirit's wisdom for the impeccable timing of Bald Eagle's arrival in my life—it's been a constant reminder of my sacred path. I greatly appreciate how he persisted after first showing up in my life in such a dramatic way.

Over the years I've learned that, whether we consciously know we're ready for the next "level" of our personal growth or not, Spirit always knows and provides us with exactly what we need to further become who we're meant to be. Regardless of what we receive to continue evolving (even situations that seem unfavourable), we can make the most of it when we trust with a greater awareness.

Having trust in life, as well as ourselves, allows us to recognize that everything is a process and that timing also plays a crucial role. When we trust that life supports us rather than sabotages us, we can navigate all experiences more confidently and persevere through the toughest challenges, knowing there's a higher purpose to everything. Our self-trust ensures that we recognize life's many forms of support and receive it, no matter how unusual the support might seem to our logical thinking. At certain times it might make absolutely *no* sense at all, but trusting it, regardless, always proves to be advantageous.

On the morning of December 30, 2012, I woke up with the strongest feeling that I had to start packing everything I wasn't using in the house! Just like that, I had this intense inner guidance that wouldn't let up. It made no rational sense whatsoever, but the feeling was so strong and clear that I didn't even ask Spirit for some form of validation. I simply acted on it, starting that same morning.

I began by taking down everything I had on the walls and packing it. That immediately changed the energy in the house, from one that felt settled to one of movement. Then I packed all the things that were decorative and in storage. Since I felt guided to keep packing, I then spent days going through a closetful of bags and boxes. These contained payroll statements from previous employers and donation receipts from various charities, accumulated for over a decade. They also contained stacks of miscellaneous papers that were no longer useful in my life. Amidst all my shuffling and sorting, four beautiful monarch butterfly wings suddenly fell to the floor beside me! They must have been in a stack of journals that I had moved, although I didn't see the source. I was truly amazed, for this was exactly what had occurred two years before, when I'd started going through my things, knowing I had to leave my old life behind me. However, those particular wings from two years ago were still securely taped in my journal. This was a different set. The butterfly had been a power animal and essence sign of mine for years, especially the monarch species. It was so uncanny that both sets of monarch wings suddenly showed up in the middle of winter, while I was preparing for a move, without knowing yet that I would be moving!

I then went through my clothing, footwear, accessories, and everything else, making piles to give away and packing what I would keep. At that time I was going through a major test of faith that Spirit had guided me into—I had found myself in a financial storm with no end in sight. (I share the full story in chapter 10.) Going through all my personal belongings, however, made me feel I was overflowing with abundance. Since I was extremely discerning about what I was keeping, I ended up with much to give away, and this felt so uplifting. Many people were overjoyed to be the recipients of these quality items. Interestingly, I was always guided to find the perfect individuals to receive specific things. I would contact them and they would be looking for exactly what I was offering them! It felt blissful to give so much and to liberate my space of things that others could make better use of. Just as I was running out of boxes, I discovered that a soul sister had stacks of them in her basement that she wanted to give away—perfect for both of us. I kept packing until I was down to what I used every day. I even dismantled the kitchen table to create a convenient space to neatly pile my packed boxes. I was so pleased to see how little space I needed compared to when I'd moved in. It felt empowering to me.

Interestingly, when I was washing the dishes one day, I suddenly noticed that my favourite glass (which had unexpectedly welcomed me to the house almost two years earlier as a clear sign from Spirit) was now cracked! It had a large fissure down the length of its thick, transparent glass. I hadn't even heard it crack in the sudsy water. As I lifted it up to the sunlight shining through the kitchen window, I noticed a brilliant rainbow appear along the crack! It felt like a perfect confirmation of what I had been feeling—that my soul contract with this miraculously manifested home was now complete. To see a rainbow at this time, in this unusual way, felt highly significant to me.

Then I received the biggest confirmation that trusting and following through with my sense of inner guidance was exactly the right thing to do. Three weeks after I started packing my things, I was told by my soul sister Anna that the house I was renting from her parents had to be torn down! Changes were happening with the property, and the municipality would only allow one house on it. It only made sense to take down the century-old house I was renting rather than the new one that she lived in. Anna felt so upset about having to tell me this. However, since I already had most of my things packed, I was actually relieved to receive the news and did not feel that it was the end of the world. I thanked her with joy and reassured her that I already had known somehow, so it wasn't bad news to me at all. Spirit had always provided what I'd needed, so I trusted that everything would somehow work out. In the meantime, it was truly wonderful to know that I wasn't crazy to have started packing my things, based on just a *feeling*! I realized how much stronger my intuitive abilities had grown over the course of just one year.

Divine timing is a gift that unlocks possibilities. Our intuition allows us to tune in to this sense of timing and know when to act or when not to. There's immense value to trusting this. When we have a greater understanding of the importance of timing, we don't force anything to happen. Instead, we allow ourselves to go with the natural flow as things unfold, even if this can test us beyond our limits at times. When we're aligned with the timing of our own truth and personal path, everything unfolds and flows with greater magick, miracles, synchronicities, and opportunities.

Trusting ourselves and the process of our journeys enables us to enjoy life more fully, to eliminate all the *should*-ing because we know better, and to handle the challenges with a greater perspective. It enables us to persevere through the unknowns, and it allows us to be more fully present to what we are called to experience.

We all have specific lessons to learn and experience to gain. When things don't *appear* to be for our benefit, having this greater perspective allows us to *trust* that everything is exactly as it should be. We can then better accept the changes and challenges rather than fight them. Changes are actually a natural part of life. In Nature, everything is continuously changing—every day is unique. We can't personally evolve without change or challenges. Challenges are the greatest catalysts for us to transform, giving us opportunities to learn more, quickly. They enable us to become greater expressions of ourselves, aligned with our divine essences (if we're willing), instead of remaining who we, or others, think we are. When we face challenges, we can choose to act from a place of empowerment or disempowerment. Knowing our own essence language and fully trusting ourselves and our intuitive abilities gives us access to our personal inner power.

There's so much information bombarding us every day about what we should and shouldn't do (regarding homes, various trends, diet, exercise, health, relationships, raising children, making a living, banking, travel, shopping, marketing, etc.), how we should and shouldn't feel, and what we should and shouldn't think or believe. There's so much judgment from people who profess to know better, including people from our various social circles as well as leaders, professionals, gurus, experts—or those who like to believe they are. It's easy to feel overwhelmed by it all.

Developing a strong sense of self-trust is really *all* you need to do. You have so much personal wisdom and higher knowledge accessible to you. That's all you require to confidently make the choices that are best for *you* and to live your life as you're meant to, as you navigate your unique path.

There will always be those who thrive on making you believe they know better, or that you're doing something wrong, especially during hardships or challenges. However, when *you* know without a doubt that it's part of your path, and you're aware it has a higher purpose, it doesn't matter who those people are or how convincing they seem.

There will also always be those who profit from your doubts, fears, and worries. Nevertheless, your sacred heart *always* knows your personal truth, and no one can take away your truth unless you allow them to. When you trust yourself, you always know what to do. If you do feel you would benefit from someone else's expertise in some form or other, then it comes from your inner guidance and wisdom, which empowers you, rather than coming from a source outside of yourself that disempowers you. You do it with awareness from within, knowing it will benefit your unique path. *Self-trust* is truly the most valuable source of empowerment you can acquire.

The Power of our Heart Desires

Sacred seeds invite divine fulfillment.

At the centre of your being you have the answer; you know who you are and you know what you want.
—Lao Tzu

Follow your bliss and the Universe will open doors for you where there were only walls.
—Joseph Campbell

Our heart desires are the magickal keys to living the fulfilling lives we're meant to live. They not only open doors, they co-create the doors themselves! They're the true desires we feel in our hearts, not because they meet someone else's expectations, not because they give us what someone else has or does, not because they keep us safely in our familiar space, but because they come from a divinely sacred place within us. We have them for reasons far greater than we can fully understand. Together our heart desires form our soul's divine compass, guiding us to experience *all* that we've come here on Earth to do and be.

Whether it's to follow a calling, to create a garden, to produce art, to take a certain vacation, to become the guardian of an animal, to travel the world, to decorate a room, to follow a course, to get a tattoo, to hike a mountain, to purchase a particular vehicle, to master a discipline, to meet a certain person, to compose a song, to live in a specific environment, to get a gold tooth, to establish an institution, to write a novel, to change hair colour, to become a parent, to design a special piece of jewellery—whatever—*none* of our heart desires are for us to judge or dismiss. However, it's always up to us to choose whether to pursue these desires or not—we have the freedom of choice. When we do choose to honour them, the mystical unites with the mundane, and we experience the possible.

When you commit to a heart desire, this activates countless opportunities so it can be fulfilled. In the process of fulfilling it, you learn invaluable lessons, you gain a deeper understanding of yourself and the world, you receive wisdom from experience, you discover what you're capable of, you expand your perspective, and you evolve. Your heart desires are catalysts of transformation and fulfillment to the highest degree.

It was 1991, and everyone was talking about our upcoming high-school graduation. Grad was a very big deal at our small-town school. It was the biggest event of the school year—like a rite of passage into adulthood. We prepared for it all year. Our class was small, with only a dozen graduating students, who had known each other since kindergarten. It was customary to have a grad escort for that special event, whether you were dating someone or not. At this school, the girls greatly outnumbered the guys, and we felt like family, having spent 13 years growing up together. Therefore, escorts were usually guys or girls from other schools. Many girls in my class had boyfriends from other towns, so their grad escorts were already automatically chosen. I didn't have a boyfriend, so I was really feeling the pressure of finding someone to fill that important role.

I actually already knew a year in advance who I wanted to fill that special role for me. However, he happened to be the best looking and most popular guy in the entire town (of course)! While Alex had graduated the previous year, I still saw him occasionally at local events, and our parents were good friends. I also knew he was single, which made him available as an escort. While I did have a big crush on him, I was focused on leaving my home province for post-secondary studies, so I didn't plan to date any guy at that point. I simply wanted to have a memorable graduation celebration with the only guy I could imagine being my special one-time date.

However, I felt like a classic ugly duckling, with my dental braces, pimples on my face, and girlish figure, so it seemed like absolute wishful thinking. Regardless, I was willing to take the risk to see if my desire could become reality. I didn't want to settle for anyone else. The one thing I did have going for me was that Alex was a very nice guy. He was very personable and never let his reputation inflate his ego. In fact, he was a bit on the shy side. That gave me courage and a glimmer of hope— just enough motivation for me to attempt to honour my desire. I simply needed the perfect opportunity to ask him—before anyone else did.

The perfect opportunity *did* manifest, in the form of a friend's party. Everyone was invited to this party, including Alex. I just knew this was my chance to ask him to consider being my escort, since graduation night was fast approaching. It was a case of now or never, and I felt terrified. From the moment I arrived at the house and saw him, my heartbeat was on overdrive. I could barely socialize with anyone, never mind enjoy myself, since all I kept thinking about was how to ask him. I would be asking the most popular guy if he'd like to accompany *me* at this important event that most of the town would witness! I almost felt sick just thinking about it. I kept reciting different lines in my mind and feeling that it was too much for me to do. Maybe I could just go to graduation by myself and start a new tradition instead.

Well, cowardice had never been part of my nature, and my heart desire wouldn't allow it. I had to at least see if it was possible, so I agonized over how to ask him—for hours—until he was leaving the party! I had to either seize the moment or let my perfect opportunity slip away. I threw myself out of my comfort zone and followed Alex outside to the parked cars, throat dry and palms sweating. I managed to call out his name. When he turned around to face me and our eyes met, I felt so hot all over, and I went absolutely blank. My mind (and heart) were racing—this was my chance, and I *had* to ask. As he silently looked at me, I finally blurted out that I wondered if he might consider being my grad escort. Then I quickly added that he could take some time to think about it—I didn't need an answer that night.

Alex looked at the ground in silence for a moment, and all I could hear was my heart beating loud and fast. When he looked back up at me, he smiled and said ... *yes*! I smiled in disbelief and asked him if he was sure, to which he nodded and replied yes with a bigger smile. While I felt as if I might burst into a million stars of absolute joy and wanted to scream with delight, I simply expressed a huge, wholehearted thank-you and headed back to the house so he could leave. I felt as if I were walking on air. I could not believe I had a grad escort and it was *him*! I pinched myself to make sure it wasn't a dream. I couldn't stop smiling.

That night changed *everything* for me. Alex's on-the-spot yes transformed me in ways I hadn't anticipated. By courageously going for what seemed like an unrealistic desire and seeing it realized, I had shifted something within me. I suddenly knew, without a doubt, that anything was possible if I desired it from my heart and committed to it. I knew that if I was willing to risk everything, for something I deeply desired, I could achieve it. In this case, I had risked experiencing rejection, embarrassment, humiliation, and a crushed dream. It was a very big deal for an 18-year-old at my school. However, that risk to me was better than not trying and always having to wonder: "What if ...?"

On graduation day, I felt like the happiest girl on the planet, and I'm sure I glowed. I wore a beautiful eighties-style "princess dress" that my mom had made just the way I had envisioned it, in a shimmering amethyst-purple satin, with jewellery and a wrist corsage to match. My entire family, including aunts and uncles, were there to witness my handsome Prince Charming picking me up at my parents' house, dressed up in a black suit. Alex was a dream come true—even if it was for just one night. I felt like Cinderella going to the ball. He even surprised me with a beautiful gift to mark the occasion! He knew somehow that I loved anklets and he got me a special one of 14k gold with a grad charm on it. I had a gift for him also, as a gesture of gratitude, but no gift could thank him enough for saying yes.

I was in heaven the entire celebration, which included the ceremony, dinner, and dance. Alex was fun and an absolute gentleman. He made me feel so special. Since he was someone my parents knew and trusted, we were able to just relax and fully enjoy ourselves with everyone present. I couldn't have picked a more perfect escort, and I've always felt so grateful to him for doing that for me. It made all my school years, even the horrible ones, worth it for just that one day. It was a pivotal moment in my life.

A heart desire is not a logical phenomenon. It's simply a sudden *knowing* that exists in your heart with the potential to become physical reality. You recognize that you truly desire something, and it ignites you when you think about it, regardless of what it is. It might feel a bit scary or intimidating, yet there's that special excitement along with it. Just the act of focusing your awareness on a desire, giving yourself permission to have this desire, and fully enjoying it, without judgment, activates its potential to manifest.

The quickest way to achieve your heart desire is to acknowledge and feel your desire in your heart, with eager anticipation and free of judgment. Leave the *how* up to Spirit, remain aware of any type of guidance you might receive, and follow through with it. The timing, of course, is always relative to each desire and always perfect. Sometimes all that Spirit requires you to do is to simply *believe* that your desire *is* possible, regardless of your current circumstances. And then the magick flows.

It was the beginning of 2013, and I was in need of a financial miracle. I was in the thick of a test of faith. I had absolutely no money to spend when one of my dear soul sisters, whom I had connected with serendipitously through my business mentor, launched her new lines of jewellery. Laurie created her unique pieces with love, intention, and genuine materials. I had always felt a special love for soulful creations. Their energy was so divinely vibrant—the opposite energy of mass-produced products. I always preferred to surround and adorn myself with objects that had been created with loving inspiration.

Upon her announcement, I went to Laurie's website to browse her online store, and I completely fell in love with one particular necklace. It was connected with the energy of the magickal elementals which felt dear to my heart. It featured a gorgeous, dark-green tourmaline pendant, and everything about it felt so good to me—it resonated highly with my spirit. I desired immediately to have it for myself. However, I didn't tell anyone about this heart desire—not even Laurie. Since all her new pieces were beautiful, I praised *all* her collections. In order to connect with this particular necklace, until I could buy it for myself, I indulged in its beauty and energy by looking at the online photograph. It ignited my spirit, which was especially wonderful to feel during my test of faith.

Two weeks later, I received a package in the mail from Laurie. In her card, she wrote, "One of my guides, an elemental, asked that I send this to you." As I looked inside the beautiful pouch, I was astounded to see that it was—that gorgeous necklace I had fallen in love with! Wow—what a special surprise gift to receive! I felt immense love and support from so many as I held the necklace against my heart and then put it on. Spirit and the elementals had definitely heard my heart desire for this treasure, through the pure energy of my heart, thoughts, and emotions (for I hadn't vocalized nor written about it). Then, through my generous soul sister, they magickally manifested it for me. It empowered me on my journey and is another reminder of how amazing life really is. We're all co-creators, whether we're conscious of it or not.

All heart desires are sacred, and treating them as such is an act of gratitude to the Divine. They're like treasure seeds that the Divine has planted in our hearts so that we may fully blossom into our greatness. New ones are continuously being added as we grow and evolve. None is less important than another. Some people might not understand our heart desires, but they don't share the same path that we do. When we accept and respect that we all have different lives to live, with different paths to experience, we're better able to deal with the biggest culprits that try to stop us—our own fears and inner criticism.

Some heart desires might take much longer than others for us to commit to, but they're always there, even if we forget about them or ignore them for a while. I've known a staggering number of people over the years who've described their heart desires along the lines of "it's not possible"; "it's not realistic"; or "it's too late." I've felt the unhappiness, resentment, regret, disappointment, sadness, bitterness, anger, or even disease in their energy as they've solemnly expressed this to me.

Our hearts yearn to show us all that's possible for us in this world. They don't believe in limitations—they know we can manifest anything with the Divine. We don't receive heart desires unless we have the ability to realize them. It's the Divine's loving wisdom at work in partnership with our own divinity.

When things don't seem to be unfolding in a supportive way, it can be a sign that we're not following our *true* desires (we're compromising or settling for less). It can also be a sign that we need to learn things along our paths that opportunities, sometimes disguised as challenges, are facilitating. It's never too late to acknowledge and honour a heart desire. Everything is always exactly as it should be, and there *is* such a thing as divinely perfect timing.

A good indication that it's time to honour a heart desire is that it moves to the forefront of your attention, and it becomes difficult to focus on anything else. It becomes a burning desire, impossible to ignore. As soon as you make the decision to commit to a heart desire so that it can manifest, opportunities start to appear that allow you to embark on the journey that it invites you to experience.

For 25 years I had a heart desire that I judged, and judged, and judged. Ironically, this was the main lesson I needed to learn through this heart desire—that while all forms of judgment are detrimental, self-judgment is even worse than judgment from others. It's only when I suddenly realized I was judging myself that I was liberated to honour my desire for what it was, and things suddenly, seamlessly, fell into place. It was amazing. I also realized how truly sacred our desires are. When we treat them as such, with intention, we can manifest anything.

I've shared the following with only a select few until now, for the simple fact that it deals with a subject of controversy. Like anything else, it's always a matter of perspective. For me to simply tell someone about this heart desire's manifested result, without the full story, would not honour the sacredness of it and my personal journey. I've been guided to now share it with you in its entirety, and I'm doing so with a wide-open heart.

Please understand that what I describe is my personal journey to resolve a burning heart desire about my own body. It does not reflect how I feel about other women's bodies. I feel that one of the greatest attributes of beauty for a woman is exuding confidence and self-love. My journey (to attain my heart desire), effected this at a level that I yearned for yet couldn't achieve otherwise.

For over two decades, I had desired to have the breasts of a mature woman instead of the chest of a young girl. Since my late teens I had felt like a woman trapped inside a girl's body. I even prayed for my breasts to develop, but to no avail. To make up for this, I started to wear padded and gel bras in my early twenties, just so I looked as if I had breasts. I was unable to feel feminine without that. It gave me confidence as a woman when I was in public. However, at the end of the day, when I undressed, I was back in my girl's body. I didn't wear a bra when I was at home, since I didn't need one, so if someone visited unannounced, I wouldn't answer the door until I had slipped on one of my heavy bras under my shirt. If I spent the night where friends or family might see me sleeping, I kept a bra on under my shirt (which was highly uncomfortable for someone who usually slept in the nude).

Shopping for clothing, bras, and bathing suits left me feeling disempowered and dejected. I could never wear the clothing that actually appealed to me, since I couldn't wear my bras with these feminine styles. Instead I wore tops that covered my chest area, so people couldn't see I had no cleavage despite my bra size. I always felt I was lying to the world by presenting myself with a woman's body that I actually didn't have. The only nightmares I had were of me being out in public without a bra, so people could see my true body, which didn't match who I was within. Every now and then, I would get inadvertently insulted by people, sometimes even friends, who made remarks about "flat-chested" women, not realizing I was one of them. This really stung, and it taught me the importance of being conscious of our words at *all* times.

For over two decades I tried to convince myself that such a heart desire was wrong. I recited thoughts like "I should be satisfied with the healthy, fit body I have"; "I'm not being spiritual to desire a different physical body"; "I'm being vain to desire breasts and consider cosmetic surgery"; "What would others, especially my family, think of me if I did that?"; or "What kind of example would I be for others?" On and on these thoughts would repeat themselves. Whenever I thought I had finally convinced myself that I needed to just accept it and live with it, I would have a nightmare about it.

Then the cysts started to appear in both my breasts. I was told by medical experts that only older women usually got those benign cysts, yet I was getting them regularly. The female doctor who drained them for me with a syringe joked that the cysts gave me cleavage. While I laughed with her, that remark actually hurt me more than the needle. I knew in my heart that the cysts had appeared because I was unable to love my breasts. I resented them for not developing, and that made me feel sad for them. This greatly disturbed me, for I felt that if I didn't find some way to resolve this, sooner or later the cysts might become other than benign.

As the years passed, I became aware of many women who had had cosmetic surgery for different reasons, including breast augmentation. I found it interesting that if someone had cosmetic surgery due to an accident or disease, it was generally acceptable with most people, but if it was a personal choice for other reasons, it was more likely to be judged negatively. For the longest time I had felt too ashamed to even mention anything about my personal dilemma. However, when I finally started to talk openly with non-judgmental people about this subject, I felt so liberated. I did some research and discovered that this industry had evolved greatly over the last two decades since I had first looked into it. I even received referrals for surgeons through my conversations. Yet, I just couldn't acknowledge that I was even contemplating it. I felt that thinking of altering my physical body in an unnatural way was betraying my spiritual awareness and not being grateful to the Divine for what I had. So I let a few more years pass, and then my heavy bras, which I despised to begin with, started giving me rashes. It became obvious I had to resolve this somehow.

One day in the summer of 2012, over a year after beginning my new life, I suddenly received a flash of insight while I was meditating. I had the clear realization that all this time I had been judging myself and my desire—quite harshly! I was stunned. I had always done my best not to judge others, and yet I had been judging myself! I was within the sacred space of my heart, and I received the Divine's message that the pure heart has no judgment. Love in its purest form doesn't judge. When I let that sink in and truly felt what it meant, it released all the self-judgment I had imposed on myself for so long, and something completely shifted within me. I realized that in order for me to be who my heart and Spirit were calling me to be on Earth, I needed to honour *all* my heart desires. Each one had a divine purpose, including this one. I had fought it persistently, without success, long enough. I realized that being spiritual was not about thinking and trying (based on meeting others' expectations of what spirituality means to them), but about knowing and being (based on honouring our personal truth with love and awareness). The sacred heart always knows—it's our direct spiritual connection with the Divine.

I had always been a highly sensual being. However, I had never felt able to express my feminine sensuality as a woman with my girlish figure. I silently tuned in to this heart desire for breasts that would allow me to fully express and experience who I was in a physical way—with confidence and a self-love that would include all of me. I discovered something else I hadn't been aware of. I realized I had been doing everything I could to keep the actual size of my breasts hidden from others, for it had been too painful for me to tell the truth. Yet I knew that if I had breast implants, I would be open and honest if someone asked me about them in a respectful way—I wouldn't lie about it. I realized I would no longer be afraid of being judged by others if I had breast implants. That in itself was an empowering realization.

I looked further within and discovered that my greatest fear surrounding this desire had to do with surgery. All my life I'd had a very healthy, strong, and resilient body that healed quickly, and I had never desired to have children, so I was a stranger to anything medical or surgical. I'd also always avoided medication and needles as much as possible. Another big concern was that having surgery might change my energy body somehow. Since I physically felt energies through my body, from Nature, Spirit, the Divine, people, animals, storms, and environments, I needed to know that surgery wouldn't damage this sensing ability somehow.

I decided to look into both of these sources of worry. I first consulted with Spirit about my energy and was reassured that nothing could change that—it was part of who I was. Then I booked a consultation with the surgeon who felt like the right one for me (and noticed that the numbers 33 and 11 were prevalent in the contact information and address of the clinic—very significant for me). I was actually able to see the surgeon's assistant within a few days! I was so impressed by how smoothly everything went, and it all felt so divinely perfect with my inner knowing. I even chose implants that same day, with her knowledgeable assistance! I chose a size that would suit my body, giving me breasts proportionate to my figure. That's all I had ever desired. When the consultant gave me printed information for my specific implants, I noticed with surprise that the logo was another highly significant symbol for me—a flying monarch butterfly! I felt *so* empowered as I suddenly realized that everything was flowing to assist me.

For the first time since being a teenager, I felt excited and joyful about this heart desire, for I was no longer judging it or feeling fear about it! I felt so liberated to know that it could actually manifest into reality, and I could finally have the body I had always desired. It seemed so surreal after all those years of agonizing.

My last hurdle to tackle was financing. Although I had enough money in my bank account to pay for everything, I wanted to keep it to pay the monthly bills. Instead, I began searching for an alternative and requested the assistance of Spirit. I knew that if this was fully aligned with my sacred path, the money would show up somehow, as it always did. And it did. While working out to my favourite music one day, I suddenly received a flash of insight from Spirit. It was a clear reminder that I had cancelled a credit card the previous year since I had never used it. I felt guided to contact my bank by phone and see if I could reactivate it with a credit limit amount of just what I needed to pay for everything. To my amazement, after only 10 minutes of conversation I had a bank representative sending me my new credit card by express post! It was *so easy.*

When I later shared this financial experience with a few soul sisters, I was told that stuff like that didn't normally happen. In fact, one of them had had the complete opposite experience while trying to apply (in person) for the same credit card, despite her good financial record! I was astonished. Clearly, a lot of magick was unfolding on my behalf. When I received my new card within a few days, I had another delightful surprise— the secret code behind it was 133, a number that started showing up regularly for me when I had started my new life. In the language of angels, it signified complete support from the ascended masters. And again the 33 had shown up.

I booked my surgery and chose August 3. Supposedly it wasn't astrologically favourable for surgery that day, but I felt strongly that it was perfect for me, so I kept that date. I trusted my inner guidance. My dear soul sister and neighbour Anna, agreed to accompany me for the surgery, and I just knew I would be fine on my own afterwards. I had set up everything in the house so I didn't have to lift anything for a while.

Just to be absolutely sure that this heart desire was fully aligned with my sacred path and highest good, and that the surgery and healing would go well without complications, I requested from Spirit a clear sign in Nature to confirm this. Although my heart knew all this already, my mind needed reassurance. For very important decisions, I liked to request signs outside of myself to confirm that my inner knowing was accurate. I began a Nature hike and asked to receive this sign before I returned to the house.

I was on my way back and just reaching the driveway bordered by forest when I suddenly heard an unusual vocal sound from the sky. I looked up and saw a glistening black crow flying above the forest, coming from the southeast. It flew to where I was standing and stopped directly above me, hovering with loudly audible beating wings. Then it flew in a wide circle in the east, and returned above me, where it hovered again. Then it flew in another wide circle in the east, returning to hover above me a third time. The sound of its wingbeats was so impressive in the silent environment. Suddenly it flew back to the southeast, calling out three times. I was filled with absolute awe, for not only was the crow's display impressive in itself, but as a spirit guide, its appearance was related to manifesting desires, among other things. Also, the number three was related to creation, and the east direction signified healing and new birth. I simply stood there awhile and thanked Spirit and Crow from my heart. When I entered the house, I saw 3:33 on the phone. When I was journaling about this experience outside a little later, I noticed a beautiful red-tailed hawk soaring low above me. The appearance of this beautiful power animal felt like one last sign of reassurance for me. I now felt fully ready, with my mind at ease and eager anticipation in my heart.

As if that weren't enough, the day before the surgery I received a statement in the mail for my new credit card. I contacted the bank to see if I could make my statements paperless, like my other bills. The representative I spoke with informed me that this option had just become available the previous week. We talked a bit and I briefly told her about my business Sacred Earth Connection™. Then, just like that, she actually increased my credit limit to $13,300! She said she loved that I was a Pisces like her as well as what I was creating through my work. I was dumbfounded. Since one of my journey's big lessons since 2011 had been all about learning to receive, I simply thanked her with appreciation. It was interesting that again 133 showed up, for she didn't simply double my available credit amount—she chose a random figure!

On the day of the surgery, I was amazed to discover that the moon was in the zodiac sign of Pisces and the sun was in the zodiac sign of Leo. When I was born, the sun had been in Pisces and the moon in Leo—exactly the opposite. This felt like a profoundly fated day for me—like a rebirth. I also found out that astrologically I couldn't have chosen a better day, since it was the most powerful healing moon of the year! I was so grateful to have kept that date despite the information I had received advising against it—it had been mixed-up, false information. This was another reminder and confirmation for me that my wise heart always knew what was best for me, and made better decisions than my mind could.

As Anna and I left for the city, I noticed 333 kilometres on her vehicle's odometer reading, and a rainbow was shining on the seat. Then Red-Tailed Hawk surprised us by flying across the road directly in front of the vehicle! I felt so much loving support from Spirit surrounding me. My wristband at the clinic had 33 in my ID number, which delighted me. Since I had chosen this, it was a positive experience for me. All the staff was wonderful. As the surgeon's gentle and humorous assistants prepared me for the surgery, I felt a calm excitement, despite the needles. Suddenly, a wave of divine-love energy unexpectedly flowed through my entire body, filling me with bliss! I heard beeping and realized that these ecstatic sensations had actually registered on the heart monitor—which the staff interpreted as stress. *Oops!* I simply smiled and reassured them that I was more than fine.

The surgery went perfectly well, and I woke up with a new figure. I was ecstatic. As Anna drove us back to our homes in the country, the sky was dark with storm clouds. Just as we were leaving the city on the first highway, I turned my head to say something to Anna. Through the driver's window I suddenly saw a single strike of beautifully brilliant lightning touch the ground in the south! It felt exquisitely significant to see that for two reasons. I had a special connection with lightning so its presence felt like a gift from Spirit. It also felt so symbolic of my true essence finally fully grounding into my physical body after all this time—the woman's body I had desired for so long. Even though the implants had to be placed underneath my pectoral muscles, I healed very well and quickly, without even requiring pain medication. My body welcomed this change instead of rejecting it. I had anticipated that after healing, my breasts might feel like a foreign object inside my body, but instead they felt as natural as my heart and lungs and everything else within my body. I felt so grateful to Spirit, my sacred heart, my healthy body and everyone who had played a role in making this heart desire manifest the way it did.

It was also amazing to see that no plans came up with family or friends that entire month after my surgery. It felt like another blessing from Spirit. I was able to simply let my body fully heal and not have to tell anyone. It was such a personal and sacred experience, I felt the need to simply nurture myself and fully savour being in the space of love and appreciation in my Nature sanctuary. Besides, not many would have truly understood my journey and choice, especially without knowing the full story. We can't fully understand anything without experiencing it for ourselves.

Anna later told me I had made that entire experience look so easy. The truth is that by finally honouring my deep desire, I had liberated myself to receive all the possibilities that were just waiting to help me fulfill it. I was ready at that point to receive everything that desire yearned for me to experience and to learn from it, which included the lessons about judgment. The timing was also perfect, even if it had taken 25 years. I had needed to experience certain things before I could make a decision from a place of awareness and wisdom in my heart, and could fully appreciate everything that manifested. I switched from letting my mind lead (and drive me crazy), to letting my heart lead (and liberate me).

I'm very grateful for all I learned and experienced through this journey. After all those years, I *finally* feel at home in my body, and that feeling is priceless beyond measure. It feels so divine to finally love my physical body in its entirety. There are no words to describe that feeling. Every aspect of my life was transformed by honouring this one desire.

My ability to feel and channel energies wasn't negatively affected either, but instead has kept evolving to incredible levels. It seems that by finally fulfilling this desire, I actually became an even clearer channel! I released the energy blocks of the denser, negative energies I had felt for so long, surrounding this desire. I had never even considered that possibility when I'd made my decision. The realization of my heart desire was a multi-dimensional gift.

Letting go of judgment—of others and of self—liberates us to more fully experience all that life wants to offer us. It doesn't matter what our heart desires are; they're all essential to our paths. While some heart desires are easy to judge as being superficial, the journeys we must take to manifest these true desires are spiritual.

Our heart desires also support us to be our best on our sacred paths. Commitment to our desires, with awareness, allows everything to flow miraculously into place, including all forms of abundance. By honouring this desire, I had obviously cleared a channel that allowed for more magick and abundance to flow through.

Shortly after my surgery, I received an invitation for an event occurring the following month near Phoenix, Arizona. During that event, I was scheduled to attend a cocktail party and was told to plan on dressing up for it. I had no idea what to wear. My soul sister Anna, who used to attend cocktail parties, showed me many dresses she had that were my size. She would have gladly lent one to me, but the one I loved was pure white, which I preferred not to wear. However, now I knew what style was appropriate and what to look for. Two weeks before flying to Arizona, I decided to go shopping for a dress. I didn't feel like spending a lot of time for this. It would be my first time driving since my surgery, and I had never been one for shopping, especially in large department stores. I preferred small boutiques and quaint shops, or the Internet. As I drove to the city, I asked Spirit to assist me with finding the perfect dress for me. I specified the style and the colours I desired and left the rest up to Spirit. I suddenly had a sense of which area of the city to go to.

As I drove by a shopping mall, I felt strongly guided to go into a large department store that I normally avoided. However, since I was on a mission and I knew better than to doubt when I felt guided, I parked the car and walked into the store. I noticed a section of formal dresses near the entrance, which was ideal. As I began to look at the selection, only one small, circular rack of dresses looked to be cocktail dress, and they were not at all what I desired. I circled this rack a few times and suddenly felt guided to walk in another direction, by the change rooms.

There, I actually ended up face to face with a small rack of dresses in *exactly* the same style as Anna's white one that I'd loved! It also comprised not only some of the colours I had specified to Spirit, but *all* the ones I had mentioned, together in a very attractive way. I was stunned! It was so perfect—even better than I could have imagined. They had only five on hand, in different sizes, and the first one was my size. I tried it on, and it fit as though it had been custom-made for my new body. As a plus, it was a very reasonable price. I couldn't stop smiling with amazement. I thanked Spirit for such a delightfully quick and beyond-successful shopping experience.

That entire trip to Arizona, including the cocktail party, felt like a celebration of my true essence emerging. It brought me back to Sedona, where I experienced so many unexpected, magnificent gifts, especially in Nature. The event near Phoenix brought more connections with my soul family and so much more. (I talked about this experience in detail in chapter 3.) The cocktail party itself was highly enjoyable with an assortment of fine hors d'oeuvres and beverages, great company and wonderful music to dance to. I just felt so happy to be alive and savoured every moment.

A few weeks after I returned from Arizona, I received another unexpected magickal blessing that further empowered me on my journey. I had been giving away more of my clothing to family, friends, and charities, since most of it had never felt like *me*, and I was more than happy to let it go to others who would enjoy it more. I had always desired to wear clothing that expressed my true essence, so I created a large space inside my wardrobe to be filled whenever Spirit felt it was time. Just letting go of everything that didn't suit my authentic self, felt so uplifting, and I enjoyed this new space for possibilities. Like all of Nature, the Universe seemed to love filling voids!

One day, while I was running errands in the city, I was guided to a specific second-hand store, where I could donate multiple quality items. Their profits went towards children's charities. That day I felt guided to have a look at their clothing in the large store. I was so surprised and amazed to discover that this particular store had a lot of like-new clothing from my favourite Canadian brand! I never would have expected that.

Aside from my cocktail dress, I hadn't purchased clothes for a very long time, and I ended up having the most fun I'd ever experienced while trying on clothing. I couldn't stop smiling! I was bursting with joy with every piece I tried on. I felt so blissful. I was also able to fill the large void I had created in my wardrobe with clothing that felt perfectly *me*, all for a fraction of the usual cost of brand new. I found eleven new tops, which interestingly totalled $55.53. That 555 number sequence kept showing up in different ways. Knowing I was helping charities twice, through both my donations and purchases, also greatly enhanced my shopping experience. It was perfect in every possible way. I felt so blessed, abundant, and deeply grateful. (As I added this story to my book manuscript, I noticed the word count was 65,553, matching the total price of my purchases and revealing yet another numerical synchronicity of 555—another "wink" from Spirit.)

Sometimes our heart desires are simply meant to have us experience more of life's wonders and greater expressions of our interconnectedness with All. They serve to expand our hearts further so we can embody love on a deeper level (hence, be more of who we truly are). The more love we embody, the more love we experience in all ways imaginable.

When I was on the island of Hawai'i in 2013, during one of my sunrise hikes I noticed a gorgeous horse on a property by one of the roads. It was kept in a large field of various tropical plants and was quite untamed. Most mornings it would be galloping freely through that field when I saw it, and it was never near the road. However, I had a secret little desire in my heart to make a connection with this free-spirited horse before leaving the island. I had always loved horses, and this one felt particularly special to me. I'm sure that the mornings I didn't see it, it was very aware of me nonetheless. I could feel its presence even though many of the large plants in the field were big enough to hide it. I simply greeted it with my heart, sending it love and appreciation for its beauty and free spirit.

As I was hiking back up the mountain only two mornings before I was scheduled to leave Hawai'i, I heard what sounded like this horse munching vegetation near the road! I couldn't see the property yet, due to the surrounding forest trees and foliage, but I slowed down my pace and calmed my state of energy (that uphill walk was quite a workout!). I calmly walked by the field and was amazed to see this beautiful horse feeding at the fence right beside the road, observing me! It gave me the perfect opportunity to attempt a connection with it. As I watched, it didn't seem to mind my presence, so I decided to give it an offering of grass. I picked a handful of long grasses near the fence and extended my arm to it, while sending it love and admiration from my heart. The horse looked at me awhile and then slowly moved towards me. It sniffed the grasses and then ate them, all the while looking at me. I felt overjoyed. It remained standing there, looking at me. So I gingerly stepped towards it, maintaining eye contact and sending it love. It lowered its head slightly towards me, so I reached out, and my heart completely melted as it let me gently stroke its white "third-eye" patch and the bridge of its nose—wow! I felt so honoured by this beautiful being and blessed by this manifested connection. I thanked the horse and Spirit, and after a while I stepped back and continued on my uphill journey, feeling so elated. It was such a gift.

When our desires are aligned with who we actually are, rather than with who we or someone else think we are, everything lines up to manifest them as soon as we make a decided request. No desire is too great or too small, too complicated or too simple, too radical or too controversial, too practical or too mystical. No heart desire is insignificant or extravagant. Each one has a purpose and possibilities to manifest it. It's not for you to judge whether it's worthy of your attention or not. If it's in your heart, it's part of your unique path.

Most of us have experienced desiring something and then receiving that exact thing we desired or something even better—even if it began with absolutely nothing to show it was possible. This is how life was meant to be, for all of us, and this is how everything in existence is created. Creation in its purest form is not a logical process.

In 2006 I decided I would prefer having a vehicle that was smaller and more fuel efficient than the one I had—one that was more *me*. The one I currently owned was a massive, old, used model that I had purchased because the price was great and I could pay cash for it. It did serve a wonderful purpose I hadn't foreseen. It was luxuriously comfortable and a very smooth ride, so my grandparents had thoroughly enjoyed the drive when I had chauffeured them to my parents' house on special occasions. They felt like royalty as they sat on the wide, plush back seat. While I had the chance, it delighted me to be able to give them such a simple pleasure that put wholehearted smiles on their faces.

Now it was time for a change, and I had saved up enough money so I wouldn't have to settle for anything less than what

I really desired. After some research, I found exactly what I had imagined as my perfect vehicle. There was one disadvantage— this particular model no longer had the two-door style that I preferred. The company had stopped manufacturing them this way, just before the new millennium. It might be a challenge for me to find one for sale in good condition. Regardless, just the thought of having one of my own thrilled me. It was what I desired, and the unfavourable odds of finding it didn't sway me. I made my decision and opened up to the possibilities.

At that time, I jogged every morning at sunrise, before the city came to life. I greatly enjoyed the trails bordering the parks and natural areas of the neighbourhood. This was my Nature time before I spent all day downtown in a large office building. It invigorated and inspired me. Interestingly, I began to notice while I jogged that the exact same vehicle I desired was starting to appear around me! It became so frequent that it was comical. I had never seen any until I'd had that desire. Now they were constant companions during my morning jogs. They also showed up in so many different colours that I knew it wasn't the same vehicle zooming by repeatedly. What an unexpected synchronicity. It felt like a confirmation from Spirit, which fuelled my desire even more.

A few weeks later, one Sunday morning, my husband at the time suddenly announced that he had found that exact vehicle model, and it seemed to be in perfect condition. It was at a dealership in the city. Adam and I went to see it immediately, and as soon as I took it for a test drive I knew it was my vehicle. It was so comfortable to drive, and I loved that it was compact like a car and yet high up like a little truck. It was silver and black, with large windows for excellent visibility. It was even better than I had envisioned it to be. The asking price was also just within my range—it was perfect! After all the paperwork was complete, the dealer handed me the keys. As I was getting into my "new" vehicle to drive it home, he received a call on his cell phone. It was someone inquiring about the vehicle I had just purchased. The dealer informed the caller that it was being driven off the lot as they spoke. I drove away smiling. Interestingly, after I purchased this vehicle, I stopped seeing the others like it during my morning jogs.

Throughout my life, so many of my heart desires have manifested instantly or within a short period of time. Those that have taken longer have taught me greater wisdom. All of them have manifested in a way that highly exceeded anything I could have imagined. This has taught me to always trust the process and to practise patience. The process is unique for each one of us, and timing is everything.

Due to my highly artistic and creative nature, it's always been important for me to be creating something on a regular basis, to keep this energy flowing. In 2007, I decided one day to create special photo albums for my four nephews and one niece. They would be keepsakes of their childhood journeys (since I had boxes of photos for each of them). I can be very particular with certain things, so I desired large square photo albums to fit many photos and other things on each page. At that time scrapbooking wasn't that popular yet, so finding such albums was difficult. I looked at the typical photography stores and couldn't find what I was looking for. While some were close to what I had in mind, I chose to wait until I found exactly what I was looking for before purchasing anything.

Since nothing was showing up, I finally just surrendered to Spirit to guide me, so I wouldn't waste more time.

One day while I was still working downtown in a corporate building, I went for a walk during my lunch break. All the downtown buildings were connected with skywalks and underground tunnels that were filled with stores of all sorts. As I got off the office building's elevator on the main floor (a retail floor), I suddenly felt guided to go into the greeting-card store next to it. When I stepped inside, I was amazed to discover exactly what I had desired—but even *better*! The store had on display a collection of square photo albums with beautiful windows in the covers where I could insert photographs. What's more, they had five different colours that were so *perfect* for the four boys and one girl: a royal blue, a light blue, a sage green, an ivory white, and a hot pink! Those were actually the only colours they had, and they seemed to be made just for me. I smiled with wonder when I also found out from the clerk that they had just received and unpacked them that morning. I never would have thought of looking in that type of store. I had found what I was looking for when I wasn't even thinking about it. I thanked Spirit once again.

Our heart desires provide us with guidance for every aspect of our lives—the practical, the physical, the spiritual, the intellectual, the emotional, and the mystical. We're multi-dimensional beings with opportunities to experience *all* of ourselves, if we choose to do so.

When you honour your heart desires, you honour your reason for existing and being here on Earth. When you do so in partnership with Spirit, there's no limit to what you can manifest along your sacred path.

Honouring Ourselves

Radiant energy fields are magnetic.

The most courageous act is still to think for yourself. Aloud.
—*Coco Chanel*

Thousands of candles can be lighted from a single candle,
and the life of the single candle will not be shortened.
—*Buddha*

We all have particular environments and activities that make us feel more clear-minded, feel more heart-centred, and feel a higher sense of well-being. These empowering environments and activities are different for everyone and perfectly suited to each of us. When we honour what makes us feel our best, we each align ourselves with our essence and become a vortex of possibilities.

These environments and activities also promote a greater flow of higher information to be perceived by our intuitive senses. When we're immersed in what makes us feel our best, we're naturally more open to experiencing the divinity of life.

We function from our hearts, which magnetize everything aligned with our purpose. This is much more effective than when we operate from our minds, which seek from a limited perspective. We accomplish more in less time when we allow ourselves to invest in what makes us feel our best.

Nature has always been the environment that makes me feel my best. I spend time in natural environments and choose to walk barefoot, as much as possible. Our feet have evolved so that when they make direct contact with the ground, whether standing, sitting or walking, we discharge any excessive static from our bodies and receive the beneficial energies from Mother Earth. Nature naturally balances our energy fields. Whenever I start feeling less than my best, I spend time in Nature. In no time at all, I feel a sense of well-being again.

I receive a lot of my information and guidance from Spirit when I'm in Nature. I actually received the title for this book during a sunrise hike in Nature on the island of Hawai'i. I was simply enjoying my surroundings and feeling so alive as my body was fully engaged with my uphill climb. I was fully present to my challenging and exhilarating path, when I suddenly received a flash of insight. My mind was liberated of thoughts, which invited higher wisdom to flow through. I had been thinking about a book title for a while, since I knew the right one would be the powerful catalyst I required to begin writing the manuscript. However, nothing had felt like it was *the* one, so I surrendered it to Spirit, letting it go from my mind. Shortly after that, I received a book title that I knew was perfect, for not only did I feel it within, but it also came from a place of higher consciousness. It was an efficient and effortless process, and it ignited the flow of writing within me. Months later, I received further confirmation of how perfect this title was for my book when I discovered, with great surprise, that it was available as a domain name on the Internet!

Incorporating our personally empowering environments and activities into our daily routines (as much as possible) keeps us centred in our personal zones of power. This encourages our energy to circulate freely, maintaining a higher frequency and level of awareness instead of falling into stagnation (which blocks energy). This enables us to handle anything with greater efficiency. We also affect others in a positive way, without even attempting to.

When I worked in the corporate world for 15 years, I felt like a fish out of water. I've always enjoyed natural surroundings the most, as well as silence, sounds of Nature and my favourite music. However, during that time, I was working in high-rise buildings surrounded by concrete, indoor fluorescent lighting, static-inducing carpets, electronic equipment, and the noise of traffic, mixed with office technology. Spending most of my days in such large artificial environments made me feel as if I were in a cage. To keep my sanity, over the years I transformed every desk space I had into a small Nature oasis. I surrounded my spaces with potted plants, large granite rocks, crystals, and favourite images of Nature from my travels and from calendars.

I was the only one who did this, which made my space stand out considerably from the other work stations. However, I noticed that, regardless of which office or department I was in, co-workers loved to spend time around my desk spaces, which looked like green islands amidst mazes of cubicles. By naturalizing my space, I managed to keep my own energy as high as possible and uplifted others also—co-workers and clients alike. I even earned the name Sunshine from an individual who few got along with. I brightened people's days without trying. I simply created environments that best supported me under unfavourable conditions, and in doing so supported many others at the same time.

When we honour who we are in all situations, we create an energy field of powerful possibilities that supports us and our heart desires. We claim our own power, and doors open for us in the most effortless, magickal ways. We also notice that doors related to our old ways of being now close, allowing us to step further and with greater commitment into who we are being called to be. Opportunities show up to release what no longer serves us, so that space is created to invite in what does. We feel aligned with a special flow of support. All that's required is to allow ourselves to go with it and follow the guidance we receive from within our hearts. Inspired action creates incredible results.

In 1991 I was graduating from high school, and every classmate had the usual plans for post-secondary studies. It was customary to move from the small town we knew so well to attend a college or university at a nearby city in central Canada. However, I personally couldn't even imagine doing that. I greatly desired to break free from the society I'd been raised in, so I could meet people who hadn't known me from birth. I yearned to have my own identity instead of being known as so-and-so's daughter, sibling, niece, cousin, grandchild, or friend. I wanted to spread my wings in a completely new environment, where I was free to discover and experience who I was without association to all that was familiar to me. I longed to know who I would be if I stripped away every form of identity and expectation that had been layered on me over the years. Just the thought felt so liberating and exhilarating.

One day I happened to tell my biology teacher about my desire to pursue studies in marine biology. I had always felt a connection with dolphins, whales, and the ocean environment. I felt this was the best career choice for me at the time. To my delighted surprise, she told me she was from a city on Canada's east coast that had an excellent university, which offered such courses in my native tongue. I couldn't believe that no one had ever mentioned this French university before. I discovered that no one was aware of it—no one I knew had even heard of the city it was in! I suddenly knew without a doubt that this was the answer to my burning desire. I submitted an admission application to this university only—I didn't apply to any other institution. I didn't have a backup plan. This was where I desired to go, and I focused my intention and energy on it with all my heart. In the meantime, all I could do was wait and see whether it would work out. Since I had done poorly in mathematics and I needed a certain grade to enter any university, my math teacher had given me extra merit points for all the effort I had put into barely passing. I was so grateful to him for that.

Shortly before graduation day, I received an acceptance letter from the university! The complete unknown awaited me, and I was ecstatic. Then it got even better. Since the course I was going to pursue wasn't offered in my home province in my language of choice, I qualified for bursaries to help me fund my studies (which I applied for and did receive)!

Unbeknownst to me, by daring to leap out of the familiar box to follow my heart desire, I became a trailblazer for many who graduated after I did. I gave others of that school more choices in post-secondary studies. Another unanticipated effect of my choice was that two of my three siblings also ended up studying in that maritime city and met their wonderful spouses there! I never could have imagined that our family would so greatly benefit from a decision I made at 18 years of age. Life is even more amazing when you can look back and see how many lives you've benefitted by living your own life with your heart leading the way!

Interestingly, while I had aspired to become a marine biologist, all the courses with numerical sciences made that dream vanish for me. When I saw a councillor after my second year of university and did aptitude tests, I was told that my mind didn't think linearly but spatially, so I should try fine arts rather than sciences. I ended up having the most enjoyable and best academic year of my life in fine arts—it was a breath of fresh air, since I succeeded effortlessly. However, I didn't pursue it past that one year. While being creative and artistic would always be a part of my life, I didn't feel the need to acquire an expensive piece of paper to say I was an artist. What I gained instead from that experience was worth much more than a diploma. I finally realized that there was nothing wrong with me intellectually. I now knew that I didn't lack intelligence; I simply had different strengths than those who excelled in physics and calculus, and these strengths were just as valuable. That in itself was priceless to me.

Years later, as the new millennium approached (with a lot of drama surrounding Y2K and possible technical mayhem) I found myself desiring to travel. Then I discovered a wonderful ecotour that was taking place in Costa Rica through a US environmental charity I supported. The purpose of this ecotour was to raise funds for their Latin American counterpart. I booked my flight despite people's warnings about planning a trip so close to the date of possible mass technological problems.

Shortly after the year 2000 arrived (without even a glitch), I spent two incredible weeks travelling all over that glorious small country and became good friends with the founder and president of the environmental foundation. Raul happened to be our personal tour guide, and our group was small enough to personally connect at the heart level. He was so impressed by my deep love and appreciation for Nature, he told me I could volunteer for his projects anytime. I decided to take him up on that offer in 2002, while I worked for an international corporation. I sold my downtown condo and moved into an apartment so I wouldn't have any attachments. I was always ready for the unexpected and even considered the possibility that I'd decide to live there.

Since university, when I was forced to change course, I had always wondered about being a marine biologist. Nearly a decade later, I was being offered this golden opportunity to participate in marine biology research as an intern, with all lodging and meals covered. I would be overseeing the project with someone else. It was truly a manifested desire. Not only would I do work that I had aspired to do, while benefiting the environmental foundation and sea turtles, but I would also live in a beautiful tropical country for three months. I had acquired just enough different certifications over the years, including Spanish language and an online environmental course, to submit the required paperwork for the intern position. Normally only university students or graduates could qualify as interns, so this was a divinely orchestrated gift I was being given. My dear friend Raul, who was making all this possible for me, told me that skills could be taught, and he would much rather train someone with my qualities than hire a highly qualified individual who lacked passion. I felt so much appreciation for him and his wisdom.

I was now all set, except for one significant detail—getting time off from work. This was never an option in the multibillion dollar corporation I worked for at the time. It was unheard of. The employees were paid very well, to work. Time off work was restricted to the bare minimum, required by law. However, I was so determined to do this volunteer work while the opportunity presented itself that I decided to be completely honest with the Human Resources department. I submitted an official request, stating exactly why I needed those months off from work. I explained that since this was a once-in-a-lifetime opportunity, I was willing to resign if I didn't receive a leave of absence (a leave meant that while I wouldn't get paid during my absence, my job would still be there for me if I chose to return). No one had ever dared to risk losing such a high-paying job, so what I was presenting to them was quite a radical approach. They knew I was serious.

I had no idea that so many departments had to sign agreement in order to give me a positive answer. After a few weeks, I was finally called into the Human Resources office and told I was being granted the months off, exactly as I had requested! The written agreement clearly stated that I could only do this one time while I was employed by that company. I was so amazed. Rumors and speculations circulated rapidly at this large office, especially since time off work had been refused to so many employees over the years. They couldn't believe I'd been granted my request, until I told them I had been willing to resign, regardless of the large paycheque.

Later I found out it was only due to certain people being positioned in the necessary departments, at the right time, that everything fell into place for me to receive this leave of absence. A very small window of opportunity had opened up. Within a month after I was granted my leave request, the director (who had given the final yes for me) retired from the company. Anyone before or after him would have said a firm no, since they all strictly followed the policy. I was told he had made an exception based on the fact that my request was for a volunteer position without pay, and he didn't want to lose me as an employee. Perhaps he was feeling more lenient because of his upcoming retirement. Regardless, he and many others, co-created a sacred possibility for me.

I was given the responsibility to manage a volunteer project for Raul, an award-winning marine biologist, for three months in Costa Rica. I lived in a stilted, open-air house without electricity, between magnificent mountainous rainforest and the vast Pacific Ocean. I was immersed in Nature every day, abundant with lush plant life and beautiful wildlife of all sorts. Several species of monkeys, colourful birds, large butterflies, and other tropical animals were regular visitors. Since it was the rainy season, I experienced glorious thunderstorms and was surrounded by blossoms of every colour, with an abundance of delicious, fresh fruit. I was part of a wonderful, small village community, with delectable, homemade meals provided daily by a local mother.

I will always be so grateful for this amazing opportunity that I received, thanks to so many individuals who made unusual exceptions for me. I felt so blessed for this experience that enabled me to discover (to my surprise) that marine biology was not meant for me after all! I realized that it wasn't my calling the way it was for my dear friend Raul. I couldn't imagine doing that work on a full-time basis. That part of my life finally came full circle in a very magickal way, and it now felt complete.

In the process, I actually met two wonderful women from the United States who lived a few miles away. They were friends, and one of them happened to have a wonderful library of esoteric books that I borrowed to read in my spare time. I absolutely loved reading those books. They provided so many insightful confirmations about aspects of myself, that I hadn't been able to openly talk about with others before. They opened my awareness even more. This was an unexpected gift I hadn't anticipated but greatly appreciated. When my journey in Costa Rica completed, another gift awaited me. On one of my return flights to Canada, most people on the aircraft were sleeping. As I looked out the window, I suddenly noticed the most beautiful celestial phenomenon occurring around us. Luminescent green northern lights were dancing in the night sky and they seemed to surround us, since we were so high up in altitude! I felt so privileged to be able to experience the auroras from the sky like this.

So many times throughout my life I've desired to do something, such as participating in a course, an event, or an adventure, and then realized it was really about so much more than that. I was guided to those things as a means to acquire something beyond what I could imagine. In the process, many others' heart desires also manifested. It's such a divinely orchestrated ripple effect. We're all so connected.

I realized that my desire to study marine biology after graduation had actually been a catalyst to fulfill many desires—current ones and future ones I wasn't aware of yet. That desire had led me to a completely different life as an independent young adult and had also given me just enough schooling to look as if I qualified for the intern position. In addition to this, so many others benefited in ways I couldn't have anticipated when committing to my initial heart desire.

When we look back, we realize that things easily fall into place for us when we feel unstoppable about something we *know* we must do. We pursue it wholeheartedly and don't think about limitations. While we can't imagine all the possibilities that await us, or how things will work out, all we need to do is open up to them by honouring our whole selves, including our heart desires and unique paths.

When we recognize the tremendous value of our own individuality and path, we're able to confidently live our lives in a way that always honours them. Everything we do comes from our sacred hearts—our divinity. This not only ensures that everything we experience is aligned with our purpose on Earth, but it also benefits many more than we'll ever know. It doesn't matter what our paths look like, what we feel called to do, or whether it makes logical sense or not. We are invaluable as part of the greater whole in this world—as we are.

Ever since I consciously realized that my own path calls for me to make my everyday life my sacred work and spiritual practice—every moment of every day, regardless of where I am or what I do, or whether I'm with people or not—I consciously show up as my best, to the best of my ability. Even if I don't go out in public, I enjoy looking my best every day, and my morning ritual makes me feel good in mind, body, heart, and spirit. I make this an act of love and appreciation to the Divine for my life. By doing this, I've learned to let my true essence shine in all situations, as a way of being.

When I was called to spend a few months on the island of Hawai'i in the spring of 2013, it was a giant leap of faith. I woke up one morning just itching to find out how long it would take me to walk down Mauna Loa to a local store by the highway and back up again to where I was staying. My body was suddenly craving extreme physical activity. I was determined to honour it by seeing if I could walk that distance within a reasonable amount of time, before the sun got too hot. No one around that area had done that before, so they considered me a bit crazy to even think of it.

However, nothing has ever deterred me when I've felt inspired to do something, so I went in spite of the lack of encouragement. I brought a packsack with enough water and snacks to last me all morning, in case it took me more than a couple of hours. I was used to walking long distances wherever I lived, to exercise and spend time with Nature. I was pleased to see that, while the incline of the uphill route was steep and challenging, I was able to complete the entire circuit in an hour and a half. I continued this Nature-exercise routine at sunrise every day thereafter, while I was on the island. It was a hike down and up the steep, hilly roads of the mountain, with brief breaks to drink water at well-chosen locations beside trees bearing beautiful, fragrant flowers. It was so exhilarating to greet the day with the symphony of the birds and invigorate my body on all levels. It was my alone time with Nature and it kept me heart-centred and fully grounded in my body. I savoured every moment of it, despite so many unknowns looming over me.

During these sunrise hikes, I got to know many locals. One neighbour, who jogged back and forth on one of the horizontal roads every morning, asked me shortly after meeting me where I worked. I told her honestly, "*This* is currently my work," meaning my hike. After pondering my answer a moment, she smiled and agreed wholeheartedly. She had grown fond of hearing my personal stories and insights, which I would share briefly with her when our paths crossed.

I didn't realize how true this *really* was until one particular morning when I was enjoying my long exercise ritual. I was steadily hiking back up a steep area of Mauna Loa when a local middle-aged woman, whom I hadn't met yet, drove uphill behind me. I always moved to the side of these narrow roads to let motorists pass. As she reached me, she stopped her vehicle, rolled down her window, and said with a big smile, "I just had to tell you that you've become my hero!" I was stunned. What a surprising thing to hear. What an honour to receive such a statement! I took a break while she proceeded to tell me that she'd noticed me every morning when she drove to work. She said she had been so amazed by my discipline and determination that she'd felt inspired to get her body back in shape. She'd started walking a short distance every day for starters, and she was determined to keep adding a little more distance every week.

I never would have anticipated that my crazy, extreme workout would have that effect on someone else. I was simply being me and doing what I felt inspired to do, to empower myself further. What she told me filled me with so much joy. I thanked her for taking the time to share that with me, for I never would have known otherwise. It was a gift for me to receive that knowledge. I had no idea what people thought when they passed and saluted me. After this woman took off with a big smile, in spirit I skipped weightlessly the rest of the uphill roads.

This gave me a whole other perspective about the responsibility I had to be me, in *all* situations of life. You just *never* know who's taking notice of you and being inspired by something you do or the way you are. It's so powerful to be aware of this.

As I transformed my fear of being seen, through work with my business mentor Holly and soul family, I was able to claim every aspect of who I was and feel safe making it visible to anyone in the world. That was a very significant transformation for me. I reached a point when I knew it was time for my photo shoot with Holly's photographer Tom. Everything I had experienced, in mind, body, heart, and spirit, had led me to this moment of having an exceptional photographer capture snapshots of my unique essence—what my mentor called "iconic" as the quality of a shining, true essence. I also had Holly, a natural in front of the camera, to coach me. It wasn't going to be a typical photo shoot, since the focus was to showcase my unique essence. It was the end of October 2012 when I flew out to work with them.

The morning of my photo shoot, I woke up early and saw weather that I highly disliked—cold and wet. It was just above freezing temperature at five degrees Celsius, windy, overcast, and rainy. It was actually part of a large hurricane system that was affecting the American east coast. Of course, the photo shoot was taking place in an outdoor park so I could be in my element of Nature! I looked outside my second-floor hotel window and just knew that somehow, this is what it was supposed to be like. I might not particularly enjoy it, but things always worked out somehow. As I thought of this and observed the trees swaying in the wind, I suddenly noticed a beautiful, little whirlwind in the parking lot below me, swirling colourful autumn leaves! How wonderful it was to see this personal essence sign! It instantly reassured me that everything was indeed exactly as it should be, and I just had to trust.

I had so much fun at the studio getting ready for this photo shoot, with my makeup and hair done by Holly's fabulous makeup artist. We also got creative with the dress I chose to wear. It was enjoyable for me since I now had the body I'd always desired. We arrived at the park we had chosen for the location, and the colours of this natural environment took my breath away. Due to the rain, every colour was resplendent! Although it was late in the year, the leaves on the ground were not the browns and greys that already carpeted the forests where I was living. Here, just a province away, they were magnificent. While there were not many still on the trees, this made for a much more colourful photo set-up. Rich amber and golden-yellow leaves carpeted the entire forest floor, vivid green mosses covered the stones and bases of the trees, and the texture of the greyish-brown tree bark was so striking.

I realized that every colour used on my business logo was represented here. It was amazing and so perfect.

While Holly and Tom had on thick jackets and gloves, I was barefoot in a strapless dress (by choice), with a warm blanket to wrap around myself between shoots. The photographer was wonderful to work with. He had to warm up his hands every now and then to continue working the camera. I was so grateful to both of them for having a great sense of humour and for being as dedicated as I was to accomplishing our goal. I was determined to make the most of it, so I focused on the beauty that surrounded me and the energy I received from Mother Earth through my feet. Tom told me encouragingly that extreme conditions usually create exceptional photographs. I appreciated that. At one point, Holly pointed out that a red-tailed hawk was soaring above us! I was so ecstatic to have the presence of this power animal. I felt blessed and supported by many, seen and unseen.

When I saw the photographs later, I was speechless with emotion. Tom brilliantly captured not only my essence but also the spectacular natural surroundings. You couldn't even tell what the weather had been like. After going through the multi-level journey that I had—beginning in later 2010 and arriving at this moment, when I saw myself in a way I never had before—I was deeply moved. It felt like the full emergence of Lucille DancingWind. After weeks of processing, my name was legally changed only a few days after my photo shoot. I received the government papers in the mail. It felt so divinely perfect to me.

I then made the decision to change my outdated profile photos on my Facebook account and website. I was astounded by the unexpected reaction from people. I had never received so many comments on a post—and this post was *me*. I normally didn't post photographs of myself, so this was another leap into being more visible. The comments I received allowed me to see how others perceived me, and it was incredible. My new photos inspired and captured the attention of people of both genders from all over the world, leading to surprising soul connections on multiple levels. Because I was willing to work through my fear of being seen by the world and show my true essence in a very visible way, magick resulted (and it has continued to)! My inner work was translated into the external world and manifested amazing, unanticipated possibilities.

The power of being and shining our authentic, divine selves is infinite. At every moment we can be a source of inspiration, empowerment, healing, and transformation for someone, usually without knowing it. We might do something so subtle that we don't even notice it ourselves, yet for someone else it's exactly what they needed to see, hear, read, feel, or experience through us.

It's not a process of trying, but simply being *you*. When you honour who you are in every area of your life, it is enough to change our world. It's one of the greatest gifts that you can give to yourself and to others. In doing so, you radiate your inner light and you become more love—and love makes everything possible.

The Empowerment
of Surrender

Miracles manifest and flow with grace.

The creative process is a process of surrender, not control.
—*Julia Cameron*

Magic is essentially the higher understanding of nature.
—*Unknown*

Surrendering a situation to the Divine doesn't mean that we're giving up or that we're being irresponsible. Rather, we're acknowledging that we're not alone and that we don't have to figure things out on our own. We're inviting a solution that we couldn't possibly think of from our perspective. Surrendering actually empowers us. We allow Spirit to work magick for us from a place beyond logic, where everything is possible. It's a sacred partnership. When we're guided to an inspired action and follow through with it, everything unfolds with grace and little effort. All we have to do is trust.

When we know that the Divine's wisdom, resources, and creativity are infinitely greater than our own, it liberates us to confidently hand over the details of our desires, such as the *how*, to Spirit. We surrender the need to control everything, so that Spirit can intervene for the highest good of everyone involved. We have faith that the best outcome will manifest even better than we could have imagined on our own. We also have trust that everything, including timing and circumstances, is exactly as it needs to be for the highest outcome to manifest, no matter what it looks like.

This can be challenging for anyone who needs to feel in control at all times. The truth, however, is that no person is ever in control of everything. In one instant, at any time, everything can change for us. I personally find this realization empowering instead of alarming. It releases us from the pressure of needing to have the answers to everything. It's reassuring to know that anytime, whether you have a desire or you're in any situation, you can count on Spirit to assist you in ways that far surpass anything that you could try yourself.

At the beginning of December 2011, I was driving to the city to do some errands. It was a very cold day, but I was feeling grateful that there wasn't any snow yet. I had purchased a used car five months earlier, and it simply was not as dependable as I would have liked it to be. Its tires were also smaller than average and probably were not the greatest in snow, especially on the country roads. I'd obviously gotten what I paid for (which wasn't much). Despite it all, I felt blessed to have found a vehicle within my price range when I really needed one—with a heater that worked. Living in the country required that I have my own transportation in order to be independent.

As I reached the highway's turnoff to enter the city, my vehicle's electronics suddenly went completely crazy. Every gauge, light, and switch was blinking on and off, the motor started to buck, and the car made terribly abnormal noises. I had just enough time to pull over onto the gravel shoulder, and then everything completely shut down! I turned the ignition switch off, and after a moment of absolute silence, I gingerly tried to turn it on again. Unfortunately, what I had dreaded was now reality—my car was completely dead. My heart sank. I just could *not* believe this was happening.

It was the second used vehicle in seven months that had stranded me on the side of a major highway! It really made me wonder what was going on. The first one had been completely unexpected. I had owned it for five years, and it had been in great condition. Then, without warning, it suddenly blew its engine on a US freeway shortly after I'd had it serviced. I needed my own reliable vehicle, especially with the winter weather about to begin. Since I no longer lived in the city, I couldn't depend on other modes of transportation. I had no money on hand for another used vehicle, and the truth was that I had been feeling quite irritated with used vehicles ever since I'd purchased this one. It had been costing me as much in maintenance every month as payments for a new car would have. I had to finally admit I'd purchased something akin to junk.

My consolation was that I had discovered a wonderful vehicle dealership by having to bring my car for frequent maintenance and repairs. The staff was always exceptionally wonderful with me, including giving me discounts on parts, service, and repair fees every single time. Perhaps my unfortunate predicament with a car manufactured by their company made them that much more compassionate with me. Whatever it was, I always greatly appreciated it.

Now, however, I was stranded on the side of a busy highway. At least I was a safe distance from traffic, out of the way of the big semi-trucks that frequented this route and made the car shake when they drove by. I suddenly remembered that when I had driven away from the house earlier, I'd had a certain feeling about the car. Now I understood, it had been a little premonition. I screamed out loud and pounded on the steering wheel to release my immense feeling of frustration. In that moment, I felt completely defeated. Fortunately I had my cell phone and was able to contact my soul sister Anna to let her know about my situation. Although she was willing to come and get me, I wholeheartedly thanked her and simply told her I would keep her updated. I felt, somehow, that another solution was in store for me. I had no idea what that might look like, but I knew that getting her to drive all that way with her children to get me didn't feel right at this point. I had to see what all my options were.

I calmed down, looked up at the evening sky, and stared at the stars that were already shining brightly. I deeply inhaled … then slowly exhaled … and expressed to the Divine that I was completely surrendering this situation, since I couldn't see any favourable solution from my perspective. It would obviously cost me a lot to revive this vehicle—if it were possible at all. I realized that I actually desired a brand-new vehicle for the first time in my life—one I didn't have to worry about when driving long distances or within the city. I had been feeling this desire for a few months already. I had always preferred purchasing used vehicles, since they were being reused and didn't put me in debt. However, the dependability factor now highly outweighed those considerations. I asked Spirit for clear guidance and for the highest outcome possible to manifest. I phoned the dealership I frequently dealt with, and they gladly sent a tow truck to get me. Once again, I was extremely grateful to the employees of this company. They had gotten to know me very well for less than ideal reasons over the past months, but now this costly "junk" vehicle was about to become a blessing in disguise for me.

By the time the tow truck had brought me and my dead car to the service department, I knew clearly what I had to do. The manager, whom I knew well, warmly greeted me and asked what I would like to do with the car. As soon as he asked me this, I confidently told him that before they even unloaded that car, I wanted to know about their brand-new vehicles. He smiled broadly and told me I couldn't have asked at a better time, since all their 2011 models were on clearance—with countless, incredible bonuses!—to make room for the 2012 models. This wonderful news instantly encouraged me. It made me realize once again that timing is everything. Perhaps my car had dramatically expired at this specific time with a higher purpose. Perhaps my heart desire for a new vehicle, even though I had felt it would take a miracle to manifest without a regular salary, was actually in the process of being realized. All I knew for sure was that anything was possible, and I felt that I was being divinely guided.

The manager took me to the sales department of the building and introduced me to a kind sales agent. Since the agent reminded me a bit of a leprechaun, I immediately felt at ease with him. I had never heard a positive story from people who had purchased new vehicles through a dealership, but despite this and my ordeal, I felt amazingly calm and focused. I noticed several of my essence language signs, including a rainbow, so I knew things were unfolding exactly as they were supposed to. Within minutes of discussing what kind of vehicle I preferred, I knew exactly which 2011 model would suit me perfectly. It was what I had envisioned every time I drove my old car—a combination of all the features I had liked best in my last two vehicles. It was uncanny. As if that wasn't enough, they actually had that model in their showroom right behind me, and in the colour I preferred! It was a shimmering, dark rusty-orange, like the beautiful Sedona landscape I loved. I was amazed and excited!

The sales agent took me for a test drive, and I knew without a doubt that I had found my vehicle—it was just perfect for me. I loved the comfort of it, its exceptional visibility, its spaciousness for a small car, and many features and little things that mattered to me. I also really enjoyed driving it. It was a reasonable price, and I was even given money for my used car, which I had purchased privately. It wasn't worth anything at that point, except maybe for parts. But since I had brought it in so often for servicing and repairs, the manager (perhaps out of compassion) signed for an amount that I could use as a deposit for this new vehicle. I greatly appreciated that unexpected gift, for I hadn't expected to receive anything for it.

I was then taken to the financing department and introduced to an agent. I suddenly realized I hadn't even thought about financing, since everything had unfolded so quickly. I had just been going with the flow. I couldn't help but smile at myself when I noticed how "present" I was to the moment (free of worry). The agent asked me all sorts of questions, which I answered with completely open honesty. I told her I didn't have a current income and had just launched my online business the previous week, with no idea whatsoever how much income I would be making. That was the absolute truth. At that point, I presented myself as a spiritual artist, since I had my first book, prints and originals of my spiritual-themed paintings and Nature photographs, available for purchase on my website. It sounded unsustainable to the typical bank or business person. Yet, she was extremely nice and non-judgmental, since her mother was an artist! After chatting a bit about my new business, she completely surprised me. She made up an estimated income for me and proceeded with filling out all the paperwork, with a smile! I saw the number 33 show up multiple times while I was with her, so I went along with it, knowing I was being guided to do this. I needed a vehicle and trusted that if that car was meant for me, everything would simply work out. If it didn't, there would be an even better solution for me.

Shortly after I had sat down in the lounge area to wait, the financial agent informed me that I was approved and congratulated me for being the owner of a new car. I was speechless and ecstatic. We finished the paperwork only 10 minute before the insurance broker next door closed for the day, so I was able to go over and get the car insured. I came back to the dealership, and the sales agent handed me a package of gifts for the car, including a valuable fuel-discount card, and the keys. He then installed the new licence plates and moved all my things from the dead car to my new one.

The wind was now blowing strongly and freezing cold, so I greatly appreciated all he did for me. I thanked everyone for their exceptional service and called Anna to let her know I was driving home in a new car! As I told her, it felt so surreal—I just couldn't stop smiling.

I drove away with my very first brand-new vehicle and felt like I was on top of the world. It handled exceptionally well on the highway, even in the strong wind (much better than my previous vehicles had). The level of gratitude and blissful joy I exuded, driving on the highway that night, was probably felt by the entire planet! I felt so relieved to have a vehicle I could now fully depend on; it even had roadside assistance (part of the bonuses I received). I must have thanked Spirit a million times as I drove the one hour from the city to my rural home. I was filled with absolute wonder. When I had been stranded on the side of the highway a few hours earlier, I could not have envisioned that this outcome would manifest for me—with such ease! Things could not have flowed more perfectly. A few days later I created a very special dreamcatcher to hang on my new car's rearview mirror, to infuse its mechanically-created space with sacred energy.

Throughout my life's experiences, I've discovered there's a divine solution for everything. It usually doesn't look anything like what we might have imagined, but ultimately it's better. We can either try to figure things out on our own or we can remain open to receiving the loving support from Spirit—an infinite amount of it. It's a form of divine teamwork based on trust, and it's always available to us. When we show our trust in this sacred partnership, through surrender, Spirit always responds immediately. Allowing ourselves to receive the support given to us, regardless of what it looks like, co-creates magick. Love is the opposite of fear, faith is the opposite of worry, and trust is the opposite of doubt.

When we practise surrender in everyday life, instead of reserving it for extreme situations, it becomes a grace-filled way of being. We don't worry about the outcome, because we're not attached to a specific one. We have faith that everything works out as it should when we allow it to. We're open to higher guidance and to the possibilities instead of holding onto preconceived notions.

In the spring of 2003, my husband at the time and I had an average-sized backyard in the city, which had issues of poor drainage and persistent, invasive weeds in the lawn. While Adam would have liked a yard that didn't require mowing, I desired more Nature in my environment. Both of us wanted a low-maintenance yard free of toxic chemicals. One day I received an insight about using native plants in our landscaping—plants indigenous to the natural habitats of our area, such as prairie and woodlands. After some research, I proposed that we transform the entire yard into many gardens of these beautiful plants. I was amazed by the hundreds of species available to choose from and even found a local nursery that specialized in true native plants (as opposed to hybrids).

I carefully selected several dozen beautiful species that would benefit our endemic wildlife. I knew these plants would be easy to care for since they had evolved with our climate and wildlife for eons. This made them hardy, resilient, and self-sufficient, with no need for special attention. This was ideal, since I didn't have knowledge about gardening or landscaping. What I had was a deep love for Nature and a talent and passion for creating beautiful things I envisioned. My inner artist and visionary saw our yard as a blank canvas of possibility and enabled me to design and create the layout. However, as far as how the plants would do, I fully surrendered that to Nature and Spirit. I felt that if any plants died it would mean they simply weren't happy in our yard, and I wouldn't replace them.

We gave our yard a complete transformation, from the ground up. We first replaced one foot in depth of the clay soil and weedy lawn with a good soil mixture. The yard's surface was now a bed of black soil, surrounded by typical city properties and streets. Before we laid down stones for the winding paths and picked up the plant seedlings at the nursery, I introduced our first plants to the yard. I planted nine small shoots (which we'd inherited from Adam's dear parents), of a beautiful native fruiting shrub found on their rural property. I added them to a corner of the yard and was astounded by what I saw afterwards.

I was admiring the red bark and new leaves of these little saplings that were no thicker than pencils. Suddenly, the tiniest butterfly I had ever seen, with shimmering violet-blue wings (each no larger than one of my fingernails), fluttered past me and up to these nine thin saplings! It circled around the plants as though welcoming them. I discovered that this type of native shrub was a host plant for this pretty butterfly. Its leaves provided food for their caterpillars, the next generation of butterflies. This diminutive winged being found them in the middle of the vast urban environment where we lived! Only energy could make this possible. These tiny plants were broadcasting their unique frequency in the environment. That little butterfly recognized their energy signature and followed it to its source. I was witnessing something truly magickal manifesting, right in my own urban backyard!

Since I had made this yard's transformation a personal project of mine, I began to consistently document my observations of its progress. I used photographs, journal notes, and drawings from the first day we began, and I continued almost every day for five years. I was so grateful I did this, for clearly I had been guided to do so—Nature had countless wonders, wisdom and insights to share with me! While I had known that the plants I chose would provide seeds for birds and nectar for butterflies, I hadn't anticipated how much of an oasis our yard would become over the seasons and years for innumerable species of wildlife, especially of the winged varieties.

I saw dozens of different species of birds, dragonflies, butterflies, and bees in our urban yard that I had never seen before, even though I had been raised in the country. It was truly amazing. Furthermore, additional species of blooming native plants started to appear among the others—very pretty and dainty species like violets, most likely introduced by the visiting birds through defecated seeds. Our yard provided shelter, water, and food for so many, in the form of seeds, small fruit, nectar, leaves, and insects. During the migrating seasons, birds found plenty of much-needed energy food, from the seed heads of the wild grasses and flowers and from fruiting shrubs and vines.

Our neighbours and visitors marvelled at the beauty of the native plants, erroneously assuming, as many did, that native plants were weeds. I loved the effect our yard had on so many and greatly enjoyed returning from work every day to spend time in this small Nature haven. Its energy felt divine to me.

I also had the privilege of witnessing the entire life cycles of several butterfly species, which was such a divine marvel. I saw female butterflies lay eggs on specific plants and caterpillars feed on the leaves of these host plants. I saw caterpillars completely metamorphose into chrysalises that hung like little jewel ornaments throughout the gardens. I observed the emergence of butterflies from the chrysalises. I saw them take their first impressive flights and feed on the variety of wildflowers available in our gardens. It was awe-inspiring and such a gift to experience all this firsthand (especially knowing that some of those butterfly species were drastically declining in numbers in the wild). Our yard unknowingly became a nursery that assisted the populations of these butterflies.

I realized that the urban and agricultural environments spanning so much of the province and beyond had replaced many natural habitats. Therefore, our use of native plants in our landscaping was such an immense service to Nature. It provided the plants that wildlife had evolved with, which otherwise were more difficult to find. So many species of plants found in our yard were also endangered due to the use of agricultural chemicals and loss of natural habitat.

Our modest urban property had become an oasis, and wildlife had found it. That in itself was miraculous. Every plant broadcasted its energy signature in a powerful way, so that wildlife, including tiny butterflies, damselflies, and bees, could find it. I had never read about this but just knew that it was another wonder of energy. Learning about it firsthand felt like an additional reward for what I had co-created. With every new visitor I observed in our garden, I felt blessed by another divine wonder. I also felt the presence of the elementals so clearly.

These guardian angels of Nature most definitely assisted in the transformation of our yard, for every person who visited felt so good there. Since I had allowed Nature to show me what was needed, rather than trying to control things, everything felt in harmony. Our yard had a very special energy that was absent in other yards. This good energy probably also had to do with its being co-created from a heart intention, centred in love and reverence.

I never anticipated what my simple desire to bring Nature to me in the city and surrendering the outcome of my inspired actions to Spirit and Nature would manifest. It brought about such a beautiful form of service and unleashed so many wonders. Our small oasis taught me much about co-creation and existing in harmony with All. The teachings I received inspired me so much. Three years after our yard's transformation, I woke up one night quite suddenly. Since I'd always been a sound sleeper, this was unusual for me. As I silently lay in the dark wondering what had woken me up, I received a surprise. An elemental, who was one of my spirit guides, suggested I create a book to showcase the best of our yard's five years, using hundreds of my best colour photographs along with my notes and drawings. I agreed to this and continued to diligently document everything for two more years.

Then, through my soul sister Flora, whom I serendipitously met in 2008 in Bimini, I discovered the perfect program to create and self-publish that book with a print-on-demand company. The company's easy-to-use program allowed me to have the creative flexibility I desired for such a special book, which I self-published in 2010. I donated many copies to local libraries. Now that book is a lasting legacy of the beautiful, sacred possibilities that manifested in response to a simple heart desire. Surrendering the outcome generated even more unexpected benefits. Through simple word of mouth, our oasis and my book ended up attracting the attention of newspapers, magazines, a radio show, and even university students who were working on a thesis. I would have done the interview with the students for free, but they had a budget to pay me. With that money I purchased a unique ring I discovered "by chance" one day, made of silver and green amber. It's a special reminder to me of all that's possible when we act from a place of love, trust, and surrender.

Surrendering can benefit us in *any* situation of our lives and in the most unexpected ways. Spirit doesn't judge, as we do. Everything we experience is valuable and part of our unique paths. It's so easy for us to judge something as not being worthy of Spirit's attention, or not important enough for a special request, or too superficial to merit assistance, etc. However, Spirit desires to support us in *all* ways.

When you let go of judgment, simply ask Spirit for support, and you surrender from your heart, your request will be received, no matter how simple or complicated or grand it might be!

During my first journey in Arizona, I had felt strongly that I would find a very special piece of silver jewellery for myself, made of green turquoise. When I was on the sacred lands of the Navajo, I did find it. It was a beautiful ring with a unique style, created by a Navajo artist. It called to me immediately amongst the hundreds of other rings all featuring blue turquoise—I felt it had been created just for me. It looked like a view of land on Mother Earth from space, being multiple shades of green with a brown matrix. Since I visited such sacred places after purchasing it, it was infused with incredible energy. This treasured ring became my personal symbol of my commitment to Mother Earth and my work in sacred partnership with Spirit and Nature.

Shortly after my journey to Arizona, I worked with my business mentor in person for two days. I was about to catch my flight back home and decided to use the washroom first. It was a small airport, and there were crowds of people, as many flights were leaving soon. Shortly after my flight took off, I suddenly noticed something I could not believe—my special ring was missing from my left index finger! It was the one ring that I wore every day. I realized with a sinking feeling in my heart and stomach that I had left it on the side of the sink after washing my hands. I just couldn't believe I had done that! I had been distracted by all the people crowding that space and had wanted to get out as quickly as I could.

I asked a flight attendant if it was possible for them or me to contact that airport immediately. I was told I would have to wait until we landed at the airport to find the phone number. I could feel panic creeping into my mind, so I closed my eyes. With all my heart I then asked Archangel Michael to please shield my ring so that no one would see it—if it was meant for me to have. There was nothing more I could do.

I stayed within my heart, with eyes closed, and fully surrendered this to Spirit. As I did this I slowly returned to feeling inner peace again. When I opened my eyes, I looked out the window and saw a rainbow halo appear and shine brightly on the clouds below the aircraft! Then I saw 333 on the TV screen as it showed the latitude and other details of the flight! What a great feeling it was to see those personal essence signs at that moment. I felt instantly that everything was going to be okay.

Upon landing two hours later, I was able to call the other airport and speak with a kind security officer. I explained my situation, and he happily went to the washroom to look for my ring. After I had waited in silence for a time, he spoke again— he had actually found it! Despite all the people that had been crowding into that washroom and the time that had passed since I'd left it there, no one had taken my ring. I overflowed with love and gratitude to all who had assisted me. The next day, the airport manager personally mailed my ring back to me, free of charge. I expressed my appreciation to her. My ring acquired even more significance for me through this, for its return was a miracle in itself.

Throughout the years, I've become well acquainted with Spirit's sense of humour. Surrendering a situation to Spirit isn't something we must save for only serious matters. We're here to experience *all* aspects of life, and that includes play! When we release judgment from all aspects of life, our sacred relationship with All becomes that much richer for it. It's always delightful to experience elation and laughter, knowing Spirit is a participant. Our heart connections deepen through joy.

One winter day, I was outside on my parents' large rural property. I was tobogganing with my four young nephews and one of my brothers, down a large snow hill that my dad had created. At one point, all the boys started ganging up on my brother in the snow, laughing with excitement. It was fun to watch, but I decided not to take part in the snow-flinging, wrestling frenzy and went walking further on the property.

As I walked through the knee-deep snow towards some trees, I suddenly heard my brother tell the kids, through his laughter, to go capture me. Of course, they all thought this was an excellent idea! As I turned around in the clearing, I saw these four supercharged, enthusiastic boys running through the snow towards me. They had spaced themselves to make sure to catch me. I had no time to escape, since I couldn't efficiently run through snow that deep, not to mention that they had way more energy than I did! They were also lighter than me, so they weren't sinking the way I was.

Realizing all this, I laughed and just completely surrendered this situation to Spirit. I decided to face them. I watched them coming towards me, wide grins on their faces and giggles escaping them with the anticipation of catching me. I smiled back and braced myself. Four boys and a lot of snow would turn me into a giant snowball in no time at all! My brother watched, smiling at his own cleverness.

Suddenly, something completely unexpected happened. When the nephew closest to me reached a distance of several yards away, he suddenly sank deeply into the snow, and his momentum made him topple over. Then the second one did the same ... and then the third one ... and finally the fourth nephew. They all found themselves snowbound and unable to reach me! My brother suddenly yelled that I had "a protective force field"—which made us all laugh out loud. I took that opportunity to escape, and I laughed with great relief at the humour of the situation. I was quite amused and so grateful for this surprising, favourable outcome.

Being brought up in a conformist society, we've been taught that things are separate and that we should automatically compartmentalize these things under attainable, possible or impossible, based on preconceived evidence and perceptions. We've been taught that things work in a linear fashion and that only the logical creates real results. We've been taught that to think otherwise is unrealistic or superstitious and we must always be in control of situations if we want to meet our expectations. We've also been taught that time as we know it dictates how long something takes to occur or to be created.

I always encourage people to find out things for themselves. If we take someone's word as fact without experiencing it for ourselves, we just might miss out on something different and extraordinary. If we accept all these things we've been taught "inside the box" as truth, they prevent us from discovering our own truth. I've always chosen to believe what feels true to me based on my heart's inner knowing, and then I've explored that for myself. Through experience, it has become a *knowing* on all levels, including the logical mind. Personal truth is powerful.

I've been shown throughout my life that when we nurture a sacred relationship with All, everything becomes possible. Surrendering any situation to Spirit when we feel we could use extra assistance, invites surprising possibilities to manifest. In the process, we're reminded that life is *so much more* than what we've been taught. The more we experience things "outside the box" for ourselves, the more aware we become of all that is truly possible to experience beyond time, space, and logic.

The Gifts of Navigating the Unknown

Magick awaits (even through chaos).

You have to take risks. We will only understand the miracle
of life fully when we allow the unexpected to happen.
—Paulo Coelho

I never made one of my discoveries through
the process of rational thinking.
—Albert Einstein

Each and every one of us is invited to experience the unknown repeatedly over the course of our life, to different degrees. It can manifest as small, out-of-the-ordinary experiences, bigger journeys, leaps of faith, or extreme tests of faith.

You know what degree of unknown it is for you by how much (or how little) fear you feel with it. It can range from feeling joyful curiosity or nervous excitement, to the other end of the spectrum, with feeling that it's somewhat terrifying or life-threatening.

When you accept the invitation to go through new experiences that don't have a known outcome, you find yourself courageously navigating the unknown. This can be as simple as "going with the flow" without a plan and being open to something unexpected. Or it might be more drastic, like changing careers, moving to an unfamiliar place, becoming a parent, answering a calling, going on an adventure abroad, beginning a new relationship, etc. Whatever this unknown looks and feels like to you, it requires that you let go of the need to know how things will turn out, regardless of the risk involved. In doing so, you can discover and receive the possibilities that are infinitely co-created just for you.

As soon as we let go of that familiar shore, fully open with curiosity to what the ocean of life might bring to us, we invite the magickal and miraculous to manifest. It's like throwing what's familiar up into the ethers to see how it lands back on our physical plane. The more of the familiar we're willing to allow Spirit to play with, the greater and more extraordinary are the possibilities. The greater the risk, the more we open ourselves to receiving something incredible. Regardless of what unknowns we choose to undertake, the rewards are always invaluable to our personal paths, whether it's physical, emotional, mental, spiritual, or all of them. Those experiences also encourage us to keep trusting.

One summer day in 2007, as I worked in an office downtown, I was feeling that I'd absolutely had enough with my job. A lot of changes were being implemented within the giant corporation, and none of them were positive for most employees or customers. The focus was apparently solely on making more money at the expense of all but the top executives. The politics; the gossip; the complaining customers, co-workers and managers—everything had made me highly irritable that day. My tolerance level had become nonexistent, and nothing could shift me out of that negative state. I needed to free myself of that claustrophobic environment. I needed something to transform this condition I felt so stuck in. Whenever I felt like this, I created what I referred to as a *storm*. I did something completely different than usual, to stir up the energies and create space for new possibilities. That day, I definitely needed to get out of the busy and noisy downtown to change my environment completely. On an impulse, instead of going for my usual walk during my lunch break, I went to the bus stop near the office building. I decided to board the first transit bus that arrived and see where I would be spending most of the next hour.

I ended up on a bus going to one of the quaint streets a little distance from downtown. It was perfect, since I could get there fairly quickly while being out of the busyness of downtown. The street was known for restaurants, cafés, boutiques, and all sorts of original, small businesses. I enjoyed the ride there, feeling happy to be on a small adventure. Already I felt better. Instead of getting off where I normally had over my years of using this public transport, I stayed on the bus until I felt guided to get off. I ventured much further down this street bordered by large trees and pretty flowers. When a store of Asian artifacts caught my eye and beckoned to me, I got off at the next stop. As I started walking back towards this store, I realized that Spirit had something even better for me to experience. I had to pass in front of another store first, one that I had never seen before, being in an unfamiliar area. I hadn't noticed it from the bus either. The store had a sign indicating its focus of personal well-being. It also had a large butterfly on the sign, which caught my attention, of course! I could smell the aromatic incense at the entrance of the store, which invited me in.

As soon as I walked in, I felt the wonderful energy of an impressive collection of crystals and stones that were on display all around. My spirit lifted at the melodious music that was playing, and my body was infused with the warm scent of the incense. The store was filled with crystals, stones, jewellery, statuettes, books, aromatherapy oils, incense, decor of all sorts, inspirational posters, greeting cards, journals, etc. It felt like home to me—a soul-welcoming place to recharge from an environment that had depleted me. Interestingly, earlier that year my favourite crystal store had closed, since the owner had decided to pursue other endeavours, so it was such a blessing for me to find this store so unexpectedly.

As I browsed the cards, I read several wonderful anonymous quotes that spoke directly to my heart, such as, "Within each of us lies the power to change the world in ways that have never been done before"; "As you follow your heart you live in alignment with your spirit"; and "All along the way there are signs guiding us to our spirit's fulfillment." I stayed for as long as I could, savouring everything that was displayed in the store—a feast for my senses that made me feel blissful.

When I felt it was time to leave, I complimented and thanked one of the owners of the store. I was then able to conveniently board a bus near the store. One actually arrived just as I reached the bus stop! It was perfect timing. I felt completely in the divine flow and left the store feeling rejuvenated and inspired.

My experience gave me the dose of magick I had been craving. I returned to the office with a renewed sense of wonder, remembering what really mattered to me and what made me feel alive and my best. I was better able to cope with this job I didn't enjoy, knowing I would be leaving soon. I knew it had served its sacred purpose, enabling me to learn, witness, and experience so much, and it was time for me to move on. It had felt so exhilarating to go off on that sudden little adventure and just see what would unfold as I let my heart lead me. I ended up experiencing exactly what I needed, and it was heavenly.

When we fully trust ourselves at the level of unwavering inner knowing, we're able to do anything with confidence, regardless of what we might face. However, we can only attain this level of trust with practice, and there's no better way to learn to trust ourselves and deepen that trust than by experiencing the unfamiliar. Experience is truly a masterful teacher. Beginning with smaller unknowns, we can gradually build to greater ones. It's an ongoing journey, and opportunities will continuously show up that allow us to further deepen and strengthen this trust in ourselves through experience—if we choose to do so.

Navigating the unknown at its most extreme, including tests of faith, requires us to trust and use all our senses even more. We're reminded of who we are and of the magnificent intuitive gifts that we're all born with, which connect us with higher wisdom. Regardless of what that great unknown space looks like to each of us, when we step (or leap) into it, we experience possibilities that would otherwise remain concealed. The deeper we delve into the unknown, with the intention and commitment to experience what our hearts invite us to, the greater is our sense of fulfillment and wonder. We learn for ourselves that anything is possible, regardless of circumstances or what we've been taught.

When 2012 arrived, it brought with it a radical invitation I hadn't anticipated *at all*. Despite not making any logical sense whatsoever—along with the endless horizon of unknowns that lay before me—it resonated so deeply with my soul, that I agreed to embark on this journey. Within my heart I felt it was clearly part of my sacred path, so to refuse would be to renounce my reason for being. While I did have the freedom of choice, I couldn't bear the thought of giving up my commitment to my soul's path. Of course, at the time I had *no* idea what I was really getting myself into. (I wasn't meant to know.) I never would have been able to maintain my commitment to this journey, had I not had my essence language to back up my self-trust and reassure my mind (when it had logically justifiable panic attacks). I had never experienced anything remotely close to this. I was about to learn a whole other level of trust, faith, and surrender.

As 2011 came to a close, I had been all set to start marketing my new online business and making money. I didn't have a source of income at that point and, logically, I needed to be able to make a living to maintain my independent lifestyle. I knew that having a regular job was no longer part of my path. Up until now, thanks to my divinely manifested rental home, I had been able to rely on my personal line of credit and my income tax refund for survival. I received a business name from Spirit after meditating one day, and one of my highly talented brothers created the perfect business logo for me. I launched my website at the end of November. It had been delayed by several weeks due to unexpected circumstances with the designer. However, interestingly enough, the date it ended up launching on was the 333rd day of the year! I didn't even realize it until a soul sister told me; she knew the significance of this number to me. It all felt as if I were going in the right direction of my path.

However, I desired extra support from a business mentor to keep me on track, since my business didn't feel like a typical one, and marketing wasn't something I enjoyed. (I hadn't even been able to sell fund-raising chocolate bars when I was in grade school!) I allowed my intuitive guidance to find the perfectly matched mentor. Then one day, I received an email newsletter from an entrepreneur whose marketing workshop I had attended in the city. In it he mentioned a business mentor who really stood out from the rest, due to her creative marketing strategies. Holly even had two of my significant essence symbols in her business logo—the rainbow and the feather. I decided to participate in one of her group programs for a few months to get to know her better, and now, in 2012, she was announcing the opportunity for us to work with her privately. Even though I couldn't logically explain it (for the investment was even more than my new car!), I strongly felt that this was my next step. However, I didn't know how I would manage it, and I needed to make absolutely sure that this was what I was being divinely guided to do.

Since this was a major decision I had to make, I asked Spirit, while hiking in Nature, to give me a clear sign that would confirm I was to work with Holly at the one-on-one level. Receiving signs outside of myself was the perfect way to override my mind (which was already spinning at the thought). Following that request, I ended up receiving *many* clear signs— every day for a week!

The most dramatic sign I received came while I was sitting in silence on a fallen tree during one of my Nature hikes. I was at the edge of the forest, facing a field and the western sky. The sun was setting but still high above the horizon, surrounded by a mostly cloudy sky. I closed my eyes and focused on my request to Spirit. I kept my eyes closed and simply listened to the Nature sounds around me, feeling deeply relaxed with a wide open heart and mind. When I opened my eyes a moment later, I was amazed by what I saw in the sky! All the clouds had cleared from the western horizon, except for five large ones that were flattened like stepping stones. They were arranged in the sky like a perfect stairway leading up to the radiant sun! I just gazed in absolute awe.

At that time, I had interpreted this as Spirit showing me the steps leading me to my business mentor, to help me shine in our world. While this was accurate from my perspective at the time, a year later (after going through everything I did that year), I realized the much deeper meaning of this incredible celestial display from Spirit. I understood that I was being shown the divinely guided steps leading to my own radiant, true essence, which Holly would guide me along. As we evolve in consciousness, our expanding awareness and perspective allow for us to experience and understand more. There's *always* more—it's an ongoing journey.

While that sign alone would have been sufficient as a confirmation, I received many more, both outdoors and indoors. One of my indoor signs happened one night while I was quietly journaling in the house. I heard a strange noise that sounded like a stone falling onto the floor from the ceiling. I walked over to the source of the noise to investigate. I found one of my polished stones, a carnelian, lying mysteriously at the base of the staircase leading up to the second floor! This stone's metaphysical properties could not have been a more significant message for me and my desire at that time. It was uncanny. All these signs made it clear what I was being guided to do. Having that clarity felt wonderful—while, simultaneously, the *how* felt overwhelming.

I now needed the means to hire Holly, and it wasn't a small investment. I used to think that a trip of a few thousand dollars was a lot. However, it was always more than worth it, so I didn't let the price tag prevent me from travelling. I just always made sure I had the money to pay for my trips beforehand, to avoid debt. The general mentality that always surrounded me was that debt was a very bad thing and paying interest was even worse. Therefore, avoiding it as much as possible was the intelligent and responsible thing to do, and I always had—that is, until I was called to completely change my life in 2011. Now, I was looking at investing the price of a car in a private mentorship when I didn't have a source of income! Of course, none of it was a logical process, and I certainly couldn't do it without divine support.

I simply expressed to Spirit that if this was truly aligned with my sacred path, I required the means to pay for this mentorship. I added that I would prefer to pay Holly in full by the deadline of only one week from that day. Doing so would enable me to receive the bonus photo shoot with her photographer. I loved his work, and interestingly, I had contacted Tom the previous year when I'd needed personal photographs for my website. Since he lived in a different province and I hadn't been able to work with him, I'd asked him for recommendations. Now I might actually get the chance to work with Tom as part of my mentorship!

I left it up to the Divine to figure it out for me, fully surrendering the financial details of this whole plan. Then, as I hiked in Nature the following day, I suddenly received an intuitive insight to ask my bank manager what my options were. I was meeting with Angela the next day to discuss the pension funds I was owed after resigning from my government job (as with the previous job, it was mandatory that I have them locked into an investment plan).

The next morning, before I left to see my bank manager, I unexpectedly heard my first meadowlark of the year singing its cheerful song. It made my day. These pretty migrating birds had arrived from their overwintering southern range weeks sooner than usual! As a spirit guide, the meadowlark's appearance signified positive news or a delightful surprise, as well as doors opening and a new opportunity for great abundance. When I saw Angela, I openly told her about my plans and how much money I required. Then I asked her if she had any suggestions for me.

She looked at my bank profile on her computer screen, and what she told me made my jaw drop open. She informed me that I was pre-approved for a business loan for the *full* amount I needed, despite the fact that I didn't even have a business account yet! She wasn't even sure herself how that was possible, yet it was. To receive this loan I did need a business account, so we proceeded with opening one. I didn't have any income projections for her, and there wasn't even a description for my type of business in the list to select from (not even close— *nothing* to do with Nature, art, or Spirit—unbelievable!), so we made up some of it. Since I was pre-approved for the loan, I didn't have to submit an application either. This accelerated the process considerably and enabled me to actually make the deadline to receive the photo shoot bonus along with the private mentorship. I was ecstatic and so amazed! I was so grateful to have Angela as my bank manager. She was another unforeseen blessing I had received when I'd moved out of the city to my miraculously provided new home the previous year. I had immediately felt I could just be myself with her—something I greatly appreciated. She was everything I could have asked for.

A few days later when I received the loan, I felt like a millionaire when I held that bank draft in my hands and deposited it into Holly's business account. What I found incredible was that Holly's particular bank was also in that small town, conveniently located just across the street from mine—I didn't even have to drive into the city for this transaction. Everything worked out so easily and perfectly! Big snowflake clusters were falling like feathers all around me when I walked out of that bank, and I joyfully felt the infinite abundance of miracles flowing from the sky. Then another delightful surprise manifested. On my way back home, I picked up the mail and discovered a beautifully magickal card of appreciation from Holly! She had sent it a few days before I had even told her I could work with her at the private mentorship level. It was such a perfect synchronicity to receive on that very significant day. It felt like a celebration of amazing things to come. I felt full support on my path and so much gratitude. I was about to discover the higher wisdom of Spirit in leading me to work with her.

One night only a few weeks later, I had one of those extremely vivid dreams that imprints in me every detail so I'll never forget it. In this dream, I was leisurely walking on a sidewalk towards a large bridge several hundred feet above a massive river. Behind me were buildings and streets, while the other side of the bridge had a natural environment, with a lush forest. As I reached the bridge, I kept walking—and I suddenly realized (too late!) that I was walking in mid-air. The sidewalk had vanished from underneath me! I fell for what seemed like an eternity and then plunged deeply into the icy-cold water of the river below. I highly disliked the sensations of falling and being cold, so this was an absolute shock to my entire system! As I swam up towards the sunlight, a large male hand suddenly cupped my chin and face and helped me to the surface so I could breathe. As I deeply inhaled my first breath, I clearly heard a strong male voice I recognized as Archangel Michael's tell me, *"You are now learning a new way of being."* I woke up completely frozen, as if I had actually been in that river. I had to soak in a long, hot bath in the middle of the night to warm up so I could fall asleep again.

Shortly after I had this dream, I was hiking in Nature and received a sudden, unexpected message, like an intuitive "download" … and it stunned me. I was asked by Spirit to now put aside my newly launched business to fully focus on deepening my self-knowledge. To answer my highly perplexed mind, Spirit lovingly told me, "You are *so much more* than you realize, and it's time for you to discover and know it for yourself." I was instructed to not focus on money(!) and to never think *I can't afford this*, regardless of what I was guided to do. I let it all sink in for a while, as Nature infused me. I silently contemplated all the messages I had received. I did not doubt that I was being divinely guided, mainly due to all the miracles I had experienced to support me in the past year under various circumstances (including some highly unlikely and incredible ones). I also knew it was divine guidance due to this being anything but logical.

I chose to accept this invitation based on my heart's inner knowing, despite my mind's strong objections to what appeared like illogical madness. This journey ended up stretching me further and further from my sense of security with regards to money and challenged my self-trust repeatedly (as nothing ever had before). I was guided to travel to different places as well as to attend events, classes, and a sacred tour, with different people from all over the world. I felt an instant soul kinship with several of them. I was also guided to maintain my exquisite self-care by continuing to purchase only the pure, organic body products and foods that I loved.

As the months passed, I realized that, bit by bit, I was being deprogrammed or deconditioned by Spirit of *everything* I had been taught about money and making a living! It wasn't just about this lifetime of conditioning either; it went back over generations. It was about eliminating all scarcity-related thinking and replacing that mentality with the innate knowledge that the Divine is infinitely abundant and the source of *all* that we need.

While this always felt true to me, putting it into practice in this material world was anything but easy. In fact, it felt quite mind-warping at times, since our sense of survival and logic is *so* strong with regards to feeling secure. In our modern society, this sense of security translates to being completely dependent on money and the rules created by our governing systems.

While I had no idea what the higher purpose of all this was, I was determined to uphold my commitment. My heart had never led me astray, so I chose to trust it and the Divine's greater plan for me, even though I didn't understand it myself. I just had faith that this radical journey had a divine purpose, and there was only one way for me to find out what it was. I had to keep the faith and keep going!

Throughout the months, I asked for clear signs from Spirit, to reassure my mind that everything was unfolding perfectly, even though I was living on credit. As I sank deeper and deeper into a scary amount of debt, I specified the essence language signs I desired as further reassurance. Aside from living in a condo for two years, I had never experienced personal debt. As I'd been taught throughout my life, I had avoided it like the plague. I had prided myself in being an exemplary citizen with regards to finances.

When I was 23 years old, I had received an unexpected opportunity to work for a multibillion dollar corporation because of an inside contact. This company paid all its employees very well and the money had lured me in. I had been hired as a bilingual customer service representative for the downtown office, shortly after moving back to my natal province for the interview. While I hadn't struggled financially before, not even as a student, I suddenly experienced a salary that was way beyond what I could have hoped for at that age. Since then, I had always earned more than enough to never have to worry about finances. I was selective about what I splurged on, like trips to special places that called to me every year and high-quality natural foods and body products. I always made sure I paid my monthly bills in full and gave generously to multiple environmental charities and other causes. I enjoyed buying special gifts for those dear to me and treating myself to massages at my favourite spa. I'd always had financial abundance and security.

Now all that had drastically changed, and I had *no* idea how far I would need to keep going. I took a leap of faith every time I purchased something, since it was all on credit. It was the complete opposite of everything I had done throughout my adult life. While it felt quite distressing at first, I quickly got over the fact that I could only make the monthly minimum payments (and was accumulating interest every month!). Since I had been asked to not generate an income at this time, I did the only thing I could do—I completely surrendered my finances to the Divine.

While this seemingly illogical madness felt quite challenging for my sense of survival, I was compensated by wonders that deeply touched me. Every awe-inspiring, divinely beautiful and soul-connecting experience I was guided to, expanded my awareness and understanding of myself, of life, and of this world beyond what I could have imagined. I also continuously strengthened and deepened my trust in myself and Spirit, along with my faith in the divine purpose of this journey. It became a continuous internal battle between my mind (triggered into panic by my basic self's need to feel secure) and my sacred heart's higher wisdom (knowing everything was as it should be). Understandably, logic was trying to protect me from what appeared to be a downward spiral of disastrous financial suicide. I was still immersed in the *old way of being* through all this, and every time I went back to feeling strongly heart-centred, I had blaring reminders about the great unknown I was navigating. I could feel the fears of the collective consciousness in everything I was facing through this—these fears were intense!

I did receive unexpected money, which allowed me to reach the last month of the year! I was actually able to keep part of the pension money I had accumulated during my government job, which was a miracle. When I was contemplating leaving my job, co-workers had told me adamantly that access to those funds was impossible (they worked in departments that apparently gave them access to such information). Yet I was able to receive what they had told me was impossible. And it had been *so easy*. All I had to do was sign a few forms and submit them! While the government did get to keep 30 per cent of it in taxes, I was very grateful for this unexpected source of income. It was so different than with my corporate job, which hadn't allowed me to touch one cent of my pension when I resigned—I'd had to lock it all up in a financial institution immediately.

I also received two refunds from my income tax filing instead of just one. My new accountant was someone I had been referred to. She was another unexpected blessing I received on my human team of support, after I left my status quo life behind me. I greatly appreciated her. Interestingly, I had discovered my second income tax refund (directly deposited into my bank account) the same day I had consciously observed how abundant Nature was when in harmony with All—and I had felt that abundance myself. I was so surprised to find that money in my account afterwards. It felt like a divine synchronicity confirming what I had felt in Nature. I also had accumulated enough Air Miles with one of my credit cards to pay for all the flights I took during the year! These were all unanticipated sources of income that felt miraculous, as well as usable currency that made good use of the accumulated credit balance. I greatly appreciated all of it during this radical journey.

Throughout my experiences, I discovered even more how glorious our world is, and I further clarified my specific role in it. With every passing month I understood the wisdom of Spirit in all that I was guided to do, including everything that stretched me further into the realm of possibilities. I learned to be very present in the moment as I navigated this journey one day at a time. I only planned ahead if I had to attend something or to book a flight and hotel. If I let my mind wander too much, it would go into a state of panic. Being in the present enabled me to sense the greater wisdom and much higher perspective governing this journey.

As the year advanced, Spirit started guiding me to share parts of my journey (including the financially-related leaps of faith) with a select few trusted individuals. It was conveyed to me that I should be very discerning about who I shared this with, as it was not something I could openly discuss with most people, for obvious reasons. Very few people would be able to understand my journey.

Money is a topic that is bound to our collective sense of survival and security. There's so much personal value and identity attached to money in mainstream society—from social classes and discrimination, to shame and self-importance. Money has been used to benefit many and used to abuse power. It continues to create and destroy relationships of all kinds, from partnerships and families, to countries and nations.

The invitation I had willingly accepted seemed completely absurd from most perspectives, and there was no point in unnecessarily alarming anyone. It was difficult enough to share this with those from my soul family; I had no idea how they'd react until I told them. I learned even more about the importance of self-trust and discernment through this.

We're always learning, regardless of who we are; unfortunately, many seem to forget this. No matter how spiritually aware people might believe themselves to be, they can still be quicker to judge others than those they criticize as being "less evolved," based on their own perspectives. They dismiss the fact that we each have our own path to follow and lessons to learn, which are different than their own and what they consider to be the right way. Many believe that our external life circumstances are a direct reflection of our state of being and use this as evidence for judgment. There's always more to appearances and there are always exceptions to everything. So many hide their fears (insecurities, wounds, worries, doubts, etc.) behind their images or spiritual facades, and if you unknowingly trigger their fears with your own experiences, they'll react accordingly.

When you know without a doubt that your personal path requires you to experience certain things (including challenges), it doesn't matter what anyone else says, regardless of who they are. You can remain confident that you're doing exactly as you're being divinely guided to do and know within your heart that you're not doing anything wrong, regardless of the physical circumstances surrounding you.

While I shared the details of my financially radical journey with a handful of soul sisters and a soul brother, I kept it secret from most people. It was quickly becoming obvious why I had been guided to hire my business mentor. Holly was not typical in the industry of business in that she also let her heart lead. She was very intuitive and connected with Spirit and Nature as well. So we understood each other perfectly. While she provided great strategies to make money, she also recognized my unique essence and path. Instead of mentoring me from a rigid business perspective, Holly tuned in to Spirit to provide me with exactly what I required to deepen my self-knowledge. She not only believed in me and my unusual path but she also encouraged me in powerful ways. We had a clear realization one day, through a synchronicity facilitated by the ascended masters. We realized I had been led to work with her for the sacred space she provided as a catalyst, guide, and witness. Working with Holly enabled me to understand my true essence with clarity, fully embrace it, and feel safe visibly living it to its highest potential. The business aspect, while valuable in itself, actually acted as an incentive for me to work with her, to support a highly spiritual journey. My sacred work would naturally emerge when I gained clarity about myself and my purpose.

I also connected with many more of my soul family through Holly, in a private group. Through these connections, I was able to further deepen my self-knowledge and self-trust, by practicing showing more aspects of my true essence and fully using and refining my gifts. What I received was invaluable to me—worth so much more than what I'd paid for the private mentorship. It was a sacred investment in myself, so I could ultimately be of service in our world, the way I was meant to be. Being seen, acknowledged, accepted without judgment, celebrated, and appreciated as my authentic self, without expectations, was such a profound gift to receive and experience. There really is no greater gift we can give to one another, regardless of the type of connections we have (with all forms of life). It exemplifies love to its highest degree.

I felt so grateful to all who co-manifested this business mentorship. Openly sharing my journey with soul family (which included Holly), as I was guided to do, unexpectedly became mutually empowering. They told me how much my experiences (especially the ones whose telling stretched me way outside my comfort zone) inspired them, each in unique ways, which I had not anticipated at all! They, in turn, inspired others by sharing my stories when they felt guided to do so. I was astonished and felt such great appreciation, for I finally understood. Through these experiences, Spirit was clearly showing me that *my life* was my sacred work. Every experience I had, how I lived my life, every way I used my natural gifts every day—I had been living my purpose all along, by always allowing my heart to lead! I just hadn't been able to know it until now. And so, just like that, I finally had a clear understanding of what my purpose involved. What a divine gift to receive, after decades of searching!

Knowing the many ways that my journey served a purpose gave me the courage to keep going instead of giving up when mid-December arrived. It fuelled me to stay focused on my heart's intention, to always keep my commitment to this path that the Divine had allowed me choose.

Tests of faith are *never* easy; they're not meant to be. They're meant to transform us at very deep levels and to reveal more of our true essences. Transformation requires chaos in some form or other. However, throughout our tests of faith we're never alone, and we're never handed one without having everything we require to succeed (whether we know it or not). A significant example of this level of chaotic transformation in Nature is the creation of the purest crystal on Earth, the diamond. Natural diamonds are created from minerals under only the most intense heat and pressure, over 100 kilometres deep within the Earth's mantle. When polished, they have the ability to reflect the purest light (rainbow frequency).

I went to one last event I was guided to attend that year, with my soul sister Anna, which we had booked in January. It was in Arkansas for the special 12-12-12 date, and we experienced a glorious thunderstorm the first evening we arrived! I fully savoured this unexpected gift in December. We connected with more soul family and impressive crystals the size of our torsos! I was miraculously able to make it through the event and pay for my luggage check-in fee. When I returned home, I had officially reached a six-figure debt! It felt absolutely surreal, to say the least. I had completely over-maxed out my three credit cards, my overdraft, and my personal line of credit, and I couldn't make any of my monthly bill payments. I had $33 cash left in my wallet after my trip (interestingly, that personally significant number).

At times like this, I was especially grateful that I had a calm and positive disposition, with a sense of humour. Within my heart I knew it had to be this way, or I wouldn't have been guided into this. I took a long, deep breath and surrendered this situation to the Divine once again. I had come this far, and I realized that if I were asked to do it all over again, knowing I would end up in this financial situation with *no* known outcome, I would still agree to it. I could never put a price on all I had been guided to experience in that past year. There had been miracles of all sorts, magick, the sacred landscapes of Arizona and Arkansas, a private mentorship with Holly, meeting and studying with my greatest mentor Drew, Sedona (twice), countless unexpected gifts, so many soul connections, various events, acquiring the body I always desired, countless adventures, a professional photo shoot, a surprise interlude, a new legal name, so many profound insights, incredible wonders of Nature—and my own accelerated personal evolution through it all! It was *priceless* to me and amazing beyond words. It left me overflowing with love and appreciation for Spirit and our world.

There was nothing more for me to do except remain wide open to Spirit. I was guided to stay at home and not go out—not even to purchase groceries, since I didn't have much fuel left in my car. I ate the high-quality organic foods I found in my pantry and freezer: quinoa, brown rice, beans, lentils, nuts, seeds, crackers, tahini, mustard, peanut butter, honey, dried and frozen fruits, olive and coconut oils, spices and herbal teas. I was also even more grateful for the good well water I had available to drink. Despite the circumstances, I felt abundant. I definitely wasn't going to starve, and I became very creative with those foods. I did greatly miss fresh, living foods, which normally made up a high percentage of my diet. So when I found small bags of sprouting seeds as I reorganized my pantry one day, I felt as if I had discovered gold! Fresh sprouts had never tasted so good to me.

I deepened my great appreciation for everything I had, that much more through this experience. There were always ever-deepening levels of experience to everything. I understood why the expanding spiral had been used so much since ages past, as a metaphor for life's evolving journey, and why so many of us had always felt a connection with its symbol.

Within that quiet, sacred space of my heart, I had always known what to do. Now I knew I had to spend as much time as I could alone, without contact, to get through what felt like an immense test of faith. Many times throughout that year, as I sank deeper into debt, I had thought about that vivid dream in which I'd been told that I was "learning a new way of being." I hadn't understood the meaning of it at the time. However, through my subsequent experiences, I understood more and more the importance of making conscious decisions based on love instead of fear (and how fear was not always obvious).

By choosing love, we choose possibilities instead of limitations. It's about following our hearts, with an inner knowing (faith) that when we do so, we are fully supported and everything we require is provided for us in various forms. It's up to us to not judge those forms of support. They're provided to us from a higher perspective.

I had been provided with the means to do everything I had been guided to do, mainly through the form of loans and credit. If I hadn't been willing to accept debt as the form of support I was being provided with, I would have missed out on the abundance of experiences that were divinely timed and orchestrated for me, and crucial to my path. I understood the immense wisdom of every opportunity I received and accepted. I said yes even though going into debt was the opposite of what I had been taught and practiced all my life. I understood more deeply the power of sacred relationship with All. I wouldn't have made it through the year without that.

Everyone's path is different and divinely designed this way. Each of us is guided to experience specific things unique to our purpose, whether through heart desires or more direct invitations from Spirit. Having self-trust enables us to know that what we're being called to do (and be) is aligned with our purpose—regardless of what that looks like. My own path happened to require that I embark on this radical journey filled with financial uncertainties and unknowns. Since I had the courage to do so, I experienced the countless forms of divine love that awaited (unbeknownst to me).

This journey also led me into a dark abyss, where every fear and doubt that people have about money and the unknown showed up! It challenged my self-trust and faith to the core and crushed my ego repeatedly. For the first time in my life, I knew what it felt like to have a fear of the unknown. I was blind to the outcome of a situation that my life (as I knew it) depended on. There was no visible horizon or glimmer of light as the financial pressure increased every day.

By going through this, I gained a deeper understanding and greater empathy for the millions of people who choose to have a sense of security instead of facing the unknown to pursue their true heart desires. I wondered about my own choice at times, even though I knew I was doing exactly what I had been called to do. While I couldn't imagine going back to the life I'd lived before, having a familiar sense of security was a temptation that I was very aware of at this time. Fortunately, my commitment to living my purpose was stronger than the temptation.

It's so easy to have faith when everything is going well, or when we have backup plans or safety nets if things don't go the way we had planned them to. Faith in its purest form has nothing to do with religion. It's a state of being that we can only acquire through personal experience. Challenging experiences allow us to learn about our personal level of true faith, for our biggest adversaries are our own minds.

At trying times, our minds automatically think of the worst-case scenarios, since that's what we're conditioned to do. It's a primal instinct to keep us safe from anything that could signal impending doom, and it's easily triggered. Transforming that becomes a priority if we don't want to become overwhelmed with fears, doubts, or worries. That's when we discover what we're really capable of. We experience so much more than just our minds and basic selves.

I spent as much time as I could immersed in environments and activities that made me feel the most empowered. I hiked outside every day to commune with Nature and Spirit. This had always been my oasis, whether I was faced with challenging situations or not. Nature reminded me of my divine essence and of my heart desire, from decades ago, for everyone to experience the divinity of life. Reminding myself of this filled me with enough determination to handle the fearful thoughts that showed up in my mind occasionally but intensely. Interestingly, a white-breasted nuthatch kept me company on most days. It would actually perch on trees near me and call out, so I couldn't overlook it. As a spirit guide, this little bird brought a message of faith, truth, and higher wisdom.

I also soaked in long, hot, candlelit baths in the dark, where I felt nurtured by Mother Earth in the middle of winter. This infused me with a deep sense of reassurance, melting away any worries that would creep up in my thoughts. I was also guided by Archangel Michael to start meditating on an ongoing basis, instead of just once in a while as I had been doing throughout the year. So I started meditating daily and discovered that it greatly empowered me. It was different than my Nature time. It was like a scheduled, intimate visit with

Spirit every day, which enabled me to deepen my connection and feel greater support in many forms amidst the chaos. When I was in that quiet space of my sacred heart, I renewed my trust in myself and my path. I deeply felt the Divine's love and let it fill me to overflowing. I also danced to my favourite music to invigorate and clear my energy field and feel strongly centred within my body. In addition to all this, I always took the time to write in my journal daily. Through journaling I experienced clarifying insights.

My need to spend time alone could have been a nightmare at this time of the year, which was usually the busiest, with Christmas celebrations and all. However, like magick I was granted this alone time through a series of unexpected circumstances that left me feeling so greatly supported by Spirit! Dinners I had been invited to by friends and former co-workers were mysteriously cancelled, rescheduled, or never materialized. Another dinner that I was invited to by family coincided with stormy weather that prevented me from going. (It was over an hour's drive away.) Due to my situation, I couldn't have attended any of these holiday functions, so I was very grateful for these outcomes. It also turned out that neither of my brothers, who both lived out of province, were coming down to my parents' with their families. Due to this, one of them suggested that we do a Christmas in July instead, when everyone would be together for our mom's milestone birthday. This meant that no one expected an exchange of gifts, which was *such* a relief. I was spared from having to decline any of the invitations and having to say anything about my situation to anyone. Normally full of holiday-related plans, my schedule had suddenly completely cleared! I was beyond grateful—it was truly a miracle in itself. I felt that so much was going on behind the scenes to assist me in ways I wasn't aware of.

For the famously prophesied winter solstice of 2012, my mentor Drew was doing a live meditation online from Sedona, for three consecutive days (prior, during, and after the solstice). It felt so empowering to be part of a worldwide group, all meditating within our sacred heart spaces, guided by this deeply heart-centred elder. The timing felt divine, and I felt even greater support from beyond our Earth's physical plane.

I did decide to spend Christmas day and overnight at my parents' country home, almost two hours away, since family meant everything to them. I also felt that being with my loving family would be a nice break from seclusion. I had always enjoyed driving, and the trip was all on highways bordered by country landscapes. Amazingly, I had just enough fuel to make it to my station of choice—the fuel tank light turned on as I arrived! Thanks to the fuel discount card I had received a year earlier, I was able to fill up my car with the $33 I had kept. I saw the number 33 countless times. I also saw very significant triple-number sequences multiple times, which were wonderfully encouraging for me to encounter at this time (such as 777, which reassures that one is definitely on the right path in every area of life). On my way I encountered ravens three times, crossing ahead of me on the highway. Raven had become a personal power animal a few months earlier. It was related to spiritual expansion, magick and manifestation, among other wonderful things. I always loved seeing it.

As I neared my parents' home, a raven suddenly swooped in front of my vehicle, closely followed by another one. I felt invited to flip up my sun visor, which I did, and I noticed that they flew up in front of beautifully brilliant rainbow patches on each side of the sun ahead of me! This was such an unexpected gift to see. Since the winter sun was aligned with the direction I was driving, I was able to easily see the rainbows while still driving. I was so mesmerized by them and felt guided to watch them. As I looked at them, I noticed that they acquired doubles on both sides—something I had never seen before. As I kept looking, the primary rainbow patches gradually became vividly radiant and then quickly got larger and brighter, until they suddenly vanished! I felt so much love energy flow through me from Spirit that my heart was bursting and tears were flowing. It was so gloriously beautiful. I had always been one to observe the sky as much as my terrestrial environment, and yet I had never seen rainbows in any form behave this way.

I arrived at my parents' for lunch a few minutes later and told them about the rainbows. We checked the sun repeatedly throughout the day and only saw clear, blue sky. I just *knew* it was a very special sign of encouragement from Spirit to remind me I was fully supported. I felt so grateful. My dear sister and brother-in-law joined us for dinner. Spending time together at my parents' was wonderful for all of us. I appreciated my mom's delicious homemade meals more than I ever had, as well as the leftovers I was sent home with. Through it all, being with them also enabled me to see that despite my circumstances, I was still able to maintain a joyful, high frequency and to uplift everyone around me (including employees at the fuel station). I couldn't have known I was capable of this without my situation. It was another gift from this experience.

By the end of the month, I had everyone calling me repeatedly for not making payments that month. Since that was a first for me, it obviously alarmed every account manager, and chaos erupted. It was maddening for me to be in this situation after two decades of being so impeccable with money and payments. My ego felt quite humiliated. At one point I was having problems with my laptop, and it was all I needed to reach my breaking point. I had infinite patience for most things, but not malfunctioning technology. I had the luxury of having the large house to myself, so I freely released every emotion and thought I had—out loud. I wasn't being guided to make money in any way or to file for bankruptcy. People were leaving voice-mail messages demanding payments, and I didn't even know what to tell them. (I just knew I couldn't tell them what they wanted to hear!) I expressed to the Divine that I required greater, perceivable support if I was meant to keep the faith and not give up. After a while I calmed down and felt strongly guided to meditate, which I did. To my surprise, an ascended master showed up clearly in my awareness, in answer to my request, and remained with me until I felt inner peace again.

As with all individuals, I had my own perception of what felt blissful or chaotic. Since I lived in a society governed by money, I was quite limited by what I could do without it. It felt like absolute chaos for me to suddenly lose the freedom to do anything financially related (including making mandatory payments). Nevertheless, I had to somehow keep navigating this storm for as long as I was required to.

While I knew from previous experiences that there was always great order at play within the chaos, being in the middle of that storm made it harder for me to keep that in mind. My best place to be was in the calm centre within myself, while the storm was swirling around me. I reminded myself that I had been guided into this by Spirit, so I had to trust that it would all work out somehow, despite the absence of evidence. At this point, sheer determination to maintain my commitment was keeping me from giving up. I was grateful to my strong will power and faith, for I knew that in order to discover the possibilities of this situation I just had to persevere. I lived one day at a time and I learned the true value of being fully present.

During this financial storm, I received another great teaching from Nature. On one particular day, I was silently spending some time with a great balsam fir that stood majestically near the house. It stood with two others, like protective sentinels. I had a special connection with this particular tree being, and enjoyed silently sitting with it. On that day, it was extremely windy and I not only understood the insight I received, but also felt it. I marvelled at how sturdy its trunk remained despite the strong wind blowing through its branches. As I sat with my back flush against its trunk, I barely felt any movement.

Trees are absolute masters of presence, and the largest, tallest ones have reached their full potential by enduring periodic storms during their lives. If a tree never had winds and storms to strengthen its young roots and tender shoots during its growth, it would definitely be damaged (or worse) the first time it experienced turbulence as a mature tree. When it endures periodic storms during its development, it grows that much stronger and becomes resilient to surrounding conditions.

After New Year's Day, I began to return the calls of everyone who was trying to reach me for overdue payments. Obviously, I couldn't tell them the actual reason why I was in this financial situation (without sounding like a lunatic). Instead I simply said that I hadn't made any art sales in December, which was true. When I had launched my business, I'd thought that selling my art would be a good start to what I thought I was being called to do. It was something people who knew me expected and could relate to. It was also acceptable from anyone's point of view. Through my work with my business mentor, however, I quickly realized that while I would always be a creative and artistic spirit, that wasn't my actual purpose. I felt greater fulfillment when I inspired people by sharing my life experiences of Nature and Spirit miracles, verbally, in writing, and through my Nature photographs. However, the art on my website did serve a wonderful purpose as a good front for me during my guided journey.

On January 3, I returned the phone call of my bank's loans recovery department. I knew the office was open late into the evening, and I had felt guided to wait until later. Suddenly, around 7:00 p.m., I felt I had to call immediately, which I did. Having experienced working with clients for years in a large corporation and the government, I knew what a difference it made to speak with clients who were kind, so I always made sure I was that type of client. I greeted the person cheerfully, refraining from any negativity or drama. I felt her energy instantly shift, and we ended up having a great conversation. I told her I couldn't make a payment at this time, and mentioned I had a lot of money locked up in pension investment accounts from my previous jobs that I wasn't allowed to access. She told me that, under my circumstances, I should be able to access some of it now. Then she paused and abruptly told me, with a strong emphasis, *"Anything* is possible, Lucille." That gave me goosebumps, for she'd used my language—it was as if Spirit had clearly spoken through her! I suddenly knew with clarity that this was what I needed to do next. It was the inspired action Spirit was guiding me to do, and it felt exhilarating.

The following day, I contacted my bank manager, who had just returned from vacation the previous day. I scheduled an appointment with her for the next available day, which was going to be the 11th hour for me. My car insurance was going to be suspended at midnight, my car loan company might be asking me to bring back my car, and one of my credit card account managers was already mentioning a collections agency! I was astounded by the amount of pressure I was receiving, despite my history of never missing a payment before. It just didn't seem right.

A few days later, on my way to the bank, I stopped in at a soul sister's house to give her a bunch of "like new" items I no longer wanted to keep. One of the items was exactly what she'd been looking for, so the timing was uncanny. She was more than happy to receive it all. She also gave me a surprise Christmas gift of a small painting she'd done of a pretty butterfly, with a butterfly ornament on the bag. I was delighted to see this power animal show up unexpectedly this way in the middle of winter. We exchanged hugs, and I left her place feeling so joyful. Then, during the rest of my drive, three ravens flew across the highway ahead of me at different times. They were all flying strongly against the forceful storm wind. I found that so remarkable and felt grateful for Raven's presence once again.

At my bank manager's office, I discovered that since I had worked for the federal government, I could make a request to withdraw some of my locked-in pension money, bypassing the provincial law that didn't allow it. I was ecstatic! We filled out the necessary forms, and Angela explained that I needed two signatures from a notary to be able to submit my request. She informed me that there was a lawyer's office at the other end of the town and that there was a charge for such a service. Since a snowstorm was starting, I decided to go even though I didn't have an appointment, and I asked Spirit for assistance.

At the lawyer's office, I was told I might be able to see the notary later in the afternoon, but he was booked solid. I told them I would wait in the lounge area. The number 33 was on his business card, along with 555—a triple sequence number that had started showing up when I began my new life. Great numbers to see! As I waited, I suddenly noticed that the country song playing over the radio speakers had "butterfly tattoo" in the lyrics. This was the third time Butterfly had shown up in unusual ways in less than two hours (not to mention that I did have a butterfly tattoo of my own!). I also noticed a magazine on the table featuring the majestic giant sequoias of California. Those tree beings had been calling to me for years already, but I knew I would just know when it was time to answer their call. As I looked at the very impressive photographs, the timely appearance of these giant sequoias felt empowering to me.

Not even 10 minutes after I'd sat down, the notary came out of his office and asked to see my forms. I explained that I couldn't pay him until I received the money, and he told me not to worry about it, for he wasn't charging me! He signed and stamped my forms within a moment's time and then wished me a wonderful day. I thanked him from my heart—I felt so grateful. I was able to hand over my forms to Angela shortly after, completely surprising her. She said I should expect to wait five business days for my withdrawal request to be processed.

As I drove the 30 minutes journey back home in a snow storm, I saw many small snowy whirlwinds near the highway. I always loved their presence! When I arrived at the house, I was surprised to find I had a voice-mail message from my bank manager. Since the message wasn't clear, I phoned her back. Angela happily informed me that the funds I'd requested had already been withdrawn and transferred into my account. They were available for me to use! I was so stunned and overjoyed. She had been able to do the transfer herself, since I had provided the notary's signatures and stamps; the rest was just paperwork. Due to this, I was able to pay everyone that afternoon from the comfort of my home (thanks to technology). I could finally feel some relief from this intense test of faith! It felt amazing beyond words. I was *so* grateful to all who had made this miracle manifest when it did. Everything had flowed so perfectly and with such ease. Through my open awareness, I had once more been able to receive the guidance that aligned me with the divine timing that facilitated this experience.

I felt so blessed for having the entire experience of the past year, including the test of faith. I now had even greater validation for my inner knowing, and this felt priceless to me. I had managed to make it through everything Spirit had invited me to experience in 2012—which felt like such a whirlwind! At the dawn of that new year, when Bald Eagle had become a new power animal for me, I'd never imagined all that awaited me in the following months! It further deepened my self-trust and my faith in my path, especially now that I had clarity about my purpose.

I had discovered so much about myself, including what I was actually capable of. Despite how mentally and emotionally challenging it had been at times, this experience enabled me to learn and transform so much in a very short period of time (making it more than worth it!). I experienced the power of love, awareness, trust, faith, commitment, and sacred relationship, more than I ever had before. While my debt hadn't vanished, I now recognized that there was a divine purpose for it and everything else—from the seemingly insignificant to the tremendous. When it was time, I would understand the higher wisdom of that, as well.

Of course, I had *no* idea that all this had merely been a *preparation* for what was to come! I thought I had experienced the most unimaginable, life-changing year of my life and that 2013 would surely be more "tame." But the unthinkable was about to unfold. There's great wisdom in not knowing certain things in advance!

Infallible Faith
(at the Bottom of the Abyss)

Agonizing ordeals reveal a divine purpose.

Great love and great achievements involve great risk.
—the Dalai Lama

Faith is a knowledge within the heart, beyond the reach of proof.
—Khalil Gibran

I never (ever) imagined that one day my faith would be tested to the extreme of 2013! I not only learned the true meaning of faith but also *infallible faith*—which takes great, great courage. It's something we can only acquire through a kind of personal experience that tests us as we've never been tested before. When we attain this level of faith, it's more than a belief—it's a strong inner *knowing* that we're fully, divinely supported, no matter what. Only this level of faith can withstand life's greatest challenges, and it's certainly a journey to attain it.

We discover our own levels of faith when we are tested through the intense pressure and uncertainty of extreme situations. These usually concern our personal sense of material security, freedom, health, and well-being (for ourselves or those dear to us). We are tested far beyond the breaking point, while we have no idea what the outcome will be or when our ordeal might end. We must choose between faith, love, and trust or worry, fear, and doubt. Sometimes, if it's part of our path, we are asked to choose over … and over … and over again.

It's by experiencing these tests, prevailing through them, and recognizing the rewards we receive from them that we strengthen our faith. We realize sooner or later that as long as we let our hearts lead us, the outcome is *always* exactly what we need for our journeys on Earth. We understand that we've gained something invaluable from the experience, something that was necessary on our personal paths. We no longer are who we were at the beginning of the ordeal. We've transformed and evolved in ways that we couldn't have otherwise. The greater our tests of faith, the more infallible our faith can become. This empowers us as nothing else can, for it takes immense trust, in ourselves and in Spirit, to reach this level of faith. This is especially true when our journeys make others question our states of mind (and people will, when something doesn't make sense to them).

Nature (as described in my "Special notes about this book" page) is such a wise and priceless teacher. It teaches us everything we need to know about life and our own paths, always supporting us when we allow ourselves to receive its wisdom. It teaches directly through messages or by using metaphors and analogies.

When I go through challenging experiences, especially tests of faith, I remind myself of everything that a butterfly goes through in order to become the graceful winged beauty that we admire. Many people have no idea what it actually takes for a caterpillar to become a butterfly. To see it firsthand is quite extraordinary, to say the least. It's such a complete metamorphosis that it requires the death of one form of life to bring forth another one! Our greatest challenges are like that. They're opportunities for unimaginable personal growth in a very short period of time.

I had the privilege of witnessing, up close, every stage of growth of the magnificent monarch butterfly when I lived in the city. When I'd transformed my backyard into a natural oasis, I had included two species of milkweed plants that the monarch caterpillars used for food. These naturally attracted a great number of egg-laying female butterflies to the yard. One particular summer, I was overjoyed to witness over 40 monarch caterpillars transform into chrysalises! They hung like beautiful little ornaments of green and gold throughout the gardens. I was able to observe with wonder, as they matured into butterflies within these chrysalises and then emerged to take their first flights. It was so inspirational!

Seeing a caterpillar transform into a chrysalis is incredible in itself—it's like watching a science fiction movie. After the caterpillar hangs upside down for a while from its chosen location, its skin splits at the head, and it gradually squeezes out of its caterpillar suit, revealing a soft, wiggling, little blob of life that eventually hardens into the form we see (the chrysalis or pupa). It's a complete transformation; there are no body parts—just a thimble-sized mass of divine life-force energy. It's magick at its best!

For a long time I wondered what went on inside those chrysalises before they emerged as fully formed butterflies, and one day I received my answer. During my daily observations (after I came home from my office job), I discovered one chrysalis that had been bitten in half by something, so I was able to look inside it. What I saw was a thick liquid the colour of the chrysalis and some butterfly parts the same colour floating in it. I was so amazed to witness this miracle of complete transformation.

The caterpillar itself goes through a type of death—death of the life as it knows it. It leaves its identity as a crawling, leaf-eating caterpillar and transforms into a casing filled with liquid. This liquid of cells magickally arranges itself into butterfly parts, eventually transforming into a complete butterfly that looks nothing like its previous form. What appears as absolute destruction and chaos is actually a purposeful process of organization and creation.

When this phase is complete, the chrysalis splits open and the butterfly emerges, fully formed, with a fat body and shrivelled, tiny, damp wings. It perches upside down on the empty casing and slowly pumps the liquid from its enlarged body into the veins of its wings, letting them expand to their full size as its own body shrinks. Then it patiently lets them dry for a while until they reach the perfect level of rigidity— and then it suddenly bursts into its first flight! Butterflies look so elated when they take that first flight—gliding, swooping, flying at great speeds, and fully enjoying their wings. They are utterly transformed from their previous lives as caterpillars. They now even have a different way of moving and feeding. They are completely different beings!

Whenever I'm going through something that makes me question whether I can keep going, I think of a caterpillar that experiences the end of its life (as far as it can tell) and, when the timing is just right, emerges as a glorious butterfly, with an acquired grace and freedom it didn't even know was possible!

Not even two weeks after I received the miracle that relieved me from my financial ordeal, my laptop completely stopped charging. I had started experiencing issues with it a few months earlier, and now it had reached non-functional status. It was my only computer, and I used it every day. I could not believe I was now facing such a considerable expense, after I had just paid all my overdue monthly bills. I had to admit I *had* secretly desired to have a better, lighter laptop, which would be easier to travel with. However, this was definitely not what I had planned. This was my second laptop in two years and it was barely a year old. I brought the computer to a reputable store to have it diagnosed and was informed that electronics of any kind are no longer made to last. I was highly unimpressed with the wastefulness of modern technology. After a few days, they told me they couldn't repair it for less than the cost of a brand-new laptop! The kind technician did surprise me by not charging anything for the work and time he'd put in trying to find reasonably priced parts—not even the basic diagnostic fee of $60. I was so grateful for that unexpected gift.

I definitely needed a computer, so I contacted one of my dear brothers, who conveniently happened to work for the same store in a different province. I wanted to see whether he could find me something like the one I actually desired, for a reasonable price. To my absolute surprise, he was able to find me something even *better* than what I desired and within my price range! In addition to being a high-quality Ultrabook, it was discounted to half the regular price, due to having been a display model with the previous year's programming (which I actually preferred!). I also noticed the number 33 printed in three different areas just on the information sticker (including barcode, model information, and dimensions). A great sign!

This Ultrabook was so perfect for me that it even fit inside my shoulder bag, which I always used when I travelled. I was amazed. Since they had my old laptop on hand, they were also able to immediately transfer everything onto my new computer for me. I felt divinely guided and expressed my appreciation to everyone who helped to manifest this for me. As I drove to my next destination, I noted that the previously overcast sky had cleared up, and I saw a beautiful rainbow patch beside the sun! Everything was flowing once again, filling me with immense appreciation. I had unexpectedly received the manifestation of another heart desire, under what had initially seemed like absolutely unfavourable circumstances.

Spirit is always highly aware of *every* heart desire you have. You don't always choose how or when your desires manifest, but you always have the choice whether to decline the opportunity or go with the flow that presents itself. When you do choose to follow what you feel guided to do, you discover what amazing possibilities await you.

March arrived, and I greatly desired a full-body massage for my birthday, to celebrate four decades of life and the profound transformation I had experienced since my last birthday. It had been an extraordinary year and life, to say the least, and massages were one of my truly favourite pleasures. However, I didn't schedule an appointment, since I had no way to pay for it. I was letting my mind lead instead of my heart! Then I "heard" Spirit ask me to focus on *joy* instead of *lack* and to schedule a massage appointment just as I desired to do. I decided that if the spa I contacted had space for me at this short notice, then I just had to have faith I would be able to pay for it. Well, they did have *one* space left, so I booked it—and immediately felt ecstatic at the thought of getting a massage on my special day.

The next morning, as I got ready to leave for the city, I felt guided to check my bank account online, which I did. I discovered that my income taxes had been processed in record time and my refund had already been directly deposited into my account! It had taken the government department only five business days to process my refund. Knowing from past years how long the process normally took, this was miraculous. I blissfully savoured my massage, with so much loving appreciation to All who gave me unwavering support on my path.

When my soul sister Anna notified me (only a week after my money miracle) that the house I was renting had to be taken down, I had already been hearing the island of Hawai'i calling me—loudly. This was also accompanied by clear signs confirming that it wasn't my imagination. Most of my travels had resulted from specific places or beings intuitively calling me, through energy, so this wasn't new to me. However, as guided by Spirit, I was still living without a foreseeable source of income. If at any time I had been asked to get a job or focus on creating other income sources, I would have done that without question.

Regardless of where I lived, I still had monthly payments to make for my car and insurance, various credit and loan accounts, and my cell phone, in addition to food, lodging, etc. Now, shortly after going through the biggest test of faith I had ever experienced, I wasn't overly excited at the thought of leaping to Hawai'i, regardless of my faith. Like a spiritual workout, my trust and faith were continuously being tested further, through new and greater unknowns. And I'd thought December had been enough.

I then received an indisputable sign from Spirit, which I could not dismiss, about having to go to Hawai'i within a month! I felt guided to return for my mom's milestone birthday at the beginning of July, when all my siblings would be visiting with their families. Despite this unquestionable sign, I was hesitant. I wasn't being asked to hop over to the next province; I was being asked to leap across the continent and ocean, to a different country, which would incur more expenses, while I had no income. I really had hoped to enjoy a break from financial uncertainties in this new year. My journey was so beyond logic at this point that my mind hurt just thinking about it!

One night, while I was soaking in a hot bath by candlelight, I had a long heart-to-heart talk with Spirit. I knew without a doubt that I had to go. I also reminded myself that things had always worked out somehow in my life, regardless of circumstances. However, the logistics of *how* were daunting, to say the least. I preferred some peace of mind regarding living expenses in Hawai'i for three months.

Only a moment after asking, I suddenly intuitively heard quite clearly from Spirit, "Your *faith* is your 'how.'" Of *course* it was! That's what I had been learning all along! However, throughout my life, I'd always had a bit of a safety net when I had taken those leaps of faith. Now I had none whatsoever—except for faith in Spirit. Oh my—I allowed my mind to indulge itself and laughingly screamed out loud, "You're *not* serious!" at what I knew to be true.

I slowly sank in the bath water up to my face and stayed submerged for a long time with a completely blank mind. Then I suddenly remembered something I had read many times the previous December during my test of faith. It was in a book written by my mentor Drew, and it had helped me tremendously to keep my faith strong and not give up. I'd had the privilege of personally thanking him in Sedona for writing his books. At that time, however, I'd had *no idea* how deeply grateful I would be by the end of that year, and now, for what he wrote about tests of faith!

After my bath, I reread that chapter as a mental reminder and then phoned a dear soul sister in Hawai'i (whom I planned to visit if I went). I could feel that there was a lot awaiting me there. It was the same feeling I'd experienced with so many other places that had called to me over the years. However, my mind was highly unsettled, regardless of all the signs I received, for I was being asked to take the biggest leap of faith in my life. By leaving the house I was renting, I was letting go of my last remnant of personal security. I was uprooting myself with no idea where my next home might be. It simply added to the sum of this great unknown I was now facing. I had to rely on faith, for I was no longer depending on the tangible but on the mystical. My heart knew I had the absolute support of Spirit. However, being able to share this with other human beings of my soul family, who understood firsthand about the demands of the material world, was an invaluable source of support I greatly appreciated.

I finally made the commitment to take this giant leap of faith and purchased my return-flight ticket. An interesting thing about the significant decisions we make is that we might get tested to see how committed we truly are—we're given opportunities to change our minds. Self-trust is invaluable then. It enables us to discern between a test of commitment and evidence that it's just not meant to be. It's about tuning in to our hearts' inner knowing. When I made my decision to book my flight, everything that could have gone awry did! It would have been so easy to allow my mind to convince me this was a sign I wasn't meant to go. However, I had an inner knowing that it was a test; it was allowing me to either commit more fully or to change my mind. I knew that life would go on if I changed my mind and didn't go, but it wasn't the direction that felt aligned with my heart. I became so determined to book that ticket, I persevered through the relentless frustrations. I had never experienced issues with booking a flight in almost two decades of travel! I was told that anyone who goes to Hawai'i to answer its call experiences an "initiation." Well, this was definitely mine.

After an evening and a morning of many long phone calls with the online travel agency, my credit card institution, and travel-insurance company, I had my flight booked and also ended up with unexpected rewards for persevering! The travel agency not only reimbursed me for an unanticipated cost (for which they weren't even responsible) but also gave me a $200 voucher to redeem for a flight or hotel because of all the hassle I'd gone through. I used it to spend the night before my flight in the city, at a nice eco-hotel with free shuttle service to the airport. Instead of staying with family or friends and disrupting their schedules, I treated myself to an evening of "me time" before taking this leap of faith. Then the bank representative I had talked with about my credit card ended up upgrading it to a high-end travel card that gave me a lot of immediate benefits—this despite seeing that I was already almost maxed out with the flight purchase! Instead of having to pay the annual fee, he also waived the minimum payment required for the following month as well as the interest for the following two months! He sent it Xpresspost, so I received it before leaving for Hawai'i.

Since I had to move out of the house at some point, and most of my belongings were already packed, I decided it was best to do the move before leaving for Hawai'i. My parents had storage space in a building on their property, so I was able to use it for my belongings. I could also have my mail forwarded to their address and park my car on their property. It was my best choice under the circumstances, and Spirit provided me with so many signs to confirm I was doing the right thing. All my feathered power animals showed up in unexpected ways in Nature, during the week leading to my moving day, including Bald Eagle! I was elated.

The night before the move, there was still a large pond of snow melt in front of my very muddy driveway, which was definitely not ideal for a U-Haul trailer and truck. I asked Spirit for assistance with that. The next morning, I woke up to a beautifully sunny and balmy day, and the pond and driveway had completely transformed into hard ground! I was astounded and so grateful for a perfect moving day. I had learned the lesson of receiving, so I graciously accepted my dad's offer to handle the move with my mom. The last time I had moved, I hadn't told my parents until it was over, and they'd wished they could have been there for me. Now everything worked out better than we could have hoped for, and everyone felt good about it. As I was driving to my parents' place, the number 33 appeared multiple times, in unexpected ways. I saw many other empowering number sequences as well. As I thought about the journey I was about to embark on, it just felt surreal.

The night before leaving for Hawai'i, I had bills to pay, but I was already into my overdraft, with little left available. I was cringing at the thought of leaping across the planet in such a financial state. However, as I logged onto the hotel's free Internet service, I felt guided to check my bank account. I was stunned to discover that I had received a second amount from my income tax refund! I was able to pay all my monthly bills, *and* this money ended up serving another purpose I hadn't anticipated. When I went through US customs the next morning, I was brought to a room and questioned as though travelling to Hawai'i were illegal. Regardless, I maintained my calm disposition and answered every question the officer asked me, including how much money I had in my bank account! I was able to look him in the eyes and tell him honestly the amount I had, which obviously satisfied him, for he let me go. I'd never been good at lying, so the timing of receiving that money was such a blessing, in more ways than one! I expressed my great appreciation to Spirit as I walked through the US customs doors, into the greater unknown.

I flew to Hawai'i absolutely wide open to whatever awaited me there. I had learned from past experiences that there was always a greater purpose to the places I was guided to go to. Hawai'i was no exception. Interestingly, during my travels that included three different flights, I ended up connecting with many different people of both genders, from youth to the elderly. Whenever I had travelled before, reading, journaling, meditating, and listening to music had been my activities of choice. I had never been interested in connecting with people except with eye contact, smiles, and a few words here and there. Being an introvert and empathic by nature, I preferred minimal contact, especially in crowded areas like airports and aircraft. However, this time was different. Through very odd circumstances (that seemed divinely orchestrated), I ended up sitting beside people who unexpectedly opened up to me about spiritual and supernatural topics which they confessed they normally didn't discuss with other people! They also expressed what a joy it was for them to talk about these things with me.

For the first time in my life, I was consciously expressing my true essence in public places, with my physical appearance as well as through my energy, and I discovered how magnetic this was to people who resonated with me! By holding sacred space within my energy field, I realized I was encouraging people to come out of their spiritual "closets" (or protective barriers). I realized more than ever, that everyone has things they secretly desire to express, share, and discuss, but they can only do so if they feel safe. By being wide open to possibilities within my heart, I attracted these connections and greatly enjoyed it. They were mutual gifts.

I had planned to stay only a couple of weeks on the island of Hawai'i, to visit with my soul sister Flora and her husband Luke. I met him for the first time and discovered he was also a dear soul brother! I'd thought I would move on to Kaua'i for the remainder of the months, since that island had been calling me for years. However, Spirit had other plans for me, and I actually ended up staying on the Big Island the *entire* time! I was clearly guided to stay there, so I did. While this was so unexpected, it had great purpose. I'd always been open to change and flexible about plans, and this served me very well in Hawai'i. An island of pure creative energy, its frequency was very high. I was catapulted into accelerated learning and teaching through various experiences and beautiful connections, human and otherwise (including the wild dolphins). It was amazing, to say the least.

Since I had already experienced being a Hawaiian tourist on Oahu back in 1999, I was able to concentrate on being present to my experiences now and following higher guidance. I was able to stay at my dear soul family's beautiful rental suite the entire time I was on the island. This was really a divine blessing. It gave me affordable, private living space and allowed me to live like a resident of the island instead of like a tourist, which felt perfect to me. Flora and Luke also brought me to special places of absolute natural beauty, on land and in the bays. Being soul family, we also learned so much from each other. The timing of my stay was clearly destined.

During my stay, I felt more and more strongly called to write this book. Yet I felt a lot of inner reluctance, since I was in the middle of my most extreme test of faith, without knowing anything about the outcome. I didn't feel I could write the book before I knew how it would end. Spirit persisted, however, so I asked for a definite sign to confirm it was time for me to write the entire book. I also asked for clear guidance regarding every aspect of it, including the cover image, the title, what to share and how to structure it.

Only two days later, I suddenly received a Facebook email in my junk folder from a group I hadn't even joined (I had unknowingly been added by someone I didn't know). The email was a notification announcing an event for anyone feeling called to be an author with a message! It provided access to calls with knowledgeable guest speakers in the publishing industry, with the opportunity to enter a contest that had incredible publishing-related prizes. I had received this notification with only two days left in the two-week event. I registered at the level that enabled me to receive the transcripts and to submit a book proposal in the contest.

I was guided to read a particular transcript first, not in the chronological order of the calls, and it was exactly what I needed to assist me in determining the best structure! A few days later, I also received the title for my book as a sudden flash of insight during my sunrise hike. This provided me with the focal point I needed to write the book. I now knew without a doubt that I had to start writing the manuscript and submit a proposal by the deadline at the end of July.

So many other significant things occurred in Hawai'i. It was evident that I was meant to be there precisely at that time. It was uncanny. Two peculiar things manifested while I was there, and although they were separate, they were also related.

Before going on a full-day volcano tour with Flora and Luke, I had been collecting beautiful, sweetly-scented *plumeria* flowers that had fallen to the ground. I was barefoot, and for the first time in my life, I was stung by a bee underneath my foot! It was such an odd sensation when I stepped on this bee, I didn't even realize what it was at first. It felt like high-frequency electrical currents shooting through my left foot. Thankfully, my body had always healed quickly and I wasn't allergic, so within 30 minutes my foot felt normal again (and I was able to hike as planned). The next day I felt guided to research the spot where the sting had occurred on my foot, in relation to reflexology points. Interestingly, I discovered on the Internet that it was in the area of the heart.

Two weeks later, I woke up one morning with a clear mark on my index finger, in the shape of a hexagon! It was a dark purplish-brown colour and almost as wide as my finger. Due to its precise, clear shape, I just knew there was more to this mark than the logically explainable. It had simply appeared during my sleep, and it wasn't sore. It didn't itch or burn; it wasn't a different texture than the rest of my skin; it simply was there, like a stamp. It was that colour for two months, and then it gradually faded to a lighter colour. It was still visible until the end of 2013.

In the days after it first appeared, I noticed that every day, regardless of where I went, I saw perfect hexagons in the strangest places: on logos, light bulbs, appliances, stickers, vehicles, buildings, even potholes on the road! They appeared everywhere. It was obvious that the hexagon was calling for my attention. As I began structuring my book manuscript's table of contents one day, I suddenly felt guided to look up the significance of the bee on the Internet. The first result brought me to a webpage with an image of the bee's hexagon-shaped honeycombs and information about the hexagon shape! I discovered that the hexagon was an ancient symbol for the heart! Interestingly, it also happened to be featured on my business logo's sacred geometry symbol. I felt that both the location of my bee sting and the mark on my finger were highly significant for me and my sacred path. While I had let my heart lead me throughout my life, this felt as if I were being initiated into something more.

Then came the day for me to leave. I had exhausted every source of currency available to me—I was *over*-maxed out on every credit account I owned. I was also unable to make any of the payments due the previous month; my situation was anything but ideal. I had my return ticket paid for, but the airline charged for luggage. For the first time in all my years of travelling, I also had two suitcases instead of one. I didn't know if they would even make it back to Canada with me. Flora and Luke had been so generous with the rent, enabling me to stay on the island as long as I was guided to. Needless to say, I didn't mention this predicament to them. Instead, I meditated that morning and Spirit lovingly reminded me that I was fully supported and told me to use the travel credit card I'd received before my journey to Hawai'i. After my meditation, I saw 9:33 on the clock. It was a symbol of many things for me. I just had to keep the faith. I deeply inhaled and exhaled and prepared to leave. I saw many reassuring signs during the drive to the airport, including 133 and 333 multiple times on license plates. I just surrendered the situation to Spirit with love and appreciation.

As the airline agent weighed my luggage, I briefly saw 555 on the scale and couldn't help but smile. Then my card was charged—and approved—and my luggage was loaded onto the belt to fly to Canada with me! I exhaled a long sigh of relief as I explained to Flora and Luke what had just happened. We had experienced so much together during my stay. They played a crucial role in my journey of Hawai'i. We shared a very special farewell on a small plot of grass underneath a beautiful tree being, before I went through security. I loved how this airport's security check area and gates were open-air, with Nature all around us.

It had been exactly five years since my soul sister Flora and I had connected in Bimini. We had both felt called to swim with the wild dolphins there for those two specific weeks. It had felt priceless to swim together with the wild dolphins again, this time off the shores of Hawai'i.

Despite my financial situation, I felt infinitely wealthy in loving heart and soul connections, and so blessed for each one. They were all precious to me—divinely provided through our hearts' higher guidance and creatively orchestrated chains of events.

As my flight left the island, I was in awe to see Mauna Kea standing majestically above the cloud line with its powerful mountainous presence. I had experienced issues with my assigned seat and ended up with this mesmerizing view. Then, as we flew over the ocean, I saw something that was pure magick. A large cloud below us in the distance was raining a beautiful rainbow! I had never seen that—instead of a sheet of rain underneath it, I saw a complete, radiant rainbow. What a gift! I closed my eyes for a long time while I listened to music, but then I suddenly felt nudged to open them just in time to see a beautiful strike of lightning in a movie that my neighbour was watching—a five-second thunderstorm scene I happened to catch. I also saw many of my significant numbers show up in amazing ways. On my last flight there was even a boy wearing a jersey with a large 33 on the front of it. I felt fully supported by Spirit and knew that everything was unfolding exactly as my path required it to.

While some people had felt the job offers I'd so easily received had been perfect opportunities for me to stay on the island, I knew in my heart that I wasn't meant to stay. I had to go back to Canada. After seeing all those beautiful, significant essence signs during my return, I now had no doubt in my mind—despite my financial predicament!

My parents had a full house when I arrived. I'd always needed a lot of alone time, so no matter how much I loved and cherished those dear to me, I also needed my own space. Now I had very little, unless I disappeared outdoors. I had lived alone for two years in a big house and had enjoyed my own suite in Hawai'i, so this crowding now required a big adjustment of me. Just as I was feeling overwhelmed, I heard ravens calling beyond the second-floor spare room where I was sleeping. I looked out the window and saw that three of them had perched atop a jack pine and were vocalizing. I felt instantly better for Raven's presence—the timing was perfect. I meditated for a while in the room and was then able to enjoy quality time with my family and focus on all the abundance and blessings I had.

Both my dear brothers lived in different provinces, so it was wonderful to see my entire family together again. Since I had always felt that at some point I would leave Canada to live elsewhere, and now I was officially out of a home, I made the most of this joyful family time. My four nephews were growing up so fast. We created wonderful memories as we all connected through our hearts and our mutual love of Nature. Interestingly, only two days after my arrival, I tried to purchase groceries using the same credit card that had allowed me to bring back my luggage with me, and it was declined for less than $40. It really was a miracle that my luggage had made it back with me.

After two weeks, everyone left—and I had to make the painful acknowledgement that I was now living at my parents' home, since I had no money to do otherwise! My dad had told me many times after I'd left my marriage that I could live with them. Although I appreciated it, I couldn't even imagine it, having been highly independent all my life, even as a young girl. I got my first jobs at the age of 10, picking radishes for a farmer and babysitting, to make my own money. This enabled me to purchase what I wanted without needing my parents' permission. The idea of living with my parents ever again had been absolutely unthinkable. Yet, for some reason, Spirit had guided me exactly where I didn't want to be! I felt betrayed and devastated, to say the least.

Despite my higher perspective that everything had a purpose, my ego indulged itself. I loved my parents dearly and had always felt they had done enough for me while raising me for 18 years. I had done everything possible to remain fully self-sufficient after graduating from high school. Going through a test of faith was one thing, but having it affect others dear to me was now the factor that sent me over the edge—repeatedly. I was now facing my ultimate test of faith, and I *had* to trust there was a divine reason I had been led here (if only so I wouldn't lose my mind). I still wasn't being guided to make money in any way. Instead, I was being guided to keep my faith strong, focus on writing my book, and see what possibilities would manifest if I managed to hold on—for how long, I had no idea whatsoever. Every week that passed felt like an eternity for me.

I had now *completely* surrendered my freedom and independence to the Divine. My heart was completely broken open as I gave up the self-sufficient life I had known. I thought about the chaotic mush inside the chrysalis—no longer a caterpillar and not yet a butterfly, and fully dependant on the miraculous! Everything now depended on Spirit to help me soar with grace out of this situation—if I were meant to. Nothing less than a miracle could transform this situation I found myself in. I had never felt more vulnerable in my entire life. To say I didn't like it was a huge understatement.

Knowing that there are no limits to what the Divine can manifest instantly, I knew I could wake up the next morning and be debt free, financially stable, and liberated to go wherever I felt guided to go. However, I had no idea what Spirit's plan was with regards to my path and this test of faith. While I now understood my purpose with clarity, I was also navigating the unknown at its most extreme. Feeling I was now a source of worry and a burden on my parents added to the intensity of my ordeal. I was in the middle of the very thing I had worked so hard all my life to avoid—being completely dependent on others! My ego was absolutely crushed!

From my human perspective, aside from having a debilitating or life-threatening health issue, this was the worst situation that I could find myself in. My dedication to my path required that I stay right where I was, with trust, faith, and surrender. I was being asked by Spirit to not hit the panic button but rather to remain centred within my heart. Yet, every time I settled into that space and felt that everything would be okay, something would show up to trigger me out of that space (like a finance-related phone call or letter). It was maddening.

That's when I learned the difference between the emotional heart and the sacred heart. My *emotional heart* felt that, because of my love for my parents, this experience was cruel to all of us and completely unnecessary. This was also related to fear in the form of doubts and worry. My *sacred heart*, however, attuned to higher divine wisdom, knew there was a great purpose for this experience, which meant gifts for everyone involved, whether obvious or not. Therefore, divine love asked that I not take away this opportunity for us to discover the gifts of the experience. (As I added this to the book manuscript near the end of November 2013, I suddenly noticed the word count was 88,555. How timely, since 555 signifies higher consciousness and huge life changes.)

One morning I felt it was the day to contact all my credit and loan institutions to let them know I was fully aware I had missed the last two months' payments and I was "working on it" but had no idea when I could pay them. It was the truth and all I could tell them. I couldn't get into the details of *how* I was working on it, since it didn't make any logical sense whatsoever. I asked Spirit for assistance with these calls and then went down my list. I just couldn't believe I was in this situation at all. As with the previous time, I made sure I was my best with everyone I phoned and used "no art sales" as the acceptable reason for my financial situation. I was so grateful to everyone I talked with—they were all so compassionate and understanding; they left me feeling amazed. One woman even went the extra mile for me, reversing the automated payment charges, applying the accumulated $100 worth of points on my card against my missed payment, and also waiving the next two months of interest! I sent her a virtual hug, which delighted her. I was so grateful to Spirit and to myself for contacting everyone, no matter how uncomfortable this situation made me feel (it felt worse since I didn't have an answer).

Every time I consulted with Spirit, I was guided to focus on things that empowered me and to work on my book manuscript. I was never guided to focus on money-related matters, to get a job, or to file for bankruptcy. I was also asked to trust that I was being taken care of as I shared my gifts and energy with others through various means, including social media. I asked Spirit to clarify the "new way of being" I had been learning since that fateful dream in 2012. I was told that the "old way" was all about trying, exerting, and chasing to get results. The "new way" was about trusting, allowing, and receiving. Instead of a dominantly "logical mind" process, it was a "knowing heart" process.

Timing is everything, and when we trust that we're being supported on our paths every step of the journey, we allow Sprit to guide us through our hearts. We're open to receiving this guidance so we know exactly *what* to do (and not to do) and *when*, making more efficient use of our time and energy. Everything flows with greater ease in all areas of life with the wise use of *being* as well as *doing* (inspired action) at the right time. Bald Eagle is also a master teacher of this way of being. The old way depletes, while the new way empowers, regardless of situations. The old way is about using our basic, primal survival instincts to dictate our decisions, actions and lifestyles. The new way is about shifting back into our sacred hearts as the leaders and using our minds more efficiently in partnership with our hearts. The shift does take commitment, since we've been conditioned by the old way and we're still immersed in it most of the time. None of us are immune to it unless we deliberately increase our awareness of our inner wisdom—and trust it.

When I moved away from home at 18 years of age, I felt strongly guided to completely cut myself off from all forms of news media, so I did. I knew that if something was important enough I would hear about it. It wasn't about choosing ignorance but rather about getting away from the fear-and-negativity propaganda, to allow myself to grow, strengthen, and maintain a personal state of empowerment. Being back at my parents' now showed me that nothing had changed with the media's focus. I saw how easily it caused disempowering effects within people. Being immersed in it again required that I stand firmly in the personal power of my heart's inner knowing, despite my outer circumstances and surrounding sources of influence. This also added to the challenge of my test of faith.

Being me, instead of gradually immersing myself more deeply into this new way of being, when I received the invitation I submerged myself in it with whole-hearted commitment and absolute trust. Our sacred hearts have no fear—our basic, primal selves do. Being a leaper of faith all my life, I realized I had been heading towards this all along.

Every week that came and went pushed me further and further. I was emptying myself of years of fear-based conditioning so I could return to that heart-centred space of *knowing*—knowing I was fully supported in all ways on my path. However, since I was a passionate person by nature, my feelings ran deep, and it wasn't graceful. My emotions threatened to overwhelm me every time I was triggered somehow. I felt as if I was going through the torturous multiple levels of a bottomless abyss.

When I first fell into this test of faith, I landed at the bottom of a dark abyss and had to deal with the demons that lurked there. Once I faced the pain, fears, doubts, and worries that surfaced in that space, I reached a point of deeper faith and trust, since I'd learned the wisdom of it and saw it from a higher perspective. As I settled into this new state of being, I was able to surrender at a deeper level and feel a wonderful inner peace. It was empowering in ways I hadn't experienced before. However, shortly after I reached that place of serenity, it was as if a trap door then opened beneath me, plunging me further down into this ever-darkening abyss, where a more challenging level of ego-crushing situations showed up. The demons of despair were an even greater threat at this new level, and I had to go through the entire process again. Then, when I'd reached that space of inner calm again, another trap door would open up and send me further into the depths … again … and again … and again. It felt as if this test of faith would never, ever end.

Interestingly, what greatly assisted me in keeping my faith strong and my attitude optimistic, so I could keep going, was working on my book manuscript! Having to go through my journals to include the different stories in this book, I was reminded how much support I'd *always* had from so many. Letting my heart lead had always ensured this support. (As I was writing this in my book manuscript at the end of September 2013, I noticed the word count was 70,444. The 444 number sequence signifies being completely loved, supported, and guided by Spirit and having nothing to fear. Its appearance was another divine synchronicity.)

I wrote my book despite having absolutely *no idea* how this last chapter would unfold. I was writing it *as I lived it!* I showed my commitment and faith to Spirit by notifying a great number of people that I was writing this book, even though I had no idea how and when I would complete and publish it. In total surrender, I allowed Spirit to fully co-create this with me.

With every emotional meltdown I experienced, triggered by my love for my parents, I asked Spirit for a clear sign to let me know I was still following my sacred path and doing everything I was being divinely guided to do. My mind definitely needed that reassurance at those times, since I was simply following intuitively received guidance from Spirit. There was nothing tangible to let me know I wasn't just making it all up in my mind. I hadn't signed a physical contract with Spirit stating that a beneficial outcome was guaranteed for everyone involved. I perceived it all in my heart, in my mind's eye, and through energetic sensations in my body. The outcome was a complete mystery to me. I was navigating a universe of possibilities, yet I didn't know what would manifest, and I wasn't allowed to know. All I could do was ask Spirit for reassurance. Every time I asked, I was filled with divine-love energy and received clear signs, as requested. I was eternally grateful.

I received one such sign as I was completing my book proposal to submit on the due date the next day. That morning I had requested a clear sign from Spirit, and the entire day went by without anything. I had worked late and finally decided I needed to sleep. However, before going to bed, I felt guided to check my emails. I was so tired that I didn't particularly feel like it, but I did anyway. I was stunned by what I discovered. Spirit obviously had spoken through one of my dear soul sisters. I had received an email from Aurora at 10:33 p.m. from across our beautiful planet, and she had written, "Here … I just found this for you. If this doesn't cheer you on, I don't know what will," and she included a glorious photo featuring a radiant rainbow and lightning striking from a cloud! Wow. I'd received three significant signs in one instant—the number 33, the rainbow, and the lightning—not to mention that her words were as though she had suddenly, clearly channelled Spirit! Aurora had no idea about my request to Spirit that morning. She was emailing in regards to the book proposal, since we were encouraging each other throughout the process. I was so grateful—to Spirit, to my soul sister, and to myself for following through on that nudge.

Interestingly, certain people asked me why I would tell a dozen others about the contest for authors, since from their perspective, this gave me more competition. That's just another example of the old way of being, based on fears. Instead of competition (which I've never enjoyed), I focus on collaboration and co-creation, for the more who shine, the better our world is for it. Those who I notified had at some point mentioned they'd like to write a book. If someone has a heart desire to write a book, it's there for a reason. I know without a doubt that whatever is meant to manifest for me always will, regardless of circumstances. I've experienced enough to know this to be true. Additionally, it's so much more enjoyable when we support and encourage each other to be the best we can be. Everyone greatly benefits from that.

I submitted my book proposal on time and felt such a sense of joy for persevering and following through with my commitment. It was such a wonderful opportunity that was handed to me, so I accepted the gift despite the many self-doubts that surfaced. These loud self-doubts haunted me repeatedly, since I was being guided to write this book about sacred possibilities while I was at the bottom of the darkest abyss of my life! Regardless of everything else I had experienced throughout my life that qualified me to share this powerful message, my mind was fixated on this one thing. However, Spirit lovingly reminded me to maintain my focus on the higher perspective and allow the Divine to keep working through me by surrendering at ever-deepening levels.

A few days later, my dad created a huge bonfire, which my mom and I enjoyed with him. He even included a surprise with it. The small packet he placed between the wood logs transformed the large, dancing flames into green, turquoise, and purple colours—like peacock feathers! It felt like a personal celebration to me, acknowledging my dedication, accomplishments, and abundance in many forms. Coyotes howled, and above us the starlit sky and Milky Way were shining brightly, with occasional falling stars appearing. It was magickal.

My car payments were now far behind and I had been given a strict deadline to make the missed payments. After some contemplation, I finally called back my car-loan contact and told her it seemed as if I wasn't meant to keep the car. My car had been a miraculous gift when I'd surrendered my predicament to the Divine at the end of 2011. Now I resigned myself to the fact that perhaps it was time for me to let it go. However, to my astonishment, she told me she would give me a bit more time to figure something out, since she didn't want me to lose my car!

Later that day, my dad asked me once again to notify him when I desired to change the storage insurance on my car so I could drive it again. I finally told him there was no point, if I couldn't keep it. I just couldn't hide it anymore. Thus he not only found out I couldn't make my car payments, but for the first time since I had become an independent adult at age 18, I had to tell my dad that I had no money. That was *so painful*. While in my heart I knew I hadn't done anything wrong, I didn't know how to tell him more without sounding like a complete lunatic, so I left it at that. I let him think I was totally irresponsible with money and credit, for that was a logically acceptable reason and easier to understand. Then we changed the subject, and neither of us brought it up again.

The next day my dad told me he would make my car payments so I wouldn't lose my car. That was even more painful for me to hear. I told him I was fine with letting the car go, but he had made up his mind. Since I had no idea what

Spirit's plans were for me, I thanked my dad with appreciation instead of resisting. He also paid for the insurance, and I felt as if every bit of independence (and pride) I had ever earned was thoroughly crushed. My parents' hard-earned money was now paying for things I couldn't pay for myself, including food. I told him that I intended to fully pay him back when I could.

I felt so utterly unhappy with Spirit—infuriated, actually. Looking back at what I'd endured in December, I saw that it had been *so easy* compared with what I was going through now! What I'd thought had been *the* ultimate test of faith for me now seemed to be just practice for this one. At least at that time I had been able to get through it without getting anyone else involved. *This* was now the ultimate test of faith, requiring that I accept things as they were unfolding and trust the Divine, regardless of how painful it felt to me. Spirit also asked that I not sell my car, despite any pressure I might experience to do so (confirming that my dad was doing the right thing).

It was so tempting for me to tell Spirit, "I've had it, and I quit!" and then file for bankruptcy to get rid of all that debt, get a regular job again, and start over from ground zero with a conformist life. *However,* I knew that my sacred heart's absolute commitment to my path would make anything else feel like the worst torture. I couldn't change that. It was maddening for my emotional heart and mind. It was a challenge to not let them overwhelm me.

While I knew from Spirit that things were the way they needed to be at this time, it was so frustrating to know I had more money locked up in bank accounts than most people make in a year, yet due to regulations, I couldn't touch it. I was now receiving a dozen phone calls on my cell phone every day from credit and loan-account managers, and the stack of letters I was receiving was also getting thicker by the week.

One day I completely shattered: I let go of my higher perspective and allowed my basic self and emotional heart to have an absolute meltdown, to fully express themselves. I felt I had given up my life, and I could no longer bear the pressure of that immense debt hanging over me with no sign of relief in sight. I didn't see any purpose in me being here on Earth if I couldn't be more useful. I was weary and suddenly felt such anger with the Divine—which turned into absolute despair. I went for a barefoot walk in Nature while my parents were at work. I felt the deepest sorrow emerge from my heart and soul and I absolutely broke down ... on my hands and knees on the ground, my entire body was heaving so deeply with soul-wrenching sobs. I had never felt such anguish in my heart and mind. I had so many thoughts and emotions going through me. I had come too far to give up now ... I just had to keep the faith that I hadn't made the biggest mistake of my life by allowing my sacred heart and Spirit to guide me. Yet, I didn't feel I could go on, either.

I surrendered myself entirely to the Divine, and through sobs, I expressed everything that weighed so heavily on me. I was in a grassy clearing surrounded by forest, near the place where I'd received my spirit name, DancingWind. It was also near where I'd received teachings from the red pine about the divine-love energy I channeled. I desperately needed some reassurance and guidance. The sky was entirely overcast, with thick clouds, yet for a moment the sun suddenly shone brightly through a small circular opening just large enough for it. It was so radiant and its rays felt divinely comforting as it shone on me. Then one of my favourite species of songbird perched at the very top of a tree near me and began to sing its melodious song, soothing my spirits. I felt Mother Earth's nurturing and loving energy flowing throughout my body; it was like a big, motherly hug.

I was told by Spirit I *was* doing my sacred work, in ways I wasn't aware of, and at some point I would understand. I was also reassured that my presence on Earth was greatly needed and that I was fully supported by so many, beyond my level of understanding. As I looked around me at Nature, which is so very dear to me, and felt the Divine's loving presence everywhere within me and around me, I gradually returned to a state of inner tranquility. I lay down on the ground, closed my eyes, and simply let myself be loved and nurtured for a while, feeling the breeze dry my tears and caress my skin. After a while I decided to spend some time with my parents' flourishing gardens.

Whenever I need to shift from feelings of lower frequency to higher ones, I throw myself into actions of love and appreciation. The joy I feel during the process catapults me into the higher frequencies again. One action I greatly enjoy is selecting someone I feel blessed to have in my life and creating a gift of loving appreciation for this person (or being). Since these are surprises for the recipients and true gifts (no expectations or occasions associated with them), just the thought of creating them fills me with bliss, and it becomes an alchemical process of emotional transformation. This is also a gift to myself because I get to express my creative spirit in a beautiful way, which always uplifts me.

On this particular new-moon day, after emptying my heart and soul to Spirit, I decided to create a beautiful salad for dinner, with love and appreciation, for my parents. One way of being of service to them while they supported me was to make dinner every evening and help out with the gardens. I chose a beautiful crystal salad bowl, filled it with lettuces, and then arranged a variety of chopped colourful vegetables on top. I visited their lovely flower bed that bordered the front of the house and selected three pretty pansies—edible flowers to garnish the salad's centre. The colourful work of art was vibrant with colours and energy. It made me smile from my heart, and it gave my parents heart smiles also.

That night, I discovered I had received many beautiful messages, comments, and emails of appreciation from different people through social media and my business email. It was like a wave of love and gratitude that showed me that, despite everything, I *was* making a difference, without even knowing it. Spirit reminded me that most of the time we're unaware of the immense ripple effects we have on others, but this doesn't mean that they don't exist or that they're less significant.

We never have the full perspective that Spirit has, and we never know all that's going on for us behind the scenes. I've learned again and again that the Divine is infinitely wise and there's always great purpose to what we experience, despite how things may seem or feel. Most of us have been taught to avoid feeling uncomfortable and experiencing inconvenience at all cost. We haven't been taught that within these fears lie our greatest opportunities for the kind of transformation and soulful fulfillment that our hearts yearn for.

I was told by Spirit that my basic needs would be provided for during my radical journey, and once again this proved true. Although it wasn't in the way I would have chosen, I was very grateful for it every single day. I had shelter, good food and water, and my parents' loving presence. I even had my own bedroom, washroom, and private living space on the second floor of my parents' home, and I was surrounded by Nature on their large, beautiful rural property. In addition to all this, I had high-speed Internet access, so I could continue to connect with others through social media, post my "Miracle of the Day" on my blog and Facebook pages, publish my e-newsletter, and make the most of opportunities that showed up for greater connections. It really was the best place I could have found myself under the circumstances, even though I didn't think so at first. Spirit had made *sure* I ended up there, so it was quite obvious there was a higher purpose for me to be at my parents' now. I soon discovered the unexpected divine gift that arose from this predicament I was in.

I always have a certain inner knowing of when it's time to do something. When I feel it, I act accordingly, no matter how challenging or unusual it might be. For some time now I had desired to tell my parents about the journey that had led me to their place, so they might have a better understanding of something that probably made no sense to them. I could only speculate how they felt to have their ultra-independent eldest daughter living with them without money, after she had been completely self-sufficient for over two decades. However, I thought I needed to get through this test of faith first and experience a magnificent miracle, so I could tell them a story with a positive outcome. This way, no matter how crazy my journey seemed, I would have the tangible, positive result that would alleviate their worries about me and reassure them that I was fine. Well, Spirit obviously had other plans (of course!).

I woke up one morning and just knew that it was time for me to share my experience with them. It was weighing on me, and I had no doubt it weighed on them also. But I had *no* idea how I could do this in a way that they would understand. After all, it had taken me two years of removing myself from the "normal" lifestyle, and a lot of different experiences guided by Spirit, to get to the level of understanding where I was now. My life now and the life I'd left behind me felt like lives on two different planets. I didn't know how I could bridge that giant gap between logical-mind leadership and heart leadership—when I didn't have anything to show for it except my current situation (which from a logical perspective was highly questionable, if not crazy and irresponsible). I needed some assistance, so I asked the Divine to please show me the best way for me to share this with my parents.

Interestingly, since I'd returned from Hawai'i I had noticed my parents reading many books about miracles, courage, trust, tests of faith, divine intervention, and answered prayers. I felt that perhaps Spirit had been assisting us already to bridge that gap of understanding. Shortly after my request to the Divine, I suddenly felt guided to randomly open the book "Flight to Heaven," by Dale Black, which was on the kitchen table (my mom had been reading it). What I read on those two pages astounded me. It read, "The Bible says ... faith is the substance of things hoped for, the evidence of things not seen ... What you see, feel, or hear isn't the final word. Don't be moved by your physical senses or the circumstances around you ... believe what God has said ... Do what you believe in your heart God is telling you to do ... Your faith must be in God and His Word ... Be on guard and ready, however, because in my experience I've learned that your faith will be tested in order to be strengthened. Understand, it is not God testing your faith, but He is allowing it to be tested to determine whether you really believe in your heart what God has promised."!

I was mute with absolute wonder. This was *exactly* what I needed to read, for it perfectly explained my journey in a simplified way, and it was even in my parents' language (directly from the Bible). This also provided me with the gift of additional confirmation that I was following divine guidance and was still on track with my path. I felt immensely grateful and relieved to have this text to help me talk with my parents.

I went outside, picked a pretty flower from my parents' flower bed and walked barefoot to my special place on their property. I expressed my deep love and appreciation to the Divine and had another heart-to-heart talk with Spirit. I explained my desire to now tell my parents about my journey but my needing to know whether this was *really* for the highest good of us all, since I was still in the middle of this test of faith without evidence of a positive outcome. As I offered my red flower, a beautiful, graceful red-tailed hawk suddenly appeared only a dozen feet in front of me! It flew low to the ground, across my field of vision. It took my breath away. I was filled with so much love. I now knew without a doubt that this was exactly what I needed to do. I thanked Spirit and Red-Tailed Hawk, and fully savoured my natural surroundings.

That night, as my mom was reading that book in the kitchen, I stopped working on my book manuscript and joined her at the kitchen table. I had written the passage from her book in my journal, so I brought it with me, along with a small rose-quartz angel statuette that my soul sister Flora had given to me in Hawai'i. The rose quartz exuded love energy and the angel reminded me of Archangel Michael, who had assisted me so many times with courage. I asked him now to surround us with love. Having a heart-to-heart talk with my parents was not easy for me, especially due to the topic I was going to talk about.

Since being a child, I'd never felt heard or understood by my parents because of my different beliefs and understanding of our world. Nature was my church, and my sacred heart and Spirit were the only forms of guidance that I trusted. This had caused unfortunate friction with my parents, and at times we just had not been able to communicate with each other. I never opened up to them after that. After living on my own for a while as an independent adult, I realized that they'd only done what they thought was best for me. Over the years we'd simply focused on the fact that we loved each other, and we didn't discuss our different beliefs or lifestyles.

Now I took deep breaths and told my mom I had something to share with her, which I had been wanting to for some time but hadn't known how. My dad had already gone to bed. I'd felt that a one-on-one talk would be better than talking to both of them together. I also felt that testing it with my mom first was the best thing to do!

I received such an unexpected gift for doing this that it left me in awe. After reading out loud what I had found in her book, I then explained my own path and the journey I had been on since I'd left my old life behind me. I said what I felt guided to say from my heart, and I never felt so deeply heard by her as I did in that moment. I felt safe to share with absolute vulnerability. She told me she could only imagine how hard it was for me to be there, having been so independent since I was a young girl. She reassured me that they were happy to have me at their house and to be able to support me while I wrote my book. She was so relieved to know the reason why I was in my current situation—to know I had faith in God. I told her I could never have made the choices I did and experienced all that I had in my life without faith, especially now. Our hearts were wide open as we lovingly hugged each other, and I felt such a tremendous relief! I lovingly thanked Archangel Michael and the Divine.

The next day I needed a little boost of courage to talk to my dad, so I asked the Divine if this would be a good day for that talk. As I asked this, a pair of large vultures suddenly, gracefully, soared into my field of vision just above the forest. They were close enough for me to see their details! They were so magnificent with their immense wingspans. Just as quickly as they had appeared, they disappeared. While for some people seeing vultures might have felt like a bad omen, they actually represented truth as far back as ancient Egypt. For me it was the sign I needed to receive. I expressed my gratitude and prepared for my dad's return from work. When he got home, he sat on the veranda swing to chat, as he usually did. I enjoyed working on my book manuscript outdoors surrounded by Nature, so we had developed this little ritual. His energy felt light and joyful, so I knew it was a good time to talk with him. I asked Archangel Michael to surround us with love, and I sat beside my dad on the swing, with my journal and rose quartz angel. Once again, I received such an unexpected gift.

I began by telling him I had a story to share with him, and he jokingly asked me whether it was a true story. I told him it was very true, and I began by reading what I had found in my mom's book (a birthday gift he had given her). I shared what I felt guided to say from my heart, and I never felt so deeply heard and understood by him as I did in that moment. It felt truly incredible! He shared some of his own stories with me and expressed how relieved he was to know why I was in my current situation and to know that I had faith in God. He had been worried about me and was very grateful for all that I was sharing with him. We lovingly hugged each other with wide-open hearts, and again I felt such a huge sense of relief! Afterwards, as I resumed work on my book, my dad walked up to me on the veranda and gave me a little feather he had found in the grass. I felt so touched by his gift and expressed my heartfelt appreciation. I also lovingly thanked Archangel Michael and the Divine.

As I contemplated everything afterwards, I realized something profound. Because of my parents' faith in the Divine, as well as their understanding of things "beyond logic" as described in the Bible and books they had been reading, they had been able to receive what I shared with open hearts and without judgment. It allowed them to understand my perspective and why I had chosen the radical journey I had undertaken. Since we loved each other dearly and sincerely desired to reach out to each other, none of us had been on the defensive. We openly connected at the heart level and allowed ourselves to be openly vulnerable in a way I had never experienced with them before. Energetically, I felt such a deep healing occur between us across the years, and even ages, past. It felt absolutely incredible and was such a divine gift! I gained a new perspective and understanding of them as my parents and felt even more grateful to them. I appreciated that they had been so worried about me yet hadn't tried to influence me in any way. They even had respectfully given me my space. I felt so much love and appreciation for them. I felt so blessed, as I thanked Spirit with all my heart.

Through this experience, I understood even more the incomparable power of love. When we do things from divine love and let our hearts lead with clear intention, we discover sacred possibilities that would otherwise not manifest. What I experienced with my parents was in itself worth everything I had gone through since my arrival from Hawai'i! I understood now why Spirit had led me there under such unsettling circumstances. Had I had access to any money, I would have visited and then left when my siblings departed. We just never know what divine wisdom is at play.

My trust and faith deepened and strengthened further. I needed this, for the pressure was intensifying daily with regards to my financial situation. I wanted nothing more than to reach some form of closure, so I could move on. However, the Divine had other things for me to experience, and once again, I saw the higher purpose of these circumstances. I was invited to multiple events involving artists, friends, and family.

I committed to being open to experiencing anything and being my best regardless of my circumstances. This invited amazing heart connections with specific people, through my presence and through conversation. This was obviously divinely orchestrated, and so unexpected, for I was simply following through on nudges I had felt, not aware that these were intuitively guided catalysts for so much more.

While these had to do with seemingly very ordinary things, they guided me into surprising one-on-one situations with beautiful souls of both genders and vast variations of ages, from youth to the elderly. When I shared my true essence through an open heart, these people received inspiration in the perfect form they needed at that specific time. In turn, I received the gift of being of service in ways I hadn't anticipated at all. When I inspired them, I felt exhilarated with love and appreciation. It was always such a sacred, mutual gift when I fully connected with transparency through my heart with others' hearts—it lit up our spirits. With every experience I had like this, I felt further empowered, knowing that everything was still unfolding perfectly.

One evening, after a day of being tested further beyond my inner-peace zone, I went for a Nature walk on my parents' property. As I reached the far end of a clearing surrounded by forest, I saw nighthawks flying low in the sky above me. This surprised me, as I had never seen them at this time of the day and had previously only seen solitary birds. I counted at least 30 birds flying above me as they fed on insects, so close to the ground I could see their every detail. I felt that their unusual presence was a message for me, so I looked up this bird in my books. I discovered that as a spirit guide, Nighthawk's appearance signified persistence with commitments. In relation to my own path, Spirit was asking me to not give up on my journey. I knew what my path required of me, since I felt it within my heart. I was definitely committed to it, so as long as it felt true to my heart, I had to remain steadfast.

Later that night, I meditated for a while before going to sleep. I felt the need to receive a little more reassurance from Spirit. I was used to having the freedom to do anything I wished and to manifesting most desires quickly, even instantly. This was an entirely new experience for me. I had to verify that this zone of financial meltdown was truly part of my sacred path, according to the divine plan for me. Self-doubts were showing up in a very big way, especially since I had to stay at my parents' house with no means to compensate them financially. I needed a reminder that I could fully trust the guidance I was receiving through my senses of perception— that I wasn't misunderstanding anything. I had built up my credit for two decades, and I suddenly no longer had access to it! It was maddening. I needed to put my panicking mind at ease before it drove me over the edge.

As I communed with Spirit, I was reassured and once again asked to keep focusing on writing my book manuscript. The irony was that I could not complete its last chapter (this one!) until I knew how to complete it. It would be as much a surprise to me as to the reader! For, while I was writing in the past tense as if the experience was already past, I was actually writing it while fully living it in the moment, day by day!

I was asked by Spirit to think of the Divine, the ascended masters, the archangels, and all others who supported me in various ways, as my *support team*, or co-workers (I called them

"Spirit" and my "sacred circle"). As Spirit communicated all this to me, I suddenly felt that wave of pure divine-love energy flow through my entire body, blissing me out in all ways. Then I heard the distinctive calls of a great horned owl from the jack pine beside the bedroom window! The calls were beautifully loud and clear, and they made my heart and spirit soar. It was the first time since I'd left my home in April that I had been in the presence of this wonderful power animal. It called out for a few minutes and then was silent. It felt so sacred to have Great Horned Owl just on the other side of the wall beside me on the second floor! I then felt guided to look at the time and then to look outside, which I did. I was amazed to see that it was 11:11 p.m., and as I looked outside, I saw a beautiful, bright strike of lightning in the distant storm clouds—the only one I saw during the time I gazed outside. All of these were very significant essence signs for me; their appearance felt very magickal and helped set my mind at rest about everything. I was also reassured by Spirit that those who had financially supported me during my radical journey would be fully compensated, including my parents. I could continue to trust my inner knowing and the guidance I received, no matter how much pressure I felt from the mundane world to act differently. I felt infinitely grateful and went to sleep.

I began every morning with my love-and-gratitude ritual and then took a break from writing during the day to spend time with Nature and commune with Spirit. It helped me remain heart-centred in the moment, as much as possible. That way, any doubts, worries, and frustrations that showed up in my mind could be objectively acknowledged without dragging me down.

I received encouragement and reassurance from Spirit through regular appearances of signs from my essence language, often in surprising ways. For some time now I had been noticing the number 633 appear to me in various ways every day. According to one source that resonated with me, it signified that the ascended masters were taking care of the situation at hand—there was no need to worry. Seeing this number was a reassuring daily reminder for me.

One day, an unexpected thunderstorm advanced from an unusual direction towards my parents' property. I sat at the edge of a little forest and watched as it rumbled continuously. The thunder was mesmerizing, without visible lightning. Then I suddenly saw one strike of glorious lightning that was accompanied with loud, cracking thunder. It lit up my spirit! Shortly afterwards, I also was given the gift of a beautiful half rainbow that suddenly appeared in front of the clouds and within a few seconds disappeared again! It felt as if it had appeared just for me. Rainbows continued to appear in unexpected ways, and this always encouraged me. (As I was writing this in my book manuscript, I noticed 3:33 p.m. on my Ultrabook—another wink from Spirit.)

Lightning also showed up in many unexpected ways, most of it not even outdoors as part of the weather. Although I was never one for television, occasionally I felt guided to watch a specific movie from my dad's extensive collection, for a movie night with my parents. Interestingly, every one of these movies from two decades ago had a thunderstorm in it that showcased incredible lightning! It was uncanny, for I had forgotten most of the storylines of those movies.

The animals that were showing up also amazed me with their messages. One day in September I was feeling extremely frustrated with being at a standstill and not contributing to this world in the way I deeply desired to. Spirit reminded me that writing my book and experiencing this test of faith were in fact a *lot* of work for me and part of my sacred work. I was reminded that my work was simply different than other work, and since I was willing to do this work, I would be rewarded soon. Of course, *soon* was a relative word and I was well aware of the difference between Spirit time and linear time, so I always took that into consideration!

As I was receiving this message, I was sitting cross-legged on the ground at my special location in Nature. I noticed grasshoppers jumping up around me and hovering in mid-air, higher than my head, with their colourful wings beating rapidly and making rattling noises. They were so mesmerizing to watch as I silently sat in that clearing. I had never seen them do this. I suddenly realized that the grasshoppers were being messengers for me—and as soon as I had this realization, they stopped doing it!

I wasn't familiar with this intriguing insect as a spirit guide, so I looked it up in my books and was astonished by its timely message. It signified everything I had been experiencing until now and confirmed what Spirit had said to me! Grasshopper represented leaps of faith, trusting one's intuitive knowing and personal rhythms. It signified being guided on journeys that progress differently than others and knowing that feeling at a standstill doesn't translate into not moving forward. I thanked Spirit and Grasshopper for their wonderful support.

I also received another visible reminder from Spirit (to share in this book) that time is nonlinear and the divinity of life is *always* aware of us. Just as I finished adding this about Grasshopper to my book manuscript (a month after it showed up in such a significant way), I went to my parents' kitchen to tidy up. When I got there, I was stunned to find a grasshopper on the kitchen counter! It made me laugh. I had *no* idea how it got there, since I'd rarely seen any type of insect in that house. It didn't even jump away when it saw me looking at it. It simply looked back at me, its antennae moving as it tasted strawberry juice on the cutting board. I thanked it and gently released it outdoors. Then I looked up at the sun and saw a beautiful rainbow shining around it through wispy clouds! After a minute, it disappeared. The timing of everything with Spirit continued to amaze me.

It was now near the end of September. Four months had passed since my last payment on any of my credit or loan balances. According to the voice-mails and letters I was receiving from many account managers, I had reached an extremely critical point, financially. Every day I had multiple calls (sometimes as many as 15), and yet I was being guided by Spirit to no longer return the phone calls until I was notified otherwise! This was very challenging for me, since I did want to acknowledge them.

On one particular day, everything hit me like an energy bulldozer. I received urgent voice-mail messages from four different account managers with commanding voices, and one message said, "This isn't going to go away, you know ... it will be escalated ... you must contact me *immediately.*" I felt how those words and tone of voice were huge triggers of a fear response. Every man and woman who left me voice-mail messages at this point was urgently insisting that I had to call back "today." As if that weren't enough, I also received a personal email stating, "I perceive a dark cloud looming on the horizon" regarding my situation and asking me to take responsibility for my parents' sake. It made it even more difficult for me to stay committed to Spirit's guidance when I felt that I was disappointing this person. The letters I was receiving were now also increasing the pressure by threatening legal action if I didn't act immediately.

Absolute trust in myself was *so* critical. The calls and insistent messages could easily have made me feel that I was being completely irresponsible and avoiding matters of great importance. In my situation, however, I knew I was following higher guidance and was required to handle it differently. I was allowing Spirit to govern my path instead of the mundane outer circumstances. This situation was not for the faint of heart! However, this is what felt true to my purpose, and this is where my commitment was.

Trusting ourselves requires ongoing practice. There will always be situations (opportunities) that allow us to further deepen our self-trust. It's not a destination but a continuous journey.

All this pressure in one morning could have completely sent me over the edge once again. However, for the first time since this test of faith began, I experienced something different instead. I was able to remain in a state of calm and not let my emotions overwhelm me. It felt so incredible. I felt guided to read an email I'd received in my junk folder, which I normally would have deleted without opening. I read the line "everything is unfolding perfectly" and saw 11:11 a.m. on my Ultrabook clock. Shortly after that, I also received two separate emails at 3:33 p.m., which were automated notifications (not influenced by any person).

When the autumn equinox arrived, it was a gloriously sunny and hot day. I brought my frame drum with me to the special location on my parents' property and did a personal ceremony to mark this significant occasion. Thinking about all I had experienced since the last autumn equinox, I felt so much love and appreciation to all who'd supported me along this journey. It was quite remarkable and I couldn't have made it this far without any of them, human and beyond. I also commended myself for persevering with so much dedication to my path while experiencing every extreme. So much had occurred in one year—it was astonishing, to say the least.

Before I began drumming, I asked Spirit to give me a clear sign to confirm that everything was still unfolding for the highest good of all involved. Shortly after my request, a magnificent bald eagle suddenly appeared from the forest and soared above me, so low I could clearly see every feather! I was deeply moved by the timely appearance of this significant power animal. I then drummed my love and appreciation to All, feeling blissful Oneness. As I finished drumming, a pair of very playful ravens called out and flew low above me, performing acrobatics together and vocalizing. Their presence also felt very special to me. A bit later, as I sat on the veranda with my parents, I received a personal email that simply showed "3:33" in the body, and simultaneously, both my parents exclaimed they had seen a whirlwind on their driveway! It felt like a very significant day for me and my path. For those attuned to the energies of Nature, the autumn equinox marked the beginning of a new year—a new cycle.

Over the next weeks, the onslaught of calls, voice-mails, and letters from financial account managers kept pouring in. While I no longer felt triggered into fear responses, having to endure this every day was taxing, especially when I did not know how or when it might end. I also felt compassion for all those trying to reach me, day after day, without a word from me. Since I was living in a world that was set up in a way that relied on the use of credit, my mind went into panic mode once again. My mind was very good at pushing my most vulnerable buttons! I had used credit cards since I was in my early twenties. I made most of my purchases through the Internet, from my favourite natural body products to everything related to travel. Now finding myself without any usable credit cards, I felt my sense of freedom being threatened. I already felt stretched *way beyond* my breaking point. I just didn't want this new onslaught of mental strain in addition to everything else. So I decided to take care of it by consulting with the Divine directly, immediately.

I walked barefoot to my special location in Nature and sat on the ground. I fully expressed my heart to the Divine and asked for a clear sign—in that moment, that would give my mind immediate peace. I also specified the sign I desired; I requested that it be a rainbow. Then I simply savoured the beautiful surroundings in silence, remaining wide open in my heart. It was sunny and warm, a breeze was blowing, and many birds were singing in the surrounding trees. Shortly after my request, a pair of yellow butterflies flew straight towards me and fluttered so close I could feel their wings on my skin! Then they "danced" together before flying away. What joy! I then felt guided to look up behind me, so I did. As I gazed at the sky, I saw a radiant rainbow suddenly appear in wispy clouds that moved rapidly beside the shining sun! It shone brightly for a long moment, and I let the image imprint in my mind so I wouldn't forget. The rainbow then disappeared as the clouds moved on and also vanished. I felt so deeply grateful for this immediate response. A little later I received an email from my soul sister Anna stating that she had suddenly felt the strongest nudge to send me a photo of a rainbow, so she had—a glorious double rainbow!

The following day I experienced wonderful, unexpected gifts that touched my heart and allowed me to feel even more the supportive divinity flowing through my test of faith. When I took a break from writing to pick beans in my parents' garden, I suddenly heard the calls of a goldfinch from the ground nearby. I looked and saw a beautiful, little bird hopping directly towards me! I noticed it couldn't fly. Since it seemed healthy as it foraged on the ground, I observed it with love but didn't touch it. However, it made its way towards my dad, who was filling watering cans, and then hopped in the direction of the forest. We suspected it might be thirsty, so my dad poured some water on the ground. Before it disappeared in the vegetation, I gently scooped up the goldfinch in the palms of my hands, and it just looked at me very trustingly without struggling. I placed it near the water puddle and it immediately started to drink, all the while calling cheerfully. It felt like such a blessing to share this moment with my dad.

Later in the evening, as I was bringing my things back into the house from the veranda, my mom put on a CD of classical music to listen to. As it began to play, we both simultaneously started to dance to the music in the living room. As she turned around and saw me, we both laughed and danced together in sync with the music, big smiles on our faces. It felt like a joyful gift to share this with my mom.

While I had been so angry with Spirit at times for my forced dependence on my parents, I now understood it as a mutual blessing for all of us. Every aspect of me knew it. It gave my parents a chance to support me in many ways that I'd never allowed them to when I was independent. It also allowed me to receive their support. It gave us the opportunity to get to know each other from a different perspective than a parent-child one. We were given the opportunity to reconnect through our hearts and to spend quality time together. It delighted me to know that preparing dinner for them every weekday reminded my mom of when she used to come back home from school as a young girl to find dinner waiting for her.

I greatly appreciated my parents' support and faith in me and my path during the most vulnerable time of my life—they allowed me to do what I felt guided to, without questioning it. While I had no idea how long I would be required to live with them, I knew that when the time came for me to move on, everything would miraculously allow me to do so.

Looking back at my life, as I wrote this book's manuscript, I realized how everything had always been divinely orchestrated for me and had worked out beyond what I could have imagined, trials and all. Yet I didn't know it at those times, not until I had actually lived those experiences and then could look back. By living from my heart, with love and self-trust, I was truly living the life I had come here to live and experienced so much more than logic alone would have allowed me to. Over the years, I gradually became more and more aware of my direct partnership with Spirit, which had enabled me to experience everything I needed to since 2011. At that point I'd needed to know that I had this extra support to be able to fully leap into the extreme unknowns.

Despite how chaotic my outer circumstances seemed to be, I knew things were exactly as they had to be, for I was experiencing abundant synchronicities and manifestations of heart desires, sometimes instantly. One such manifestation occurred one day when I was craving a fruit I hadn't had since Hawai'i—one that my parents didn't normally purchase. That day they went grocery shopping and, without knowing about my craving, returned with an abundance of avocados! They'd purchased them since they happened to be on sale. I was so surprised, elated and grateful (simultaneously)! On another day, I had used up the last of the garden carrots for dinner. I thought of how nice it would be to have more, since they tasted so much better than store-bought ones. When my mom returned from work that day, she had a large boxful of garden carrots that a co-worker had given her!

Astonishing synchronicities also occurred as I worked on my book manuscript. Different numbers and words I typed would suddenly show up around me at the same time through different means—even unusual words that were not common in mainstream vocabulary. They appeared visually as well as audibly through my parents' conversations, the radio, and television. Personally significant as well as new numbers also showed up consistently, giving me powerful messages from the ascended masters, the Divine, and the archangels. Rainbows were prevalent, showing up whether I was indoors or outside. My power animals showed up often in various ways. It felt so wonderful and reassuring to see the divinity of life at play.

When October arrived, the image for that month on the bedroom calendar was a radiant rainbow shining beneath dark storm clouds. It felt like a very significant metaphor for my journey. One morning was exceptionally magickal, encouraging me to keep moving forward as this test of faith kept stretching longer and longer. It was October 3rd and I woke up around 3:00 a.m. I normally would just go back to sleep but that morning I got up to look out the bedroom window. The night sky was so clear and the shining stars and constellations seemed closer and brighter than usual. Within one minute of gazing with wonder at our beautiful universe, I saw two impressively large and bright falling stars travel slowly across the sky towards the Big Dipper! It was such a perfectly timed and unexpected sighting—it felt like a gift meant for me.

Later that morning, I walked barefoot to my special area on my parents' property and brought flowers as an offering of love and appreciation to Spirit and Nature. As I simply expressed my heart to All, I suddenly felt guided to look directly up above me in the sky. As I did, I was so astonished to see the most *beautiful* rainbow I had ever seen, in a clear, blue sky—it hadn't been created by clouds or rain! It was a full arch of brilliant colours, like a giant, radiant, divine smile. It shone its magnificent beauty for a while, and then a graceful bald eagle flew across it towards the south! Moments later the rainbow slowly vanished. It felt like such an incredible gift from Spirit, and it deeply touched my heart and soul. Throughout that day Bald Eagle showed up three times in various ways, including indoors.

One night as I meditated, I asked about the purpose of stretching this intense test of faith for so long. Spirit lovingly explained that the entire process was teaching me through experience about my limitlessness. When I first embarked on this radical journey, just spending money on my credit cards that I had no means to pay off every month, was an ordeal that stretched me beyond my previous breaking point for inner peace. When I reached a six-figure debt with no logical means to pay off even the monthly interest, it felt like an insane predicament and stretched me beyond my new breaking point. Then, not being able to make any kind of payments for a month felt like a nightmare that stretched me further beyond my new breaking point. And then Spirit managed to stretch me further beyond my newly expanded breaking point again … and again … and again … by adding those dear to me into the equation and stretching my time of financial delinquency *and* dependency into weeks and then months!

Each new month increased the pressure while everyone was urgently contacting me about my overdue balances. I kept being stretched further and further beyond what I'd thought was my breaking point. Every time I felt as if I just could *not* possibly keep going—I felt this way every week for the first few months—I somehow did manage to keep going beyond that. Now I had finally reached a point where I knew I could keep going for as long as I was required to, since my heart's commitment to my path was stronger than my mind, and I had Spirit supporting me in countless ways, through people and otherwise. Spirit showed me that what I had thought was my absolute, agonizing limit was, in fact, just an illusion, real as it may have felt.

We really are all limitless beings; the limits we perceive are those we create ourselves. It's only by experiencing things beyond our perceived limits that we not only believe this to be true but *know* it.

My biggest fear, I realized, had always been to lose my freedom. Through this journey, I came to understand that *true* freedom is a state of being. We achieve this state of being when we no longer let fears dictate who we are and how we live. We follow our hearts' guidance and live our true essences in all ways, in all situations, knowing we're fully supported by Spirit. Our true freedom is not dependant on the material security that we perceive, which can drastically change from one moment to the next, completely altering our world as we know it.

True freedom is achieved when we're in sacred relationship with All, including ourselves, through love. This makes *everything* possible, regardless of what our physical surroundings and circumstances may look or feel like. This is another aspect of the "new way of being" that Archangel Michael invited me to learn about through experience (ranging from one extreme end of the experience spectrum to the other). The root of this is always love. It's what choosing love, committing to love, and *being* love is all about.

The entire month of October came and went, and at this point I had surrendered to the Divine in ways I'd never imagined were even possible. I started feeling as much an observer of my life as a participant, while remaining dedicated to my heart's commitment. The writing contest winners were announced, and I was surprised to discover I wasn't on that list. Since I had been guided to write my book within such a short period of time, I'd thought I might be destined to win one of the publishing packages—it made sense. Spirit obviously had other plans for me and this book.

I was sitting outside on the veranda swing, Ultrabook on my lap, the moment I discovered I hadn't won anything for the contest. I asked Spirit for a clear sign to confirm everything was still unfolding in divine alignment with my sacred path, since I felt perplexed by this outcome. Only seconds later, a little junco (a sparrow-sized bird) flew into the veranda, fluttered at the kitchen window, and then flew directly up to me. It perched on my hand, looked up directly into my eyes ... and *pooped* on my hand before flying away! Oh my! I burst out laughing and expressed gratitude for Spirit's immediate response and infinite sense of humour, creativity, and wisdom. Getting pooped on by a bird has been considered a good omen in many cultures, and I just knew this was Spirit's answer to my request—but it was a first for me! I was surprised by the weight of that small bird on my hand, and when it made direct eye contact with me, I recognized it as a messenger. Its appearance signified coming opportunities for further growth. My book had already evolved so much since I had submitted the proposal, more than tripling in size, that it wasn't even recognizable—and Spirit had a few more *very significant* surprises in store for me that I would need to include in this last chapter before it was complete.

As I continued writing, I realized how many more stories and insights Spirit wanted me to share. As I lived this chapter day by day, I began editing my book manuscript, but instead of decreasing the word count as I had expected, I kept increasing it, significantly! Many mornings I woke up with another story or insight to add, guided by Spirit. I was grateful that the contest had motivated me to write my book in very little time. Now I felt more at peace with my test of faith and was able to get into the soul of each chapter with greater openness to Spirit. I remained wide open to guidance and kept writing.

Then I received an unexpected call from a senior publishing consultant at Balboa Press who knew me by name! This was such an unexpected and welcome surprise! Somehow, my book proposal had ended up on her desk after the contest. We had such a mutually uplifting conversation, I just knew this was Spirit encouraging me and letting me know my book was destined to be published, regardless of the contest results. I was reminded that Spirit was ultimately in charge.

In the midst of increasing financial chaos, miracles and magick were also manifesting in surprising ways. To experience the divinity of life this way was such a blessing. One day I had the opportunity to see for myself how well I was handling the chaotic circumstances around me. It was Spirit's way of *showing* me, instead of only expressing it to me, that my loving light was more radiant than ever, in spite of my trials. The greater the pressure, the brighter my diamond light became, it seemed.

I was invited to visit a soul sister who had given birth to a baby boy while I'd been in Hawai'i. I hadn't met her son yet, so I went for a visit. It gave me a little break from everything. As Karen greeted me at the door, she warned me that her son would probably "freak out" and want nothing to do with me, since he didn't like anyone but his parents and grandma—everyone scared him! Being aware of how acutely sensitive babies are to energy, and how purely truthful they are with expressing themselves, I knew this was the ultimate test to see what frequency my energy was radiating. Well, when her husband brought him over to greet me, we all had an incredible surprise—this beautiful baby boy seemed to instantly fall in love with me! He spent the rest of the evening looking into my eyes with a sweet smile, cooing at me, and actually looking quite mesmerized by my presence! Karen and her husband were absolutely stunned. I was amazed and ecstatic! I thanked Spirit and this little soul multiple times for giving me this priceless gift of knowing.

Also during the month of October, my business mentor started a new group on Facebook in preparation for a new mentorship program she was launching. My mentorship with her had reached completion, and Holly announced she was no longer doing private mentorships. I realized what divine timing had been required for me to work with her when I did. I had felt then that it was crucial for me to seize the opportunity while I could, and now that feeling was confirmed. She added me to her group and invited me to post my "Miracle of the Day." It would be a way for me to share my essence with the group every day with inspiring Nature photographs and wisdom specific to the group. Since I had been so focused on writing and editing my book manuscript, I hadn't been paying much attention to what was going on. However, Holly's invitation did feel like a great opportunity for me to be more visible while I was immersed in my writing, and to make even more connections with soul family. I joyfully accepted. Well, I had *no idea* what sacred possibilities would magickally manifest because I said yes to this!

I made many more wonderful soul connections and one of them resulted in the beautiful cover of this book! I unexpectedly received the image in my mind's eye one day. I saw it so clearly that I knew I had to somehow create it—it felt divinely perfect. In this new group, I'd immediately noticed a man who stood out, not only because he was the only consistent male presence, but his energy captivated me. I also noticed he always liked my posts and often commented on them. I felt an instant, special connection with Michael that I couldn't logically explain—it really was an energy thing, and it greatly intrigued me. Then I also noticed how much he supported my work by "liking" my Sacred Earth Connection™ page and posts, commenting on and sharing my posts with such sincere words, and even purchasing an art print. We became friends, and I discovered he was a graphic artist.

Shortly after we began to have Facebook conversations, I suddenly *knew* without a doubt that Michael was the one who could bring that image to life for my book's cover. He understood and appreciated me in a way that fully honoured me on all levels; I required this in the person who would create that image for me. He had already generously offered his support, free of charge, with technical things that had frustrated me, so I asked him whether he'd be willing to create my book cover even though I couldn't pay him. He was so surprised I had chosen him for this and happy to accept my request.

The following day, as Michael wondered whether he could actually create what I desired, he unexpectedly saw an incredible phenomenon in the sky—it reflected the image I had described to him for my book! He took a picture with his cell phone and sent it to me. It gave both of us goosebumps and confirmed that I had indeed chosen well. He not only manifested my envisioned image, but he did so even more brilliantly than I had imagined it! I loved it that he suggested using one of my own photographs (from when I was hiking the Nature trail of the Grand Canyon in 2012), which made it that much more significant to me. It also felt important to me that *he* was involved. The book's cover image manifested through a co-creation between Spirit, me and Michael. It was a reflection of the sacred geometry symbol in my business logo, depicting the divine relationship between the sacred feminine, sacred masculine and Spirit.

November arrived, and I noticed the image on the bedroom's calendar was of glorious, luminescent-green northern lights in a night sky. This was another significant essence sign for me. I'd always seen the heart chakra's pure love energy as luminescent green and had used images of the northern lights in collages expressing the heart. As I admired this photograph, I was also feeling disbelief about being at my parents' home after four months. I'd never considered that I would be there that long. When I had legally changed my surname to honour "DancingWind" in 2012, I had also chosen to include my mom's name and maiden name, and my dad's name and surname, as my middle names. It was my way of honouring them and both my lineages, while also maintaining a legally recognizable tie with my siblings, their children, and our ancestors. It felt like the right thing to do at that time. Now, after all the unconditional love and incredible support I'd received from them through this challenging part of my path, it felt even more like the perfect thing for me to have done. I chose to use my "star name," Aylani, for my Higher Self instead—beyond Mother Earth's plane.

My financial situation had so deteriorated that it felt absolutely surreal at this point. My stack of letters from my financial institution and collection agencies was now one inch thick, and I was still receiving calls and voice-mails every day with urgent messages. However, I was still being instructed by Spirit to not contact anyone related to my financial accounts. I did the only thing I could—with every phone call I received, voice-mail I listened to, and letter I read, I sincerely sent love and appreciation and surrendered it all to Spirit.

At one point I was stunned by what I witnessed. I received three letters from my bank, with great detail about threatened legal action against me if I didn't pay the full amounts due for each account immediately. I surrendered it to Spirit and remained open to guidance. Two weeks later, I received another three letters and was expecting the worst—only to discover that I was being offered assistance in the form of a debt reduction by one third if I paid the reduced balance in full by a certain date! It was an incredible offer, considering how much money I owed them; however I would also require a miracle to pay even that amount. I wasn't guided to somehow manifest the money I required, and no opportunities showed up either. I realized Spirit was simply reminding me that regardless of what the physical circumstances seemed to be, even at their most extreme, *anything was possible.* I had to admit I never ever would have thought that the bank would go from threatening law suits to suddenly offering such a generous alternative. It was another important lesson for me about how outcomes are directly influenced by reactions. Had I immediately reacted to the first set of letters, I wouldn't have received the possibility of the following letters.

Holly invited me to a live "Google Hangout" event where she would showcase a select few of us who had worked with her as a business mentor. I knew that thousands from around the world would see this, either live or through the recording. So many thoughts went through my mind. It was another opportunity for me to show up as my best, regardless of circumstances, and shine my true essence. However, I was feeling completely vulnerable, since I was in the middle of this immense test of faith with no end in sight. I knew this opportunity would not have manifested without a divine reason, so after testing the technical system with Holly's assistant and a soul sister until I felt comfortable with it, I accepted the invitation with gratitude.

The morning of the event I felt a million butterflies fluttering within me. Many in my soul family were cheering me on, knowing how I felt about the spotlight and all. I felt so much loving support. I went for a Nature walk and communed with Spirit, reflecting on my journey with Holly. I realized that it didn't matter that I currently was living at my parents' home, with no available income and had a six-figure debt. My success stories weren't financial breakthroughs, yet they were of immeasurable value to me. I experienced abundance in countless forms and incredible transformation on all levels. I felt that I had acquired true wealth as I thought of it all. I was now ready to share my experiences and energy with many, in the spotlight. I dressed up to feel and look my best, danced to my favourite music, and then it was time.

Well, although we had tested the system twice without issues, that morning it wasn't allowing me to go on live. I could not believe it! Everything was set up exactly as it was supposed to be, except I just wasn't appearing on the screen with the others! It was maddening as I tried and tried, while communicating with Holly's tech support. Suddenly I had an immense *aha* moment. I realized just *how much* I actually desired to be there, to be visible, to connect with everyone, to share my heart and experiences in that spotlight! As soon as I *truly felt* that strong desire in my heart—*ta-dah!*—I suddenly appeared on the screen with the others! What's more, I no longer felt nervous, just so happy and grateful to be there! I then knew that it had been Spirit's wisdom at play again, and I couldn't help but smile as I silently expressed my gratitude. I decided to simply speak from my heart in the moment when a question was asked. It felt so powerful to me to share a bit of my journey without reservation, including some of the miracles and magick I had experienced.

It was equally powerful for me afterwards, when I watched the recording and was able to witness myself shining in the spotlight, and see the reactions to my stories of those present in the group. I also received many wonderful messages of gratitude from people, for inspiring them by sharing bits of my journey through my essence and "powerful presence." Once again, simply showing up as my best was all I was required to do. I felt tremendous loving appreciation for Spirit, for continuing to give me opportunities through so many and for guiding me so I could keep expanding my sacred work and soulful connections.

Interestingly, the longer my test of faith kept going, the more I noticed fire energy spontaneously moving through me every day. It felt like the most intense fire travelling throughout my inner body; as well I suddenly would feel burning hot on my skin, especially around my shoulder blades on my back—as if I had etheric fire wings! When I asked Spirit about this fire I consistently experienced, I was told that my heart's passionate love fire (for All as well as for my purpose) actually did create etheric fire wings. I physically felt them! It made me consider that the outcome of this radical journey could either completely incinerate and reduce me to ashes or allow me to soar like a Phoenix out of the abyss, to do my sacred work. It was entirely up to Spirit, as I held the intention in my heart to be of service in the greatest way possible.

As the month advanced, something amazing unfolded that I hadn't anticipated at all. I realized there was so much more to my connection with Michael than I had foreseen. While I had felt an undeniable connection from the start, I hadn't put much thought into *why* we shared such a connection. Now, in working together on the book cover's design, we connected every day through Facebook messages and emails. As the days went on, we quickly recognized how well we could "read" each other through energy! It was something we had never experienced with another person at this level. We were exchanging so much information between us through our higher senses, bypassing the more common forms of communication. This enabled us to naturally connect so deeply at multiple levels. It was almost dumbfounding, this level of ease and trust that we'd immediately felt with each other, despite being several thousand miles apart and never having made eye contact.

Due to our mutual ability to hold sacred space and our willingness to be vulnerable with each other, we were also learning so much about ourselves through each other. We clearly saw where we were being called to evolve further as individuals, by bringing out the best in each other as well as exposing our shadows. It became glaringly obvious that we had a sacred agreement (a soul contract) together and had agreed to reunite at this specific time in our lives. The timing could not have been more divinely orchestrated for both of us. This was confirmed further when we discovered how we both had ended up in Holly's Facebook group through a series of amazing chains of events. Ultimately, we both had let our hearts lead us there, to each other. As the days went by, things between us just kept evolving and I experienced things I'd never had with a man before.

Our multi-dimensional connection was so profound that we felt a mutual desire to share everything about ourselves. We opened up completely to each other, without secrets. It was an incredible act of courage and trust for both of us, yet so liberating to be completely transparent with each other and never feel the slightest judgment. We discovered that we'd had so many similar experiences throughout our lives, resulting in the same lessons and wisdom. This gave us a level of understanding about each other that was simply mind-boggling. Interestingly, we even discovered that we'd both acquired new bodies recently, which no other had been intimate with—not even a kiss! A year ago, Michael had suddenly decided to completely transform his overweight body through cardio exercise, weight-lifting, and healthier eating habits. I had also chosen to transform my own body the previous year, with my breasts. We now both felt we had accurate physical expressions of our true essences.

We also discovered that we both had tattoos that included butterflies and meaningful esoteric symbols! Countless incredible synchronicities began to appear between us every day. One of them involved his own personally significant body tattoo. We realized that he'd received it on the very same day I had seen those two beautiful falling stars travel across the Big Dipper before dawn. I had journaled the details. I had also seen Bald Eagle fly across the most beautiful rainbow I had ever seen in my life on that day (it had looked like a divine smile directly above me in clear-blue sky). Before I had made the connection with that day, I was amazed to learn how highly significant falling stars were for Michael. I also discovered that the flag of Alaska (where he currently resided), featured the Big Dipper as its symbol! The only other time I saw a rainbow directly above me like that was in Sedona, when I had expressed my desire to Spirit to reunite with my beloved "twin flame." Michael had also received an eagle feather as a gift from a friend years ago. While we knew these things about each other, it was only when he told me the exact date he'd received his tattoo that we suddenly connected all these highly significant and synchronistic symbols. It was uncanny!

We discovered more and more how highly attuned we were to each other, which continually left us speechless. He began to share "random" songs, images, and thoughts, and these were always so highly significant to me, either with synchronicity or resonance. The very first one he shared opened our awareness about our connection. I was editing my book manuscript up to the tenth chapter, and I decided to listen to a music album that featured vocalizing dolphins. I hadn't listened to it since I'd been in Hawai'i several months earlier. Not even a minute after I'd started listening to it, I received a message from him. I flipped screens to Facebook, and what I saw was the most glorious photograph I had ever seen of a pair of dolphins leaping out of the ocean together in a golden sunset! He had never shared anything related to dolphins before that—he'd simply felt like sharing that image in the moment, having no idea how much the timing and image deeply touched me. Like the yin/yang and double trees, two dolphins jumping together like that were such a significant symbol for me of sacred partnership with one's beloved. Every song he shared with me was from artists I had never heard of, yet the songs resonated deeply with me, like expressions of my own heart and soul. It really gave me goosebumps. He knew me so intimately without consciously realizing it (and he said the same of me)! Every image he shared also deeply touched me; some triggered memories of past lives together. Our sacred connection kept revealing itself further.

We also quickly realized we could physically, strongly feel each other's hearts and love in ways we didn't even know was possible. (This confirmed even more to us how powerful energy is, especially love, regardless of distance.) We felt waves of massive love energy flow through our heart chakras and burst beyond our bodies every time we felt love for each other through focused awareness (like thoughts). I had never experienced this before—it was like the Divine's pure-love energy amplified by our own (or vice versa) and flowing through us! It was absolute, expansive bliss, similar to my full-body divine-love energy experiences, except this was all contained in our chest areas. It felt as if our hearts were pure love radiance that expanded beyond our bodies, similar to solar flares from the sun. I knew Michael was experiencing this also, since he described it this way to me. I was suddenly reminded that it was solar flares that caused the northern lights—my personal analogy of the heart's love energy! I was quite amazed that a man was sharing with me, so much of what I was experiencing myself! This felt like an orgasm of the heart, with love expanding into infinity. I hadn't known one could experience such a thing, never mind with someone else! It felt so very sacred.

From the start we had been freely expressing love to each other, as we did with others of our soul family. Those connections were always rooted in love, so it felt natural to do so. Then Spirit decided to have a bit of fun with me. One morning, I was thinking about Michael and how special he was to me—and as I picked up a jar of coconut oil from the kitchen pantry, I almost dropped it when I saw the brand name on it—it was *his* surname, in big letters! I was flabbergasted, since I had never even heard that name until he'd shown up in my life, and here it was in plain sight!

After that, I had one of those highly significant dreams during my sleep, involving Bald Eagle, an abundance of eagle feathers, and highly fragrant clusters of white blossoms. The dream made it clear that I was actually *in love* with Michael, a man I had never even met in person! I suddenly remembered that, for the past few months, every time I'd been in Nature I had received clear signs about a form of upcoming partnership: double trees, two identical feathers together on my path (multiple times), fluttering pairs of butterflies that would circle around me, bird pairs flying above me and often appearing to kiss each other by touching beaks in flight. This had occurred every day until I wholeheartedly connected with Michael. These signs had obviously been leading up to him!

Then, before I could share how I felt with him, he openly expressed that he was completely in love with me! I could feel his loving heart and how much he meant what he said. He also not only said it, but consistently showed it with his actions in ways that astounded me and deeply touched me. Since we were both highly empathic and intuitive (which seemed highly amplified between us) it assisted our mutual desire to be completely transparent with each other and to keep the energy between us crystal clear. I loved that we were both equally willing to always be open to fully sharing, and being present with each other through wide-open hearts. That was so important to both of us and such a rare gift. We had never experienced this deep level of intimacy with anyone before. It was so unlike any relationship either of us had ever had—even more so since it wasn't even in person!

Interestingly, self-trust had been a key player for both of us in our journeys towards each other. I had known for some time that my sacred man would find me without me having to look for him. I had jokingly been told many times that I would never find a man if I didn't do this or that. Many people believe that we have to put in time and energy *outside* of ourselves to find a partner. At this point I was not interested in a partner who was not my equal. I knew he existed and that my beloved was not the type of man I would meet in a regular way—he was someone like me. This meant that our hearts and keen ability to feel energies would be key factors. Neither of us would need to do anything except honour and shine our authentic selves, and let our hearts lead us. I did not desire someone who didn't live this way. And so I listened to my heart's wisdom and did exactly what I felt guided to do, including accepting opportunities that felt aligned with my essence. This is exactly what Michael did also, regardless of what others said.

It's all in the energy, just like plants that attract their perfect pollinators. Some are so specialized that only *one* kind of pollinator will do, and yet they find each other! The more we radiate our energy signature in its purest form (by doing our *inner* work), the more likely that we will attract exactly who we desire, for all sorts of connections. The geography and circumstances are inconsequential. Energy has no boundaries.

And then, December arrived. Another month had passed, with me still living at my parents' home. I noticed that the bedroom calendar's photo prominently featured a large double tree! It felt so significant once again. This calendar's images seemed to be so synchronized with the energy of my life—it was uncanny.

Under bizarre conditions, Michael and I had both found lists we had handwritten a few years earlier describing exactly what we desired and required in our beloved partners. I was astonished, since he fulfilled almost everything I had written on my list, including things I had added as not necessary but definite bonuses! Interestingly, I had never specified superficial aspects—I'd simply written that I required mutual physical attraction. This was the *only* thing on my list that left a question mark for me. When he shared his list with me, it gave me goosebumps—it was as if I were reading about myself, in great detail, including physical appearance! What was mysterious is that we hadn't looked for these lists—they'd appeared to us among our personal things, as if influenced by Spirit. I recognized once again the incredible power of the word. It was as if Spirit were taking every opportunity imaginable to show us that our deepest heart desires had manifested in each other!

We knew there was higher wisdom at play, since we had connected in a way that left the distraction of the physical presence out of the equation. I knew we were being called to fully surrender to and explore this incredible connection we felt at the heart, mind, and soul levels. It was another aspect of this "new way of being" I was being invited to experience—that is, to love deeply despite the uncertainty of the superficial. Michael and I had experienced *love at first feeling* rather than *love at first sight*, and it was so powerful. We obviously had planned this with Spirit before incarnating on Earth, for it was teaching both of us big lessons in different ways.

I realized something about myself that I hadn't been consciously aware of. Throughout my life, I had been committed to always letting my heart lead. However, I now realized that in the matter of selecting relationships, I had not fully done that. Instead, I had mostly let my ego lead—my basic primal self, had been at the forefront in selecting my relationships. I had never considered a man I didn't feel an immediate physical attraction to, even if he'd had a beautiful personality. I realized that the visual appeal had stroked my ego and had made it difficult to choose otherwise. While I had required a deeper connection than the physical to consider anything more, including kissing, it was the mutual physical attraction that opened the door to exploring more possibilities. My previous relationships had all started at the superficial level and evolved from there. Each of those relationships had obviously been destined, bringing with it invaluable lessons that prepared me for the one I actually yearned for. Now I realized that "the one" had required a completely new way of connecting and it made divinely perfect sense.

Michael and I found ourselves fully immersed in the relationship we had always truly desired, and it was a completely new dimension of love that neither of us had considered even possible. It began with the heart and soul levels *first*—learning to love deeply without reservation from the inside out, instead of the other way around.

It had been brilliantly orchestrated, for the fact that I didn't feel physically attracted to him. It caused my mind and ego to panic once in a while, for I had never loved a man as deeply as I loved Michael, yet I didn't even know if I'd also be able to feel a physical connection with him. He knew this, for we had agreed to always be completely open with each other about everything. It wasn't easy for me to express this to him—it made me feel terrible actually. However, his non-judgmental understanding and acceptance of how I felt, melted my heart even more, and opened me to the possibility that I might feel differently in his actual presence.

Meanwhile, he realized that he had chosen to incarnate in a physical body that didn't immediately mesmerize me, for a divine reason, despite his bruised ego. He accepted this awareness in a way that made me feel even greater respect for him as an evolved man. This physical aspect had already served a higher purpose, by making us both aware of our egos' influence in our relationships. Awareness opened the door to possible transformation.

We agreed to meet in person when we felt divinely guided to the perfect place and time. Then we could explore the last level of connection—the physical presence. It seemed that as soon as we mutually expressed this, Spirit began to guide us to that very special location. In conversation one day, I happened to mention to Michael how I'd felt called for years by the giant sequoia tree beings of California. Then he informed me that his parents owned a beautiful vacation home nestled among glorious parks where those giants of the forest stood! Multiple synchronicities occurred after this and significant essence signs showed up to further confirm that this would be our sacred place of meeting. It felt so perfect to us, and we sensed it would be like a long-awaited reunion when we met. We felt so familiar to each other and there was no denying our profound connection. We already felt so blessed for all we had already experienced together.

As I found myself immersed in what felt like an intense financial superstorm, Michael reminded me every day, with his loving, strong presence, that I was surrounded by immense support and love from Spirit. Michael felt like a manifested miracle to me. I greatly appreciated the energy of all miracles, even more so at this point of my test of faith. Every financial account I had, including my personal bank accounts, was now in the hands of collection agencies. Every single collections agent was also calling me daily and leaving voice-mail messages requesting an immediate response. Every day I checked with Spirit and was advised to not return their calls and to keep my faith strong. I was asked to continue focusing on my book manuscript and to allow myself to fully experience love with Michael in every way it desired to evolve. Rainbows prevailed in those days, and so did Raven's presence.

One early morning I suddenly felt guided to look outside the dormer window on the second floor of my parents' house. When I did, I saw a raven fly across a rainbow patch by the sun! Then, in the late afternoon during my Nature hike, I once again suddenly felt guided to look up from the trail, and I saw a raven fly across another rainbow patch beside the sun! I was reminded of a year ago when I had been driving to my parents' house on Christmas day during my first test of faith. I had witnessed two ravens flying across a brilliant rainbow patch that became so magickal. This felt very significant to me. However, the previous December I had only been one month behind in overdue payments, before I received a financial miracle. Now, I was quickly approaching seven months since the last time I had been able to make the monthly payments! I was truly astonished to have made it this far and see that people were still attempting to contact me to resolve this. I desired nothing more at this point. However, I also clearly understood the divine timing factor which only Spirit could orchestrate. I surrendered the situation to Spirit every day and sent love and appreciation to those who were trying to contact me, trusting that somehow the outcome for the highest good of everyone involved would manifest.

Amidst all this, I had a profound realization. Throughout my own journey of life, I had continuously been given opportunities to choose between love or fear, love or security, and love or comfort. Sometimes the choice was easy and other times much more challenging. However, the more challenging it was, the greater was the love I experienced as a result—for myself and with others. I knew with certainty that I would always choose love in its highest form, trusting it to be for the highest good of all. I also knew that if I were now given the choice between the kind of sacred love I shared with Michael *or* enough money to clear up my six-figure debt, I would choose that sacred love. If I had to choose one or the other, I would always choose love. I understood now, more than I ever had, how love in its purest form was the greatest wealth anyone could ever experience.

While money is currently a necessity in most societies of our mundane world, it's a man-made creation. Its value changes daily and can disappear from one moment to the next. Love, however, is purely a divine creation and infinite in value, as it continuously expands. It will always be available to everyone and will always be priceless, as it creates life, miracles, magick and beauty in their purest forms.

I was experiencing the most financially chaotic time of my entire life, and yet I was also experiencing the greatest abundance of love I had ever felt in my entire life—from Spirit, from soul family, from friends and family, from people I inspired, and from my beloved. I honestly felt wealthy beyond my wildest dreams. Interestingly, as soon as I had this clear realization, I felt strongly guided to look at Michael's Facebook posts. The first one I saw was a story about three sages called Love, Wealth, and Success. It described how the latter will follow when we choose Love! It felt like such an incredible confirmation from Spirit. I felt such great love and appreciation for All.

Between the full moon and winter solstice, I was having a conversation with Michael when he shared something with me that made my jaw drop open. It was a beautiful image of a female figure in black and white, with colourful, blazing wings of fire that even included green light (like the northern lights) within them! I was looking at an image that exactly matched the way I'd described my own etheric wings to Michael! The image's accompanying text even mentioned that they were wings of passion and soul fire. He had just happened to see it posted on Facebook. It was so uncanny! It further validated my unusual experiences and what Spirit had explained to me. It was quite amazing that so many of the significant signs I was receiving from Spirit (as forms of confirmation) were now being channelled through Michael.

To some people, my experiences might seem completely crazy, yet to others they're more real than those that others would consider normal. It's always a matter of perspective based on personal experience. Self-trust is crucial so that we don't dismiss our personal truth, even when others don't agree with it. For every person who doesn't agree with us, there is someone who does.

As the winter solstice approached, the unthinkable occurred. I received a phone call from a collections agent on behalf of my bank, at my parents' home! I couldn't help but feel very upset about this. Since I had been asked by Spirit to not communicate with anyone, this was so unexpected. When my mom answered the call, I had no choice but to speak to the agent. She knew I was there and would keep calling my parents' number, which was the last thing I wanted. I was put on the spot and suddenly confused as to what Spirit was asking of me. I took the call and couldn't answer her questions in a way that made sense to her, but I did the best I could. She asked me how I had talked the bank into giving me such a large line of credit and didn't believe me when I replied with the truth—that it had simply been handed to me through a pre-approval several years ago. I was informed that if I could somehow find a way to make a minimum payment by the end of the week, my delinquency would fall back to zero, and my credit rating would not be impacted. I thanked her and hung up the phone.

A rush of emotions suddenly threatened to overwhelm me. However, my parents completely respected my space and didn't inquire, for which I was so grateful. As an added gift, Michael happened to have what he called a "random day off" that evening—the first I was aware of since we had connected. He was so wonderful, completely devoting his evening to me through Facebook messaging. This allowed me to fully process my thoughts and emotions, and express myself without reservation through writing. He was so fully present in exactly the way I needed him to be. After I'd released everything that had been weighing on my mind and heart, he even managed to completely transform my energy, by making me burst into laughter! That felt so divine to me. He helped me fully return to the sacred heart space where I felt my best. That was a gifted ability—another one of the many that I treasured in him. I loved that he enjoyed writing as much as I did and how much fun we already had together despite the distance between us. Neither of us could be with someone who didn't share the same sense of humour. I felt so grateful to Spirit for Michael and for my parents.

Later that night, I went into meditation to ask why things suddenly seemed so chaotic, when I had done everything I'd been asked to. Spirit lovingly explained that this unexpected circumstance allowed me to see how supported I was even under testing circumstances—not only by my parents but also by Michael. I had never experienced this level of absolute support from a partner before; it was everything I had desired in my beloved. No matter what I shared and revealed to him, he was fully present and committed to being there for me in exactly the way I needed him to be. I didn't even have to ask—he just knew. Our intimate connection enabled us to intuitively know what we required from each other. It allowed us to be our best as individuals and partners in our relationship.

After I'd left my marriage, my former husband told me that I had taught him so much about love and beauty. He asked me to never, ever again allow a man to treat me less than I deserved to be treated. Now, through Michael, I was witnessing and experiencing what that really meant. From the moment he had found me, he had been treating me like a cherished goddess, for he so highly and fully valued what I offered to our world, and him, just by being authentically me.

Interestingly, before leaving for Hawai'i, I had felt guided to do something I didn't usually do—make purchases in quantities that would outlast my time on the island. I had specific things I loved, such as my favourite all-natural personal-care products, my favourite pens for journaling, and my favourite supplements. I normally never purchased much more than I required. Now, after half a year of having no money to spend, I understood the wisdom of Spirit's guidance with this and was so grateful that I had listened. My supplies had lasted me until now. Then, just as I was running out of some things, Michael gifted these to me, along with a special, personal surprise that was so meaningful to both of us. The absolute irony of this became so apparent to me. *I* was usually the one who would send surprise gifts to those dear to me, and I so desired to do this for him, yet I couldn't. Instead, I was on the receiving end; I knew Spirit was observing with great curiosity.

Even though I felt some resistance, I chose to surrender and wholeheartedly accept these beautiful gifts from his heart. Michael had been so generous with me already, always reminding me that there were no expectations attached. I knew how sincere he was since I could feel his energy and his words. His gift-giving was just another way for him to show me his great appreciation.

It so deeply touched me to be fully seen and honoured this way, to be so highly valued for who I was as a soul. I had nothing physical to give in return, and yet, this did not diminish Michael's love for me. It was not contingent on any superficial assets or conditions. What a sacred, mutual gift it was to experience this higher potential of love together. As guided by Spirit, I surrendered even the smallest resistance and allowed my heart to love Michael as profoundly and freely as it desired to. While we both felt that this bond we shared was already divine beyond words, another level of possibility unexpectedly revealed itself to us. Incredible fires of passion ignited within us when we both fully surrendered to this love! The energy was no longer contained within the area of our heart chakras but affected *all* our chakras, on all levels. It was absolutely amazing to experience this deeper level of connection through only words and energy. We couldn't help but wonder what awaited us when we met in person!

All this time I also remained open to Spirit's guidance. Then, two days before the winter solstice, which was a Thursday, I woke up knowing that this was the day I could finally contact everyone who had been trying to reach me about my delinquent credit and loan accounts. I asked Spirit for assistance, and then I contacted everyone. I ended up speaking with incredibly kind people. I openly expressed my loving appreciation to them. I was told that my credit rating had not been negatively impacted yet, despite the fact that I had not communicated with them for so long and had account delinquencies of more than six months now—and a thick pile of letters threatening otherwise! I was astonished.

I did speak to one account agent who reminded me of the ego-centred systems that still dominate a good part of society. It took everything I had to stay in my heart space, for he attacked me repeatedly with harsh words, accusing me of so many things based on assumptions. He was livid that he'd had to call me every day, saying that with the amount of debt I had, any other company would have taken serious action a long time ago and certainly would not have called me for months on end. By saying this, he unknowingly confirmed that I had experienced many miracles, since every agent assigned to my seriously delinquent accounts *had* in fact kept contacting me every day.

This agent seemed infuriated that I was speaking to him in a calm manner instead of showing signs of fear or stress, which he obviously expected. I did fully understand his perspective and felt compassion for him, so I kept sending him love and asking Spirit to send him some also. I felt stuck between two worlds, since I couldn't answer his questions in a way that would make sense to him. He made it clear that he had the power to sink me if he wanted to. After a moment of silence, I told him to make the decision that felt best for him, since he clearly didn't want his name on my file. In the end, he advised me to make a minimum payment by the Monday after the weekend, and he did not guarantee that he was keeping my file. It was a risk I had to take. Despite it all, I still expressed my sincere appreciation to him and surrendered it all to Spirit. I did the best I could—and kept breathing.

I also received a surprise from the agent who had called at my parents' home and had requested that a payment be made by this day. When I informed her that I couldn't make that payment, she ended up extending the deadline to after the weekend—also on Monday. Ultimately, every agent I had spoken with wanted to help me get back on track. Each made arrangements with me to resume a monthly payment that worked with my finances.

While I had agreed to these arrangements, they were *all* based on *faith*! I had three payments to make by Monday and the other payments were scheduled to automatically debit from my chequing account at the beginning of the new year! I was able to make these arrangements in lieu of having to pay the full balances immediately—which would have forced me to file for bankruptcy.

Spirit had obviously ensured that I wasn't forced to file for bankruptcy, for reasons I was unaware of. While I knew of many who had filed for bankruptcy in the business world (and it seemed like an ideal solution for me also, from a mundane perspective), it was clearly not what I was being guided to do. I had always intended to fully repay those who had supported me since I'd stepped into the unknown of a new life in 2011 (for none of what I experienced since then would have been possible without them). However, I also always gave Spirit full permission to guide me for the highest good of all, and I would have filed for bankruptcy had I been guided to do so.

I now found myself having to come up with enough money to make payments on three accounts, within three days, if I didn't want to be labelled a "bad debt." I contacted my bank manager to discuss the possibility of requesting the withdrawal of my pension funds as I had back in January. She confirmed that I could make another request, but not until the end of the next month, in January 2014. I surrendered to Spirit. I simply asked for clear guidance and assistance with manifesting that money somehow, *if* this was really aligned with my sacred path.

The next day I woke up with a clear knowing of what I had to do. I had to stretch beyond my comfort zone again. As much as my ego tried to persuade me otherwise, I knew I had to reach out to two very special family members (with whom I'd always had a special connection). I sent them emails openly explaining that I had a few things to pay the following week and was offering my original paintings in return for any sum they'd like to pay me. I made it clear that I had no expectations—I was simply following higher guidance. I was so touched by their incredible responses. The timing was perfect, with the holidays, since we would be seeing each other before Monday! I would not only receive money I required, but my art would also be going to people who meant so much to me. They were overjoyed to have the opportunity to assist me on my path—it became a mutual gift! It felt wonderful and so worth bypassing my ego once again.

The winter solstice arrived at exactly 11:11 a.m. in the time zone where I currently resided! It felt very powerful and special to me, being on the 21st of December. It was three years ago to the day, that I had been initiated by Spirit into a whole new level of experiencing divine love and ecstatic energy. For this significant day, I created a special ceremony outdoors to honour All with great love and appreciation. I drummed in my special location and savoured this glorious day with the sun shining radiantly and the cold air crisp but calm. Afterwards I encountered every species of woodpecker endemic to that area, including an elusive, very large one that my parents and I hadn't seen yet that year. It felt so perfect, with those birds being the natural drummers of Nature. As spirit guides, their appearance signified entering a time of abundance and being protected even in times of storms. I expressed loving gratitude to them and to Spirit.

On Sunday I attended a family Christmas gathering and received the money for my paintings. Monday I drove to the nearest town that had a branch of my bank. As I walked on the sidewalk, I saw a feather on my path in the snow—very unusual for winter and a wonderful sign for me. I knew then that everything would somehow work out. The teller couldn't assist me, since I had a hold on all my accounts with overdue balances. The cheques also had to be certified. That could have been the end of it. However, the very kind branch manager took me into his office for a talk instead. He decided to assist me in any way he could. He made an exception to the policy so I didn't have to drive to the city to get the cheques certified. He was another human angel. After many phone calls to other banks, he then processed my three payments (bypassing my accounts and the mandatory hold on the funds)! I knew then, without a doubt, that everything was still unfolding perfectly with divine assistance.

Afterwards, I decided to celebrate by going to the only store that carried my favourite style of journal. I was nearing the end of my current journal and desired a brand-new one to begin 2014 on the new moon. I knew what colours were available online, yet it was rare to see more than one in stock at a store. Since my dad had unexpectedly topped up my car's fuel, I was able to use the small balance I'd received from my payments, in the form of cash, to pay for a journal. I was so surprised to see the store was carrying two journal colours—the exact two I preferred! However, even *better* than that, they had a third colour that wasn't listed online—a beautiful rusty-orange colour, like the Sedona landscape! It felt so meant for me. The journals were also at a discounted price. It felt so perfect to gift myself this meaningful reward for being fully committed to my path.

I happened to be the only one of my four siblings who was around for the holiday season, which my parents greatly appreciated. Ever since I was a young girl, I had always felt I would live outside of Canada one day and that my beloved was not Canadian. When I'd ended up with my former husband, I'd thought that perhaps I had been wrong all along. Now I found myself in the most incredible relationship I could have imagined for myself, with a man who wasn't a Canadian citizen. While he currently lived in Alaska, he was born and raised in California and loved warm weather year-round, as I did. This could be the last Christmas I spent in Canada for a while, so I made the most of it with my parents and extended family members.

On the eve of 2014 I saw hexagons everywhere—my entire environment was saturated with this ancient symbol representing the heart! It was astonishing! January arrived with not just a new moon, but a "supermoon" (when the full moon coincides with the closest approach the moon makes to the Earth in its elliptical orbit). It was a significant celestial gift of powerful energies to bless our intentions for the new year!

The following day I had a heart-to-heart talk with Spirit. I wholeheartedly expressed that if I were to continue doing my sacred work, complete my book, and publish it, as I was being guided to do, without filing for bankruptcy and starting over, I would require a financial miracle. This would have to include enough money to pay my parents and everyone else I owed money to, as well as enable me to publish my book with the publisher I was being guided to. My cell phone bill was also long overdue, and my service would be suspended if I didn't pay it within two days. In addition to this I had two collections agents asking for minimum payments, one due by the following day, and another one due the next week.

While Michael was generously willing to pay the balance of my phone for me, I asked that he wait to see what might unfold. I had always been one who thrived on manifesting and co-creating, either purely from desires or from desires with inspired action. I always knew what was required of me through intuitive perception. I knew it was all about divine timing, so I surrendered this desire to Spirit and requested a miracle by 3:33 p.m. that would clearly guide me to a divine solution.

Shortly after this, I received a call back from a pension-unlocking specialist referred to me by one of the very kind collections agents. She informed me that normally financial institutions did not allow for funds to be unlocked, which was why her business existed. They would process their clients' requests by bypassing the banks, and it did take a while before the client received the funds. She was amazed that my own bank manager had been so accommodating and supportive the previous year with withdrawing funds from my pension. She concluded that she couldn't assist me more than my bank manager could. She suggested multiple times through that short conversation that I contact my bank manager. I suddenly knew that this was exactly what I was being guided to do, even though I had already contacted her recently.

I contacted Angela immediately and was delighted to hear her answer the phone, since she had been on holidays at this time the previous year. Now I discovered that she was going on vacation in a few days and would not be returning until the end of the month. That was why I'd been told I couldn't submit my withdrawal request sooner! My soul quickened at this window of opportunity. Since she was going to be at the office the next day with an open agenda, she scheduled me in. I also required a notary's signatures on the forms, so I called the office I'd gone to the previous year and confirmed he was going to be there the next day. I couldn't schedule an appointment with him, since he was booked, so I had to take the chance that he'd be able to see me between clients. It was a much longer drive now that I no longer lived at my previous home. I preferred knowing I wouldn't be making the trip for nothing (especially since the weather forecast called for a snowstorm the next day). I did feel this was my miracle unfolding, so I planned to go, regardless. I had driven in countless storms in all seasons, so inclement weather didn't deter me. That evening I experienced something truly magickal, which let me know Spirit was definitely working with me for a favourable outcome.

I loved to decorate my journals, and I had taken a little break from editing my book manuscript to embellish my new journal even more. I decided I would leave a blank page inside the cover for the image of a glorious monarch butterfly in flight, with its wings spread wide open. My previous journal featured five successive images from a magazine in which a monarch emerged from its chrysalis and then hung upside down to dry its new wings. Symbolically, I was also preparing to take flight. This new year was feeling like the year in which I would finally spread my wings and take flight!

Not even a minute after I decided to add a flying monarch butterfly to my journal, I heard my dad calling to me from downstairs to say that he was watching a television documentary on … monarch butterflies! Usually, once I went upstairs after dinner, my parents left me alone to work on my book, so this was unusual. The timing was so uncanny that I just had to go see, and what I saw filled me with wonder.

It was footage from the special place in Mexico where these magnificent butterflies migrate to from North America. Every autumn they fly there to spend the winter. At the time when they were first discovered there (in the 1970s), the monarchs gathered by the millions! Each person being interviewed on-site kept saying it was such a spiritual experience.

What I saw on the television screen was mesmerizing—thousands and thousands of monarch butterflies were flying in front of the camera! I had desired *one* flying monarch butterfly for my journal and ended up seeing thousands a moment later! I thanked my dad for letting me know and thanked Spirit for this unexpected, miraculous moment showcasing one of my beautiful power animals and a significant essence sign.

The next morning, the first thing I saw was 77777 on a US dollar bill that Michael had photographed to share with me. The 777 had become very significant for us and the 7 itself signified that divine magick was providing support for an outcome that would exceed expectations. Then I saw 555 twice on the withdrawal request forms that I filled out before leaving. Great numbers to start off my day! As I left the house, I asked Spirit to assist me in all ways possible, including a safe journey to that town and back. A strong wind was already blowing the snow around.

As I scraped ice from the windows of my car, I suddenly noticed Raven's beautiful presence—several ravens were flying all around and above me, facing the strong wind! I felt Spirit's protective presence. I knew with certainty that I was meant to go that day and I would be safe. I thanked Spirit and Raven and left on my journey. I was so in awe to see Raven fully present with me the entire drive there and back! I had never seen so many ravens in one day. They flew alongside my car and across the highways ahead of me, and one even landed on the left side of the highway and simply stood there looking at me as I drove by. As a spirit guide, Raven signified so many things, including the magickal and the ability to travel between the spirit and mundane worlds. It felt so special to have this power animal as a companion on this significant journey.

I went to the notary's office first. As I waited no more than 10 minutes, I saw a magazine that featured incredible images of tornadoes. As I flipped through the pages, I also saw a beautiful photograph of a radiant rainbow. After the notary had signed and stamped my forms, he told me there was no charge—another gift! As I left his office and walked outside into the blowing snow, it suddenly felt so uncanny. This was exactly like the last time I had received a money miracle, a year earlier: a snowstorm, Raven, and whirlwinds!

It was so nice to see my bank manager again. She had always been so wonderfully non-judgmental with me, regardless of what situation I brought to her desk. I handed her my withdrawal request forms and she brought up my profile on her computer screen. We had to open a new account for me, since my previous one had been closed only a few days prior (due to inactivity for six months). I found it so interesting that my bank account—of almost two decades of my life—was history, and a new one was now open to receive the next possibilities of my life. It was the beginning of the next phase of my sacred work.

Then Angela offered me a new debit card that also functioned like a credit card. I had just recently heard of these types of cards. I silently thanked Spirit for this unexpected divine solution, since I required a credit card to pay for my book's publishing and professional editing. Through this journey, I had found myself without any usable cards. While the processing of the withdrawal request normally took five business days, we chose to focus on a possible same-day outcome, like I had unexpectedly experienced the previous year. After everything was complete, I told Angela that she was anonymously included in my book wit gratitude, for she had definitely been one of the human angels on my path. We exchanged warm hugs and I left for the journey back.

I drove in the storm with the wonderful company of Raven. The highways and visibility were already much worse. Once safely back at my parents', almost one hour and a half later, I went for a Nature hike and brought an offering of love and gratitude to Spirit; it was a little bundle with sacred medicine plants. I sat next to the beautiful red pine (my teacher of the divine-love energy) and expressed my loving appreciation to many. As I did so, ravens flew by, and one loudly called out just above me! It felt so magickal, and again I sensed a lot going on behind the scenes on my behalf.

Shortly after I'd returned to my parents' house, Angela contacted me and informed me I had received the *full* amount that I'd been eligible to apply for from my pension! It was all in my new bank account! I had received more than double the amount than I had a year ago. I had felt that the more money I received at this point, the better, and obviously Spirit agreed, for I experienced three miracles that worked in my favour: The money was processed immediately; I didn't get penalized for taking out the funds sooner than their maturity date; and—for reasons unknown to her—the expected 30 per cent taxes were not deducted. Incredible! I felt ecstatic as I lovingly thanked her.

I reassured Angela that the taxes were nothing to worry about, for everything always worked out somehow. I had to focus on the present moment. I now had enough money to bring all my outstanding, urgent debts up to date, as well as publish my book the way I was being guided by Spirit. It felt so wonderful, especially after I'd spoken with everyone to settle all my financial accounts. Once again I had received a big miracle at the eleventh hour! It also felt very fulfilling to be able to pay my parents for the past six months of support! They were fully compensated for their faith in me, just as Spirit had reassured me they would be.

I was also grateful to receive the manifestation of a small desire I'd had for months. I thought that perhaps the irate account manager I had spoken with before the solstice had let go of my file after all, since I hadn't heard back from anyone after I'd made the requested payment. Either way, I had to find out whether my payment had been received. As I dialed the number, I asked Spirit for assistance. I was preparing for another challenging conversation, but I was determined, regardless. I was so thrilled to hear the voice of another manager instead. He was the same one who had left me so many kind voice-mail messages over the previous months (before it had switched over to the unpleasant one). I was finally able to sincerely thank him for his persistence and kindness all those times he had called (which he greatly appreciated hearing).

It all felt so good to my heart and spirit—I was finally free of all the phone calls, letters, and voice-mail messages. I suddenly understood clearly why I had been asked during these past months to not communicate with anyone related to my financial accounts. Throughout the past half year, I had also been asked by Spirit to not get a job but instead to focus on writing my book—that's where I needed to channel my energy. I had been asked to not dwell on money-related matters, for things were being taken care of. Regardless of how difficult it had been for me, I had done as asked. I now realized this had given me the time I'd required to focus on my book without having to do other work. Had I spoken to any of the account managers or collections agents during that time, I would have been expected to provide at least the overdue minimum payment, which I didn't have.

Every manager and agent had been aware of all my financial accounts. They had known that someone else was making my car payments for me. By remaining silent, I'd been able to stretch the time I needed until I was able to request the pension withdrawal and make the payments. Everything just fell into place after I received that phone call at my parents' home. It was miraculous in itself that no one had called my parents' home long before that, or written off any of my accounts as bad debts during the half year of silence! And now, just like that, the storm was calm, as if the past six months had never occurred. Having trust in myself and Spirit, with absolute commitment to my path, had been crucial for this to work out the way it did. It was wonderful to suddenly see all this with clear understanding!

And finally, I received confirmation from Spirit that I could now complete my book's final chapter! All along I had no idea how this chapter might unfold or when it might have some sort of completion. I just had to persist through my test of faith to find out what possibilities desired to manifest through this experience. I had surrendered everything to Spirit, so I had nothing to lose. (As I wrote this, I noticed the word count was

103,777. I always loved seeing 777, signifying that you're on your illuminated path in all areas of your life.)

In return for my commitment and dedication to my purpose, I received the most precious gift I could have ever desired. Of course, Spirit knew exactly what that was and lovingly exceeded my desire once again.

Throughout my experiences since I'd left my marriage, I had been reminded of what I strongly felt was divinely possible in a relationship, as a couple. I realized that my greatest heart desire was to receive the full experience of this sacred possibility, with my "twin flame," in divine timing. I felt I had experienced every relationship I was required to on my path leading to "the one," and I was ready in all ways to be with him, regardless of my circumstances. I knew my beloved existed on Earth, for I had this desire to be with him. I felt that every other aspect of my life (and his) would be enhanced by us (re)uniting, for we were divinely matched in all ways. Only amazing things would result from us being together as two equally purposeful, heart-centred individuals dedicated to love and our sacred work. Therefore, being together would benefit both our purpose here on Mother Earth. I believed in this possibility with all my heart.

Then Michael showed up in my life in the most unexpected way—like a rainbow that suddenly appears through a storm and just leaves you speechless! Wow. As I wrote this I just had an *aha* moment—the image I had seen on the bedroom calendar for October, had actually signified Michael entering my life. *He* was the rainbow in my storm on that image! At the time I had interpreted it as simply a symbol for my journey. Life is so amazing.

As I write this in January 2014, we haven't even spent time together in person, yet what we've been experiencing is so much more magnificent than what we both desired as a possibility! To be able to experience each other's multi-dimensional connection in so many divine ways, before we've actually met has been such a gift. Spirit also keeps showing us, in various jaw-dropping ways on a regular basis, how sacred our relationship really is (in case we had any doubt!).

One such confirmation was an unexpected synchronicity in which I had suddenly felt guided to visit Michael's timeline on Facebook, out of the blue. He'd happened to "randomly" find a video about twin-flame relationships and he was sharing it on his timeline just as I arrived there. That post literally caught my attention by appearing on my screen with impeccable timing. In this video there was an extensive list of attributes a couple might experience, to strongly indicate that they are twin-flame partners. Both of us ended up with goosebumps, since we'd already experienced everything on that list! The video even included two of our personal essence signs that had actually felt like essence signs for our relationship from the start. It was incredible.

Spirit has already manifested so many of my heart desires through Michael and is obviously delighted to continue manifesting beyond my wildest dreams! It now feels as if a steady flow of divinely orchestrated blessings is celebrating my commitment to my path. It's a path of being, living, and experiencing love in as many divine ways as possible; a path of allowing my heart to lead. One of my heart desires has been to have two weeks as a complete "time out" from the Internet, my computer and phone, before my book publishes. This will give me a transitioning break between what was and what's coming. It will enable me to spend all my time immersed in and fully savouring the Divine's many beautiful expressions of love, in a completely different environment of Nature (and warmer climate).

This heart desire will actually manifest when March arrives, as a birthday gift from Michael! He expressed that he's already missed enough of my birthdays and intends on making this one very special for me. It will be, for we'll finally meet in person and be able to spend time together! We'll be staying at his family's beautiful vacation home in California for two wonderful weeks. It's surrounded by glorious parks and ancient tree beings that will hold sacred space for us. It will be incredible to finally answer the call of the giant sequoias, in the company of my beloved. Michael's attention (purely from intuitive knowing) to even the most subtle things that are meaningful to me, never ceases to amaze me. Who knows what spending time together in person will be like, after all we've experienced together to date. I already have butterflies fluttering inside me with the anticipation of our finally being together!

Since we realize that we might need to adjust to each other's physical presence, we've agreed to simply hold sacred space for each other, with open hearts and minds, to allow what is meant to unfold to do so, naturally. Because I'm now aware of how strongly my ego can take over, I've promised myself that I will not let my mind lead. I'm keeping this relationship's leadership centred within my heart. We know this is only the beginning of something significant, for we were clearly destined to come together at this time. What that will look like for us remains to be seen. So many possibilities await us. Regardless of how our sacred connection is destined to unfold, we have already experienced the most incredible-beyond-words relationship with another that we could ever have desired! I am eternally grateful to Spirit for this.

One day in January, my parents received a surprise in the mail—a magazine that they were no longer subscribed to. Since it was a magazine with beautiful Nature photographs throughout, I decided to look through the pages. I suddenly burst with delight to find a full-page photograph featuring … a glorious monarch butterfly with its wings spread wide open! It was *perfect* for my journal, just as I had envisioned it with my desire!

When I look back at all that has manifested in my life from love and heart desires, and all the divinity that I've experienced in countless ways, I feel *so* privileged to be here on Mother Earth. Every day, the divinely phenomenal lives through us and our surroundings. Life, in all its different aspects, is truly a sacred gift.

AFTERWORD

There are two ways to live: you can live as if nothing is a
miracle; you can live as if everything is a miracle.
—Albert Einstein

The person who says it cannot be done should
not interrupt the person doing it.
—Chinese proverb

When you trust yourself, you're able to confidently live the life your sacred heart yearns for you to experience. You're able to courageously follow the path your soul desires to travel here on Mother Earth. You feel fulfillment in its most divine form.

Had I not had self-trust from a young age, none of the stories in this book would exist. I could never have experienced all that I have. I would not have wanted to miss *any* of it—it's been such a priceless gift to live it all.

I'm left in awe when I still see ripple effects from experiences of decades ago. It is a testament to the divine power of our heart desires when just one heart-led action, after two decades, keeps benefiting so many (not to mention others that we don't know about)! It has all been possible only because I've had the courage to live my life as I've felt called to do.

There's an overabundance of information in the world now, and self-trust is invaluable in eliminating the excess and overwhelm. With self-trust, you know exactly what's best for *you*, regardless of what others might say.

Interestingly, I never felt the desire to read the popular or highly recommended books of well-known spiritual teachers of our time. My two greatest mentors are actually not as popular, but they resonated strongly with my heart when I discovered them through divine guidance—and their books were perfect for *me*. They provided so many confirmations and allowed me to continue expanding my understanding of my own truth with confidence.

Now that I've completed my own book's manuscript to submit it for publishing, I recognize the wisdom of my heart and Spirit once again. All my life, I have felt guided to experience things for myself. In doing so, I've gained the same insights and wisdom I now see expressed by so many spiritual leaders. It's amazing to see that while our paths may be different, we eventually arrive at the same intimate understanding of life.

Reading is a wonderful thing. I've been an avid reader of non-fiction since I was old enough to read. However, nothing substitutes for personal experience when it comes to gaining true wisdom and discovering our personal truth. I now understand that my soul desired to discover everything firsthand. Thus my book was born purely from my own heart and Spirit, without the influence of others' writings.

Now that *Sacred Possibilities* is complete, I've been finding quotes that confirm many of the things I've discovered for myself! I've included many of those quotes, from highly respected people, in this book. It's so fulfilling. It's comparable to when you see a photograph of a beautiful place on Earth and think to yourself, *Wow—I've been there! And it really does look like that!* This is a completely different feeling than seeing that image and not being able to relate to it personally. Now I see those quotes and I can honestly say, "Yes, I *know* that to be true, for I've experienced it myself!" and my entire being smiles along.

"Life is a journey, not a destination." I've heard and read this quote by Ralph Waldo Emerson countless times. Those words are timeless; there's such wisdom to that simple phrase. This explains why my book doesn't have a typical ending but rather opens up to more possibilities. My life's journey continuously evolves with endless possibilities, as I allow my heart to lead me in sacred partnership with Spirit. Rather than being a linear path, it's an evolving spiral of transformation, where endings are new beginnings.

Throughout my life I've received gifts beyond any I could have imagined, because I've allowed Spirit to manifest the highest possibilities. The higher the risk factor, the greater the trust, faith, and surrender required to allow for the most amazing-beyond-words manifestations. Spirit ensures that even the more painful experiences are opportunities to gain something of immeasurable value to our personal growth.

The most divine gifts I've received throughout my life have been manifestations of love that Spirit has orchestrated for me to experience. By surrendering to the Divine, I've been blessed with rewards that fulfill the heart and soul like nothing else can. Consciously co-creating with Spirit is such a sacred experience.

My entire test of faith was such a profound catalyst and teacher for me. It enabled me to master so many levels of self-discipline in a very short period of time. I was able to connect deeply from the heart with so many people, due to being broken wide open. It gave me the opportunity to see how strongly I could hold sacred space and be a great source of inspiration and empowerment for others, despite the oppressive ordeal that infused my life for months. That was such an incredible, powerful gift in itself. Without going through it, I would never have known what I was capable of. While it was definitely not easy, what I've gained from the experience makes it *more* than worth it. I don't even have a full understanding of how much this experience has benefited my life and others'. As with other experiences I've had, I keep discovering their ripple effects as time goes on. As I keep moving forward on my sacred path, I feel more empowered and abundant in love and support than I ever have—and it feels absolutely divine.

Trust your sacred heart, for it *always* knows the truth of who you are. Commit to your heart desires—the stepping stones of your unique path—and discover what sacred possibilities await you.

Acknowledgements

My deepest love and gratitude goes to divine Love, Spirit, and Nature, my greatest teachers and unwavering sources of support throughout the years of my life.

I also send great love and appreciation to *every* person who has played a part on my path, from fleeting to significant, since I became an individual on Mother Earth up until now and beyond. There are so many. I'm truly grateful for the roles each has played to co-create all my experiences (invaluable to my personal growth) and to assist in manifesting my heart desires. If you're reading this, you're also part of this group.

I wish to give very special thanks to the following (not in order of importance): my dear soul sisters, soul brothers and beloved Michael Leon Rockwell; my dear parents, Victor and Gisèle, and family, including Mitch, Alain, Joanne, Rosie, Lucie and paternal grandparents; Georgina Carter and her family; John and Ann; Lori A. Andrus, of www.journeyjewels.com; Eva Annaluna and Lee Wakefield, of www.homehearthawaii.com; Laura Hollick, of www.soulartstudio.com; Drunvalo Melchizedek; Randall Arauz; Maria D.; Dr. Turner and his staff; Ted Andrews; Kevin Thom; Gail F.; Serge B.; the Bydak family; Christine Kloser for the TAE contest; my high-school English teacher Gisèle V., for igniting my love for writing; and the staff at Balboa Press and

Hay House for making the publishing of this book not only possible but also such an enjoyable experience.

Lastly, immense loving appreciation goes out to all who have made exceptions for me along my journey of life. You willingly risked getting into trouble or relinquished personal gain, simply because you acted from a place of love. In doing so, you created miracles for me.

Glossary

Shamanism (in chapter 1)

The following definition has been derived from different parts of the book *Shamanism as a Spiritual Practice for Daily Life* (1996), by Tom Cowan. It best explains Lucille DancingWind's own way of being.

> Shamanism is timeless and universal, concerned with the health of the planet and its many species of inhabitants ... As the Native Mind deems worldwide, the shamanic practitioner sees all life as inherently holy; recognizes a Divine Being who permeates the cosmos and sanctifies it; heartily accepts responsibility for living harmoniously with the Earth; expresses gratitude; sees the universe and everything in it as alive, dynamic, and changing, yet animated by some unifying life force; understands the circular nature of time; accepts the mysteries of life; finds kinship and empathy with all creatures; celebrates joyfully its personal life and the Greater Life of which it is an integral part ... Shamanism is the intentional effort to develop intimate and lasting relationships with personal helping spirits by consciously leaving ordinary reality and journeying

into the non-ordinary realms of the spirit world ... where the spirits of the natural world and the animals, deceased ancestors, ascended masters, deities, angels, elementals, and other spiritual entities dwell ... to gain knowledge, wisdom, guidance, protection, empowerment, practical healing methods, and other vital information to benefit one's life and the life of others ... One of the most universal methods for altering consciousness for the spirit journey is a persistent, mesmerizing drumbeat ... the drum is a universal language ... there is something so familiar in the drum and the drumbeat, which mimics the sound of our heartbeat ... it takes us very quickly from the everyday beta state to the alpha state; some may even feel like it has taken them to the theta state, the state where we are when we are dreaming ... The Native American style is called the one beat, one heart, one mind drumming ... it promotes a sense of calm and transforming energy, which allows the drumbeat to carry the listener and the drummer into other realms.